Breakup Girl TO THE RESCUE!

A Superhero's Guide to Love, and Lack Thereof

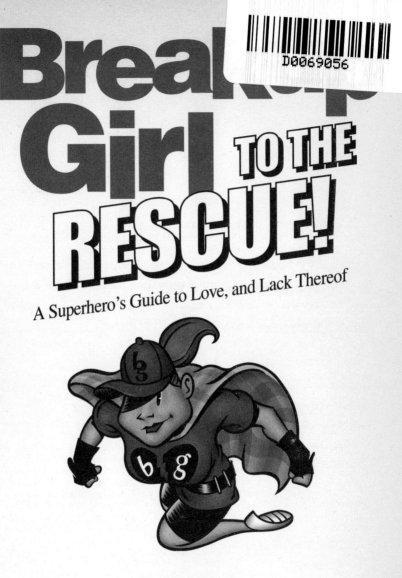

Lynn Harris

Illustrated by Chris Kalb

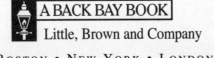

A BACK BAY BOOK

Little, Brown and Company

BOSTON • NEW YORK • LONDON

Library of Congress
    Catalog Card Number
    99-069828

10 9 8 7 6 5 4 3 2 1
MV – NY
Printed in the United States of America

The buzz on Breakup Girl
and BreakupGirl.com:

"Breakup Girl is a modern-day superhero who dispenses funny, irreverent, and consistently intelligent relationship advice." — *New York*

"Fun and flip, geared to the unabashedly hip." — *USA Today*

"You'll love BreakupGirl.com." — *Newsweek*

"She's faster than a snail-mail Valentine, sassier than the average superhero, and can mend a broken heart with a single quip." — *San Francisco Chronicle*

"The Web site for the hip lovelorn." — *Boston Globe*

"Perhaps the only Ivy League–educated on-line love adviser with a background in standup comedy . . . A staunch foe of simplistic 'Mars and Venus' dating drivel."
— *Elle*

"Breakup Girl is a chance to heal fresh wounds or revisit old ones, and laugh through the tears. Bring it on home, Breakup Girl. You feel my pain."
— *Seattle Times*

"What sets Breakup Girl apart from Dear Abby and Ann Landers? About 50 years and a wicked sense of humor." — *Time Digital*

"Breakup Girl is a superhero of a classic stripe. . . . But unlike Superman . . . Breakup Girl can give advice. Damn good advice, at that."
— *Philadelphia Weekly*

"Ex-girlfriends and ex-boyfriends of the world, meet your new guardian. She's strong, she's sassy, she's (ta-DAH!) Breakup Girl, heroine of heartache."
— *New Haven Register*

"Breakup Girl is fast becoming très hip." — *Citysearch.com*

"Hip, funny . . . A safe, compassionate place to take your broken heart where everybody understands." — *San Jose Mercury News*

"Graphically sexy, witty, fun . . . A way to try laughing your way out of the gloom." — *St. Petersburg Times*

For Breakup Mom, Breakup Dad,
Breakup Auntie Bess, and Breakup Dog
— Lynn

For Chris Mom, and Chris Family
— Chris

CONTENTS

ACKNOWLEDGMENTS

Profound thanks to everyone who helps Breakup Girl fly:

- ♥ Betsy Fast, Breakup Girl Friday, Employee of every Month, who will always get the headset.

- ♥ Colin Lingle, our hero, who crossed the country in a single bound to join forces with Team BG.

- ♥ Paul "Paul the Intern" Sullivan, who stickers better than Betsy.

- ♥ Mike Lee, animator genius, who brings BG to the screen and joy to the team.

- ♥ Oxygen Media, Inc., particularly BG-believers Kit Laybourne and Sarah Bartlett, plus BG-TVers Machi Tantillo and Sue Hollenberg.

- ♥ Belleruth Naparstek, Official BreakupGirl.com Psychotherapist-on-Call (http://www.healthjourneys.com), who is always unsparing in wisdom and wit, compassion and coolness.

- ♥ Mike Liss, Editor Boy, a hero whether or not he ever gets written into the comic.

- ♥ Conan Smith, who puts the "integrity," "loyalty," and "heart" in "agent."

- ♥ Ken Treusch, who believed even when this was all just a Breakup Gleam in our eye.

- ♥ Nancy Rose, fierce and graceful protector of BG's best interests.

- ♥ Claudia Cross, who makes the book business a pleasure.

- ♥ Julina Tatlock, ever steady and sharp, whose talk we will always walk.

- ♥ Rob Paravonian, who makes Breakup Girl — and everything else he touches — rock.

- ♥ The Associates — cast, crew, and creatives — whose voices, talent, and friendship make BG's world a better place.

- ♥ Chris Mazzilli, of Gotham Comedy Club, who brings class to comedy and *Breakup Girl LIVE* to life.

♥ Greg Young, who puts l'amour in gl'amour through the boozy magic of Gregoire.

♥ Jennifer Cunningham, Jeremy Gold, Jaime Panoff, and Robert Morton, of Panamort Television, who saw big small-screen things for BG.

♥ Rita Rosenkranz, Breakup Girl's original—and most loyal—literary den mom.

♥ Heidi Swanson and chickclick.com, who make the difference between cute hobbies and realized dreams.

♥ ComedyNet.com and Michelle Ferguson Public Relations, who streamed up a storm and pitched up a fit.

♥ And, of course, Breakup Girl fans, supporters, and visitors worldwide. We built it, but you came. Back, even. Thank you.

INTRODUCTION

I am Breakup Girl.

I am the only superhero whose domain is love . . . or lack thereof. My job is to fight crimes of the heart, stop dating indignities, get your stuff back, help your mom through your breakup, make good relationships great . . . all the while trying to find time to have romantic problems of my own, if you know what I mean.

My headquarters: the Studio Apartment of Justice.

My virtual headquarters: the award-winning Web site BreakupGirl.com — where thousands of visitors go every month to follow my adventures and, ideally, my advice.

My motto: "I'll be right there . . . *'cause I've been there!*"

My core belief: We can make our breakups, and thus our relationships, and thus our bad selves — *and thus the planet* — better.

Breakup Girl's Vision for World Peace

How do I make the jump from our own little worlds to, like, the whole world?

Easy.

First of all, I can fly.

But more to the point, "relationships" (lust, romance, dating, courting, "concentrating on me," whatever you want to call it) are not merely the fluff piece at the end of the evening news. Love — or lack thereof — is right up there with Supreme Deity of Choice as the prime mover/shaker behind most wars, voyages, art, and really tall buildings. Relationships are our comeuppance, our downfall, our overlord. The floods may come, the bombs may drop, the market may crash, but we are rarely a moment away from thinking, "Did he call?" "Will she say 'Yes?'" "Which tie should I wear?" Or even "I can't believe I missed my Nobel announcement. But I just *had* to check my voice mail."

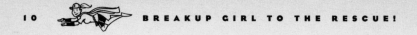

So that's why saving love lives isn't so far removed from saving the world. And that's where I come in. Natural disasters, criminal masterminds, and global conspiracies — they've got their own superheroes. Why not a superhero for relationship issues ... you know, natural disasters, criminal masterminds, global conspiracies?

I'm not offering simple answers to such massive questions as "What, besides razor design, are the true differences between men and women?" "How *can* we all get along — no matter what our persuasion/orientation/position on the ketchup-on-eggs question?" "Why would anyone marry Dennis Rodman?"

But I do know this: When it comes to social change, our social lives are an excellent place to start.

. . . And Where You Fit In

You fit in to my vision because you helped shape it. *Your questions* are my primary source of answers. The letters forming the spine, if you will, of this book are the actual missives submitted to my online advice column by the world's inquiring hearts: male, female, gay, straight, married, single, hopeful, jaded, and everyone in between.

That's right, *everyone.* Breakup Girl is an equal-opportunity superhero. I'm a girl because I was born that way, not because I take gender- or other-based sides. My fundamental mission and message is this: We can all transcend icky, limiting stereotypes; we can be dignified and respectful; we *can* all get along. In certain combinations, maybe, for only three months at a time, but still.

True to that mission, BG works hard for:

- ♥ **Both sexes.** Men are not from Mars, women are not from Venus; breakups are from hell. If you're not with me on that last one — even regarding the kindest, gentlest, mutualest splits — I don't know what planet *you're* from.

- ♥ **All ages.** Teen love is different from grown-up love mainly in that teens are more likely to measure their relationships in lunch periods, and adults are less likely to use Scotch tape on their walls. Teens are wise beyond their years; grown-ups play house and buy Hello Kitty. Let's listen to each other.

♥ **All sexual preferences**. Gay, straight, curious, tri — no matter what our lifestyle choices, we all manage to achieve our shared goal of freaking out our parents.

♥ **All political persuasions**. I will treat you according to how you treat others, not according to how you treat Jesse Helms. (Keep in mind, however, that how you treat others is sometimes directly linked to how you treat Jesse Helms.)

♥ **All phases of attachment**. Lots of people write to me to say, "Dear Breakup Girl, I wish I'd had a breakup because that would mean I'd had a relationship." Sure, but the goal here is not to Get a Relationship. If you think that once you do, your work is done, you've got another think coming. Like, think about packing. The goal here is to have a *healthy* relationship — especially with that hottie named Numero Uno. You know, *you*. Because Numeros Dos, Tres, et al. are *icing*. Gravy. Hot chipotle mayo on your sweet potato fries. Not essential, but . . . *yum*.

Love, or Lack Thereof: The Pep Talk

COME *ON*, BREAKUP GIRL, HOW DO I FIND SOMEONE? Okay, okay. It's actually a good question. Does the real thing come only to those who wait to be tapped by the wand? Is "trying" a jinx? Or does finding love — like keeping it — simply demand hard work? People do approach this love thing with rules and lists and "if . . . then . . . " functions and spreadsheets. Which are not necessarily a bad way of organizing your thoughts and plans.

But you can't organize people. Or feelings.

I mean, one advice-seeker lamented to BG that she kept getting led into relationships "by the heart."

Um, that is how you get there.

All your missives to me — and all the minutiae, all the micro-introspection, all the madness therein — are part of the whole great big crazy messy love thing. So yo, make room. When your head's buried in Compatibility 2.0 for Palm Pilot, you might not notice the stranger asking you to dance.

And if questions come up, just write to Breakup Girl and let her take some superpowered guesses. Oh, and read this book, where you'll find:

♥ A curl-up-with-it compendium of BG's advice, derived from and

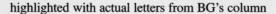

highlighted with actual letters from BG's column

♥ "Getting the Digits" — statistics from surveys answered by visitors to BreakupGirl.com

♥ All-new episodes of the comic Adventures of Breakup Girl!

Remember, Breakup Girl is only a superhero, not a psychologist. So who comes to the rescue when I call for a pro? Belleruth Naparstek, Official BreakupGirl.com Psychotherapist in Residence, author of *Your Sixth Sense: Activating Your Psychic Potential* and creator of Health Journeys, a best-selling series of guided imagery audiotapes for mind-body health. Her virtual headquarters are at www.healthjourneys.com.

I'm not promising to trim and buff the world of love into some creepy, perfect Disney village. Lame dates, bad good-byes, mixed signals, grody rebounds: *This is the messy stuff of life, not the sloppy kiss of death.* So go concentrate on you: enjoy, love, regret, respect, live, laugh. I'll concentrate on you too. Which is the same thing as concentrating on my career. And as "concentrating on me." Which actually explains a lot.

Love,
Breakup Girl

1

Relationships:

If my super–job description covers all elements
of relationships — even happy ones — how
come I'm called Breakup Girl? And how come
I'm starting the book at the end, as it were?
Isn't that a bit of a downer?

Not if you do it my way.

You'll see.

DOING THE DEED

A STEP-BY-STEP GUIDE

Here's why my name is Breakup Girl, as opposed to Take Things to the Next Level Girl, or something else less cumbersome but equally as hopeful sounding. A breakup is not only an ending. It is also a beginning. The first day of the rest of your love life, as it were. How you handle your breakup, especially if you're the dumper, will help determine how you set yourself up for your next relationship — with another human or with Martha Stewart (as in, all the creative projects you'll have time for now that you're on your own).

You act like a jerk now, and guess what's going to be stamped all over the baggage you claim at your next port? You act respectful, humane, and forthright now, and, well, you'll be packing lighter. I promise.

So now what? Well, this is not the part of the book where you spend a lot of time figuring out whether or not you should break up. You've got entire relationships to do that. By now, I trust, you've figured out that the feeling you've got to follow is not the one in your head that says, "But statistics show that my chances of finding someone else will decrease dramatically if I become single now." It is not the one in your heart that says, "But I can't hurt my love's feelings!" It is not the one in your elbow — 'cause that's how smart this one is — that says, "I can live without passion, intellect, and shared interests." It is not the one in your childhood that says, "I don't deserve to be loved, blah blah blah." It is not the one in your loins that says, "[Unprintable matter.]" It is not the one on your shoulder — you know, that little devil guy — saying, "But it's almost my birthday, and I could have sworn I saw a receipt from Alfa Romeo."

It is the one in your gut that says, "OW OW OW OW OW OW OW, but this is the Right Thing to Do. OW OW OW."

If you promise me that *that's* the feeling you're following, then it's time for this.

⚡ In Defense of the Dumper

Dumpers, like lawyers, are universally reviled in an unfair, knee-jerk way. Contrary to popular belief, however, dumpers are people too. Isn't it meaner and more evil to stay together out of principle, to live a lie in the name of fear? Or laziness?

You, dumpers of the world — if you are kind — are brave. Risk takers. Bigger-picture seers. Self-trusters. I get just as many letters from agonized dumpers as I do from their (ex-) counterparts. Your mission is next to impossible. Someone is standing there, loving you (or not loving you enough, as the case may be) and you are saying, "I hate to say this, but no." You are saying, "I hate hate hate to hurt you, yet I am hurting you, and I have to live with having done that." Wow. That's hard. So the bottom line, dumpers, is decorum. It's not *that* you do the deed. It's *how* you do it.

Which, put another way, is an

IMPORTANT BREAKUP GIRL MAXIM

LET YOUR EX BE MAD BECAUSE YOU BROKE UP WITH HIM / HER. NOT BECAUSE OF *HOW* YOU BROKE UP WITH HIM / HER.

To wit:

⚡ Breakup Girl's Pentagon Papers: How to Drop the Bomb

Unless this "breakup" is pre–third date — in which case, though a polite call might be in order, it's not really a "breakup" and you two should lighten up — then you do need to do *something*. Laissez-faire breakups are no fair. Do not just stop calling, coming home, etc. (Betsy, Breakup Girl Friday, calls this nonmethod "being disappeared.") It's impolite, and actually, you're the one who gets stuck with the guilt.

So here we go:

The medium is the message

And you — ideally — are the messenger. So choose wisely. Rule of thumb: Unseal the deal the way you sealed it; choose the medium that matches and honors the relationship.

Your options, in theory:

■ The written word
E-mail

A thousand times no. Unless you want your cybergood-bye forwarded around the world a thousand times. Exception: If you've never met in person, guess now's not the time.

> "I was dumped via e-mail, in about three sentences containing many words that are banned by the FCC. And this was on New Year's Eve."
> -- ALEXANDER

A letter

An epistolary breakup is a little too Bram Stoker for Breakup Girl's taste; according to the above rule, it's appropriate only for dumping a pen pal. But if you must:

♥ Handwrite it. In pen (don't get cute with color). I don't care how bad your penpersonship is. Handwriting adds a personal touch and allays suspicion that you cut and pasted a breakup.txt file.

♥ Be prepared to follow up in person, or at least on the phone. The pen is mighty, but it will not protect you from Having to Deal.

♥ Make it sound / look like a *letter*, not a treaty. Or a living will.

♥ I don't have to tell you not to fax it, right?

■ The spoken word
Now we're talking.

On the phone

Phone breakups are not inherently rude, as long as your phone manners aren't. You may, for example, use the phone to tell your Psychic you want to be Friends. Sure, phoners are iffy after the proverbial three-month mark, or after you've moved in together, but they are under-

> "She called me and said, 'Look, my parents don't want me to be dating you, so we need to break up. Oh, the washing machine just went off, I'd better go.' [Click.] She didn't answer the phone when I called her back."
> -- NICK

rated as feelings- and scene-sparers. They grant the dumpee the privilege of hanging up, gathering his / her thoughts (also, your things), and calling back. The phone breakup also circumvents the awkward exit, the ride home, letting them see you sweat / cry. So if circumstances — say, "snowbound!" — dictate that it's the best way to go, don't rule it out on unfounded principle.

In person
See "Location, location, location?" below.

A third party.
Avoid this method. The whole Romeo-and-Juliet thing could have been avoided if they'd simply left out the middle man. Also, do not use the third person to "show, not tell" that you've moved on. As Katharine writes:

> When I was shopping with a friend, I saw my boyfriend of three years holding hands with another woman. When I approached him, he actually said, "I'm sorry, do we know each other?"

Location, location, location?

Where should ground zero be? Some swear by the "Dear John dinner" restaurant breakup, but I'm not so sure; in any case, don't expect to go dutch. The most obvious — yet also delicate — breakup locus: one of your homes (preferably not the vacation home where you've just arrived for a romantic sojourn, and preferably not under the covers).

As far as Breakup Girl is concerned, the home-based breakup is among the least of many evils. And I say, if you're going to go there, go *there*: to your ex-to-be's pad. As Carol suggests:

That way the dumper can leave and the dumpee can just crawl

> "When I was fourteen, my boyfriend had his twin brother call on the phone and break up for him*!!* I didn't figure out it was the brother until halfway into the breakup*!*"
> — MAYA

> "I was broken up with right after midnight on . . . well, New Year's Day. He waited until after we had rented a hotel room together to begin ignoring me, hoping I'd get the message. I had to push him to tell me; otherwise, he'd never have done it himself."
> — JENNI

HEARTBREAK!

into bed and cry instead of trying to navigate their way home
through a mess of tears.

Exes don't let exes drive sad.

Still you should be aware of the biggest at-
home breakup risk: early — *very* early — back-
sliding. This is legalese for "sexual relations."

> Dear Breakup Girl,
>   What do you do if you have a vaca-
> tion planned with your significant
> other but you want to break up with
> her?
>   —Pete

> Dear Pete,
>   Few things are less romantic than a romantic vacation
> with someone who's planning to dump you. Do the deed; take
> a buddy.
>   Love,
>   Breakup Girl

> "Let me suggest
> the supermarket.
> The dumped may fill
> the cart with the
> necessities of
> recovery (choco-
> late, caviar,
> Kleenex, tiny liquor
> bottles), and the
> dumper has to pay,
> because he / she
> invited."
>   -- MELANIE

Breakup scheduling

> Dear Breakup Girl,
>   My friend wants to break up with her boyfriend, but he
> got laid off the day she was to do the deed. She opted to
> wait for a more "suitable" time to let him go. What's the
> holdover time on breaking up after a layoff?
>   —Shady

> Dear Shady,
>   When Breakup Girl was thirteen, Breakup Mom had a rou-
> tine checkup with a doctor who wasn't convinced that she was
> getting enough rest.
>   MOM: It's just because my daughter's bat mitzvah is com-
> ing up.
>   DOC: Mrs. Breakup, *there's always a bat mitzvah.*
>   Yes. There's always some intervening concern, some
> source of angst that can conveniently explain why we haven't
> joined the gym or spent quality time with family or...gone
> through with a breakup. So. Your friend was right to spare

him the brush-off the day of, but really only a few more days
are required. The layoff shouldn't become a stalling chip.
What, she should wait until he's happy?

    Love,
    Breakup Girl

Line, please

While planning your speech, keep in mind this

IMPORTANT BREAKUP GIRL MAXIM

THERE'S NO SUCH THING AS "BREAKING UP WITH SOMEONE" WITHOUT HURTING THEIR FEELINGS.

Of course you're hurting their feelings; you're breaking up with them.
Now, how can you *spare* some of their feelings?
By remembering this

IMPORTANT BREAKUP GIRL MAXIM

MEAN IS BAD, BUT BLUNT IS FINE.

Don't sugarcoat: NutraSweet has that saccharine aftertaste. Don't patronize; it will make your ex-to-be (a) mad, and (b) say, "Well if I'm that great, then how come you're dumping me?" Don't say you think it's best for him/her. Don't talk about being friends. Do talk about how you feel, what you need, where you feel your life should go. But don't expect him/her to, like, *agree*. Just do the best you can. Which may still lead your ex to the conclusion that you're the worst person on earth, but it doesn't mean you messed up.

    Also, get to the point.

Dear Breakup Girl,
    I want to break up with my boyfriend of five years, but
I don't know how to broach the subject. I have thought of an
approach where I discuss:
    1) The current situation (i.e., everything that's
going wrong)

2) His future plans and mine (i.e., they're incompatible)

3) Therefore, we need to split.

What do you think of my approach, Breakup Girl?

—Hermetica

Dear Hermetica,

With all your whereases and therefores, it sounds more like you're breaking up with Parliament. He'll get the point by the time you get to Section 1, Item b, so you may as well skip straight to Section 3. But other than that, DON'T try to make him *agree* with you or tell you that he thinks you're a Good Person who's doing the Right Thing. Just read your bill gently, then take questions.

Love,

Breakup Girl

Avoid not only parliamentary procedure but also clichés. Here's the problem, though. *At no time are all those cliches more true than at this one.* Heck, this is the place they came from originally, before they became clichés! I mean, you're right: It ISN'T fair to the dumpee to be dating someone whose heart's not in it. You're right: It IS you; someone else will find your ex-to-be's irritating habits adorable, perhaps sooner than you'd like. You're right: you do love, but are not in love.

But do not say any of that.

If a cliché pops out, you must follow it up immediately with, "I know that sounded like a total cliché, but it's true."

Oh. Also a cliché. Never mind.

And let's say you spent all night constructing an elaborate Downy-soft, April-fresh "explanation" specially designed to prove beyond a reasonable doubt that you are Right and Good and oh, yes, so is your delightful, wonderful, best-thing-that-ever-happened-to-you ex. When you use it, you will get one of two results:

1. Your dis is so feathery light that your ex-to-be will call you three hours later and say, "Okay, have you had enough space yet?"

> "He just told me, face-to-face, that he'd tried to make it work but that the relationship was just not what he wanted. An honest version of 'it's not you.' I respected him for that."
> -- JESSICA

2. Or, s/he will be offended by your condescension and BS-ification, and may even write to BG to share the ridiculous thing that you said.

> Dear Breakup Girl,
>   What do you think of the statement, "I broke up with you because I love you so much and was afraid that you might become unhappy with the relationship"?
>   —Julian

> Dear Julian,
>   HA HA HA HA HA HA HA HA HA HA HA HA HA HA HA HA HA HA HA HA HA HA HA HA HA HA HA HA HA!!!!!!!!!!!!!!!!!!!!!!!!!!!!
>   Love,
>   Breakup Girl

Skip the preaching, skip the patronizing, and tell the truth. Well, most of it.

> Dear Breakup Girl,
>   How do I tell my guy I want to break up without hurting his feelings? He has bad breath, bugs me about if I like him or not (which I did until he started bugging me), and he wears makeup to cover acne. What to do?
>   —Darlene

> Dear Darlene,
>   Two things do not work: (1) bugging someone about whether they like you, and (2) tinted Clearasil. In fact, they both backfire.
>   But about you. Your job is to tell him nicely but firmly that you're terribly sorry, but it's just not a happening thing anymore. Even if he presses for details—which he will —don't you dare mention the breath. Or the makeup. Those are things that a well-intentioned close friend or tactless aunt —not an about-to-be-ex-girlfriend—should say. You can't not hurt his feelings, but do him a favor and cover up a few of yours.
>   Love,
>   Breakup Girl

Then again, as long as they get the point — you might not have to say much at all. As BG's intern Paul says, "I hear 'We have to talk,' and I collect my CDs, no questions asked."

Post-Breakup Maintenance

Dear Breakup Girl,

What do you suggest for someone who is dealing with the guilt of being the dumper, so they don't go back to heal the broken heart?

—Scott

Dear Scott,

Splendid question. Being the dumper feels rotten, especially in the case of those hideous gray-area, gut-feeling breakups where just because you don't see yourselves together in forty years doesn't mean you don't care. But.

IMPORTANT BREAKUP GIRL MAXIM

EXES DO NOT HELP EXES THROUGH BREAKUPS.

It's too close, too much, too weird—like dating your therapist in reverse—and it doesn't work. (Sleeping together does not "help," either.) The humane thing to do is to hear your ex out—Say nothing! Don't defend! Don't justify! Bite your forked tongue and just listen!—and then see your ex out.

As long as you have been fundamentally kind, respectful, and human/humane, your ex's reaction is not something you did. Exes are entirely capable of feeling out of control and miserable all by themselves. You can't go fix it. Sometimes the best way to take care of them is to leave them alone.

Besides, as much as you feel your ex's pain, Florence Nightingaling is mainly about absolving *your* guilt. So don't send mind-gaming "I miss you" cards and e-mails; don't call to see if your ex is "okay." That's what spies are for.

Love,
Breakup Girl

And finally, make no major decisions about the future right now — and certainly don't take any back. Remember this

 MIXED FEELINGS ARE PART OF A BREAKUP,
NOT NECESSARILY EVIDENCE AGAINST ITS
WISDOM.

When you wake up in the morning, you feel tired. Of course you feel tired; you just woke up! Same thing: Of course you feel crappy; you just broke up!

But at least, if you follow the BG plan, you will feel bad about what you had to do, not about how you did it. Right?

OTHER BREAKUP LINES (ACTUALLY USED IN HISTORY!)
THAT WORK INSOFAR AS THEY WILL ASSURE THAT YOUR EX
REALLY WON'T WANT TO DATE YOU ANYMORE

- "I have had a transfer of affection."

- "My father has been married three times. . . . it runs in my family. . . . It's not my fault I'm not good with commitment."

- "He says that because of calculus he just doesn't have time for anyone."

- "The only reason he gave me was he didn't like me as much as I liked him and it wasn't fair to me."

- "It's not fair of me to string you along while I am trying to fig-ure out what to do with my life, when I'm scared that my deci-sion may not leave room for you."

- "He said I was too beautiful for him!"

- "I'm already juggling two girls and I just don't have time for a third."

- "I don't like the whole corny idea of holding hands and going out."

- "He said he would rather date a goat than go out with me ever again!"

- "The reason? He didn't want to lose me, but he could see that if we stayed together any longer, he'd lose me forever."

- "We should break up for the right reasons rather than be with each other for the wrong."

- "You're too good for me. You're understanding. I don't deserve how good you are to me. I could never give back to you what you give to me."

- "He hands me a five-page letter about how he wants to 'date others' and says, 'Read this while I go shower.'"

PREDICAMENT of the CHAPTER!

A Breakup Technique DON'T Wall of Shame

Dear Breakup Girl,

After three years my girlfriend broke up with me on the phone — and then refused to talk about it because she was late for a movie! When we finally spoke, she said, "I'm going out with someone else now, and there is no chance of us getting back together." Her new boyfriend, she said, was a "real man" who could provide for her financially and emotionally in a way I could not (he has a $45,000 job and a $35,000 Jeep, and I am a grad student). I e-mailed her to ask for my stuff back — and her new boyfriend responded, saying he was her soul mate and that she never wanted to see or hear from me again. Then she dropped off a box containing every gift I had ever given her, except the stuffed animals, which, her note said, she'd given to charity.

I don't understand what has happened. I was always kind, caring, and understanding to her, and then she ended the relationship in such a callous manner. How could she continue saying 'I love you' till the end, then two days after breaking up with me jump into a new relationship, claiming this person as a soul mate? All I know is that I am really hurt and...

— Confused

Dear Confused,

Does it make you feel at all better — in a heaving, hollow sort of way — that your ex has violated just about every breakup rule there is?

1. Phone breakups are not allowed in three-year relationships.

2. While it doesn't work to talk your dumpee *through* a breakup, you at least owe it to him / her to talk *about* it. Time-management tip: If you're going to be late for the movies, dump him / her afterward.

3. No follow-up calls involving the words "new boyfriend" or "real man" or actual dollar amounts.

4. Gift return is permitted if deemed a necessary purging and healing process, but only with a note saying something like, "I'm sorry, but it will be easier for me to move on without these."

But BG is not in the business of making people feel better by saying, "You're right, s/he is very, very bad and wrong!" and leaving it at that. So. What happened? It's possible that she and Mr. Soul Mate were already shagging and she got tired of the complicated scheduling. Or, she wanted a way out — for whatever reason — and happened to see this guy in a Jeep with a big red "Exit" sign over his head.

And sometimes, callous is easier than careful. You behave badly, you don't have to make the time or effort to deal. You rationalize twistedly: "Well, maybe if I'm a huge troll, s/he'll be glad to see/let me go."

All of which hardly makes you feel better right now, but in the long run, it will. So will this: If he really makes $45,000 and spent $35,000 on a Jeep, he has only $10,000 — well, $6,600 after taxes — left for everything else, like food, clothing, and...rent. She says he "provides for her"; I say they live in his car.

Love,

Breakup Girl

Having the DEED Done to You: WHAT TO DO?

What's the opposite of *euphemism*? (Maybe *eeeeeuuuw-phemism?*) Reason I ask is this. Corporate America has come up with all sorts of cushion-the-blow terms like downsizing and reengineering — heck, even the slips are "pink." Nice, clean, slick terms for very dirty work.

But Breakup America doesn't even try. Sure, we drag all sorts of cumbersome clichés into our actual breakup conversations (unless we've read the preceding chapter), but we don't have even a faux-kind word for *dump*, or *dumped*. Even the slightly more objective "I've been *broken up with*" wouldn't pass muster with Strunk, White, or Churchill (and suffice to say, we'd much rather that sentence end with a *proposition*).

There you go. *Beyond euphemism.* Getting dumped is *that bad.*

How do you deal?

In this chapter, we'll cover pretty much just the immediate reaction, the dump-and-response; you've got the rest of the book for rebounds, reunions, and rethinking the whole enterprise to begin with.

And when you're at rock bottom, the rock-bottom line is this:

⚡ Maintain Personal Dignity (MPD)

This is more than a Breakup Girl Maxim; it is a way of life. One borrowed from BG's friend Lucy, actually, who coined the term as a way of dealing graciously with her — unfortunately — true-to-stereotype mother-in-law. "I imagine that my behavior is being recorded and will be played back on giant video screens in front of thousands of people," Lucy explains. "This terrifying thought helps me behave more magnanimously." I'm not appealing to some higher moral plane; I'm just telling you to *make sure you look good in front of your ex.* Begging and badgering, throwing a tantrum, threatening to write a memoir — all of the above make you an unattractive candidate for a reunion.

But one of the main challenges to MPD is that dumpees will usually feel that this thing is being done *to*, foisted *upon*, dumped *on*, them and that they have no say in the matter. That, of course, is the nature of the beast. And that is also why dumpees are driven, in the chill of the

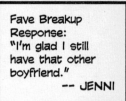

Fave Breakup
Response:
"I'm glad I still
have that other
boyfriend."
-- JENNI

moment — or in a series of late-night phone calls — to respond by asking — or at least wanting to ask — all sorts of unanswerable questions. Undignified questions that often risk undignified answers.

So let's run through them now — complete with BG's answers — so you won't have to do it then.

I. "WHYYYYYYYYYYY?"

[Director's note: exaggerated whine.]

DO NOT ASK WHY.

```
Dear Breakup Girl,
     I am trying to move on from a recent breakup, but I am
haunted by the question of "why." Last night I talked to him,
and the subject came up again as to why I'm "not his type" —
not attractive enough, not thin enough. Now I have the left-
over feeling that I was dumped because I'm unattractive. I'm
terrified of meeting anyone because I fear it will happen
again. And my self-esteem is zilch. Will I forever hear him
in my head saying that I am unattractive?
     —Crushed

Dear Crushed,
     I am totally sorry about your breakup. But let's break
```

things down a bit here. You say, "The subject came up." It did? All by itself? I don't think so.

The major breakup lesson I hope you're learning here—though it is the hard way—is Do Not Hound Your Ex for a Reason Why. I am not saying your ex is right or that you don't deserve a basic explanation.

But is there actually anything he could say that will make you say, "Oh! Got it! Thanks! Bye!" No.

And what actually happens when you do press him for a reason? The real risk is that you will drive him to say something that YOU DO NOT WANT TO HEAR. Worst of all, *you probably already know what that thing is*.

And you don't need to hear it from him.

But try not to fear next time, Crushed. You'd have the willies right now no matter how much you weigh, no matter how pretty or ugly you feel. Breakups are not known as self-esteem boosters; simply stated, *this is your brain on breakups*. Don't make it worse by bugging him; make it better by writing to me.

Love,
Breakup Girl

2. "What do you really mean?"

Don't bother doing close readings of The Breakup Speech. I'm not saying that dumpers are necessarily lying, but they are speaking Breakup. Most of what they say is well-meaning/butt-saving Breakup Filler. So forget vain attempts at lit crit/close readings. You should listen to it like that dog in the "Far Side" cartoon; all you should hear is, "Blah blah blah breakup blah blah blah." Otherwise, you'll drive yourself nuts. As Bereft wrote:

My girlfriend of three years recently broke up with me. I don't know what went wrong. I tried calling and e-mailing her to talk, but she avoids me. All she says is that her feelings for me were fading, and also that she wants me to "find someone else"!?!?!? Why would I do that when I love her?

She wants him to "find someone else," huh? That, of course, is a Line (also see page 23). Come on, didn't it come in the form of "I want you to be with someone who'll love you the way you deserve to be loved"?

That, or she really does want him to find someone else...so that he'll stop e-mailing and calling her.

(Especially because—just a side note— dumpers generally do not want their dumpees to find someone else. *They* want to find someone else. They want their dumpees to remain, nobly and indefinitely, alone.)

Moral for everyone: Take everything dumpers say with a grain of NutraSweet.

Oh, except the part where they say they're breaking up with you. On that, I recommend you take their word for it. Which brings me to:

> Dear Breakup Girl,
>
> Two days ago on a park bench (cliché!) my boyfriend broke up with me. I think. His grounds? Law school. He explained that his first year has monopolized his time and that he can't be good to anybody else right now, blah blah. All said through tears. He then insisted that this was not a breakup but a hiatus; he closed the deal by saying he loved me. What the dilly? Am I dumped or what?
> —Law School Widow

> Dear LSW,
> Yes. Truly sorry. But at least he said it through tears. Not through, say, an attorney.
> Love,
> Breakup Girl

THE "MUTUAL" BREAKUP

There are two types of "mutual" breakups:

1. Mutual of Omaha's Wild Kingdom

The kind where a couple actually agrees -- together -- that being apart is for the best. Certainly not extinct, but they are elusive beasts, rarely observed.

2. Mutual Image Consultants, Inc.

> Dear Breakup Girl,
> If I have just dumped my boyfriend, will he tell his friends that he dumped me?
> —Heartbreaker

> Dear Heartbreaker,
> Probably. If he's a prince of a guy, he'll say, "It was mutual."
> Love,
> Breakup Girl

3. "Don't I have a say in the matter?"

Well, no. You don't. This is a breakup, not Debate Club. Not fair at all, but it is the nature of the breakup beast.

And specifically, I do not recommend that you argue, plead, or otherwise question a decision that has — we hope — been a difficult one for its issuer. Your dumper's response will be, with hands over ears: "LA LA LA LA LA!!!" At this moment, at least, you will only make him/her dig in the heels of those made-for-walking boots. Trust me. It's not about being a doormat; it's about maintaining personal dignity.

But remember, there is a difference between expressing your feelings and trying to change someone else's. If you are hurt, say so. If you are confused, say why. If you think s/he is giving up the love of a lifetime, say, "I think you're giving up the love of a lifetime." Instead of accusing or badgering, try to stick to "I" statements. "I think," "I hope," "I want" . . . "I feel . . *that you suck.*"

4. "Couldn't we have worked on it?"

Missing Her wanted to know:

> How can her feelings for me change so quickly?

Well, they didn't. Her feelings didn't change quickly; she just told MH about them quickly. That fadin' feeling was probably percolating for a while, and either — to give her the benefit of the doubt — she was just giving herself the chance to be sure of how she felt, or — to withdraw said benefit — she's known for a while but, given the way she dumped him (e-mail, if you must know), she just didn't feel like getting around to dealing.

So in some cases, of course, breakups are hasty, speak-too-soon impulses attributable to mood swings, mood rings, etc. But in most cases, yes, your dumper will have gone through the second-hardest part without you: figuring out what s/he wants, or doesn't want (which, all too often, are the same). Sometimes, no, there truly would have been nothing to "work on." Sometimes, no, there's no couples-therapy "project" to be done. Sometimes it's not about how the two of you interact, how the two of you communicate, how the two of you disagree over old versus young Elvis. Sometimes it's about how *one* of you feels. Sometimes, when it's "just not working," it's just not worth "working on."

Console yourself — hah! — in this knowledge: Even though a sudden blow smaaaaaarts, it's better than a slow Band-Aid peel on a raw wound. What would have been the alternative? Stressing yourself out over passive-aggressive hints and warnings from the dumper-to-be? Feeling like you tried . . . and failed? Prolonging of agony? It may not be "better this way," but it's not necessarily worse.

5. Caveat: "Huh?"

You *are* allowed to seek clarification. As Brett wrote:

> Dear Breakup Girl,
>   My girlfriend of one year broke up with me, then e-mailed saying she thought she still loved me but couldn't deal with the distance (she moved two hours away). I told her I couldn't deal with e-mails saying she thought she still loved me and asked her to take some time to figure out if she did or didn't and to get back to me. Now I'm starting to get upset that it's taking her so long to decide. Should I push her?
>   —Brett

> Dear Brett,
>   She's allowed to be confused, but she's not allowed to send you confusing e-mails. If there's something specific that you two need to work through together, then fine, you should talk; but writing, "hi, might still love u but not sure, bye! :)" <SEND> doesn't count. You need to <REPLY> with, "ok, let me know by [specific deadline]."
>   Which *you* should be prepared to stick to.
>   Love,
>   Breakup Girl

6. To self: "How will I get him/her back (reunion)?"

YES, you may reunite in the future, but — you know where this is going — *now* is not the time to broker that deal. Here are two things that do not work *in media dump*:

1. Bugging, badgering, begging, bargaining. See "LA LA LA!" and MPD, above.

2. Sleeping together. The general wisdom of sleeping with an ex — your garden-variety relapse — is something we'll get to later (page 55). Sleeping together as a Reunion-Chances Enhancer — especially as part of an, um, "bargain" — well, as ends go, it's pretty dead. Why? I'll spare you the indelicate buy-the-cow versus milk-for-free homily. You nurse false hopes instead of wounds; s/he gets all the cake, none of the commitment. Totally counterproductive.

So if you're going to hold out for Numero Dos, at least look out for Numero Uno first. Like Forlorn.

Dear Breakup Girl,

Boy of My Dreams (BOMD) dumped me last week. He said he's happy 95 percent of the way, but he doesn't see that last 5 percent. He says he loves me. Our sex life is beyond the beyond. We enjoy the same things. Everything was peachy. But he just isn't sure.

BG, I love this guy. Enough to understand that if he truly doesn't love me "that way," then I need to let him go, for both our sakes. But now, I want to hang on. I feel like— sheesh, 95 percent.

So: I'm giving him all the space he needs. I've told him that the door is open. I love him so much that I have to hold out hope right now, but I won't let him string me along.

Am I behaving desperately? Should I just swallow this bitter pill? (I'm definitely already going through the motions; what with the movies rented, books devoured, and stenciling project I've started in the hallway.)
—Forlorn

Dear Forlorn,

Desperately? HARDLY. Stenciling? Go, girl.

Cautionary note: Everyone reading this who has EVER been in BOYD's position—of loving someone dearly but not being able, for whatever *il/elle ne sait quoi* reason, to go the extra 5 percent—is thinking, "That's exactly how I felt: mixed up, yet sure I was doing what I needed to." He might be back, but I wouldn't bank on it. Mainly because banking on it won't bring him back. Which you already know. (Unless you're stenciling his initials.)

So if it makes you feel any better, stencil your bad self onto some oak tag, 'cause you are now BG's poster child for How to Deal.
Love,
Breakup Girl

7. To self: "How will I get him/her back (revenge)?"

Mastermind an evil, elaborate revenge plot involving the mob, the Spielberg people, Limburger cheese, and that Celine Dion song. Then: Don't do it. *Then:* See the "Back Atcha"chapter.

The 4 Cs of Being Dumped

Dear Breakup Girl,

My girlfriend told me that we don't "click" anymore. I've always tried to be there for her, and I loved—still love—her more than anything in the world. I was in the jewelry store the other day learning the 4 Cs of diamonds, hoping to present her with a ring. I want to be with her so badly. Our friends thought we were made for each other.

What do I do? Crawl back to her, begging her to not call it quits? Ask friends what she says about me? Live by the adage that "if you love something set it free?" This is tearing me apart.

—Owner of a Broken Heart

Dear Owner,

Not that there's any reason Breakup Girl should know this, but in case anyone's wondering, the 4 Cs of diamonds are Cut, Clarity, Color, and Carats.

More important, it's clear that you are a gem of a boyfriend—and your letter is one hell of a heartbreaker. But I want you to know that Crawl is not one of the 4 Cs of breakups. Neither is Check with friends.

These actions may, in the immediate, satisfy your restless, frustrated urge to do, fix, or know something about the relationship, but they are not guaranteed to bring her back. I'm guessing that the breakup was a tough, gray-area, gut-feeling decision for her to arrive at and stick to. Any pressure in the opposite direction may, at this time, only diamond-harden her resolve.

So here, unfortunately, are the 4 Cs you need to learn today:

1. Confusion. Ultimately, you're not going to fully understand what "doesn't click" for Miss Ringless. That's partly because she probably doesn't quite understand either. You may just have to live with that for a while.

2. Centuries. How long it will seem to take to get over her—or at least for her to have had enough "space" to be able to turn around and reconsider from a new perspective.

3. Clemency. Let her know—once and for all—that you are merciful and all-forgiving. That if she all of a sudden hears that click, she knows where you live. Then leave her alone.

4. Carnage. The effect that all of the above will have on your heart and mind. Just so you know. Be brave.

Love,

Breakup Girl

KNOWING YOUR Stuff AND GETTING IT BACK

We can track the development of any relationship on the basis of who leaves what stuff where, when. Never mind sex, meeting the parents, going away together; the real signifiers of seriousness are: the Second Toothbrush, Drawer Allocation, Total CD Commingling. You know: "She left her gym bag in my car! This really could be going somewhere!" (Caveat: If she also left the keys in your car, running, she may just be absentminded.)

That is why the act of reallocating items after a breakup is also fraught with meaning. Stuff, much like (or including) children, can be a pawn in the Who's a Good/Bad Person game, a drama enhancer, a complication adder, an agony prolonger. (Not to mention a "reason" to stay together. As in, "I was feeling restless and unfulfilled in the relationship, but who wants to move a piano?") See how Dane got bogged down?

Dear Breakup Girl,
   I broke up with my girlfriend almost three months ago: no tears, no calling just to "hear your voice," no attempts at reconciliation. Just silence. Two weeks ago it was her birthday. I sent a card to show I didn't hate her and that I do have some class. No response. All I wanted was a simple acknowledgment/thank-you. So now I'm mad. I still have some things of hers—should I send them back? I thought of including with the package a note letting her know how classless I think she is.
   —Dane

Dear Dane,

Yes, in the world of non-breakup etiquette, it is tacky not to acknowledge a well-meaning missive. And yes, in the world of breakup etiquette, it is tacky — though understand-able — not to acknowledge a well-meaning missive. Understandable? Yes. You don't know what her healing M.O. has been. She may still need a communication moratorium. Maybe she's too sad? Too mad? Or she's just tacky. Who knows?

Your motive, not hers, is at issue here. What you sent with that card was a big yellow stickie saying, "SEE? I AM A BETTER PERSON THAN YOU ARE." So if you would like to return her stuff, fine. With a note that says, "Hope you had a great birthday. I'm sending this because it's easier for me not to have it around — hope you understand. Would be delighted to hear from you, when/if you feel like it." *That's* the classy thing to do.

Love,

Breakup Girl

And that is why BG recommends making this transaction as timely and as ... *meaningless* as possible. (In an ideal world, you would meet and make the trade in a neutral place, like a parking lot, or Switzerland.) Because as much as commingling your stuff symbolizes the evolution of the relationship, demingling your stuff can symbolize, sadly — and quite tangibly — its end. As rituals of closure go, it is — if handled appropriately — pretty effective. You can also use it to jump-start some other winter-of-your-discontent cleaning. Which frees up space. You know, for shopping.

BETTY CURRIE-ING FAVOR: USING A THIRD PARTY

Barring certain sexual prac-tices that are entirely your business, reallocation of stuff is the only situation wherein you are allowed to enlist the involvement of a third party. That is: no fair sending an emissary to ask someone out, break up with someone, etc.

But.

If the act of returning / retrieving is deemed (a) immediately necessary -- because you two *could* elect to wait until things (e.g., the Sharper Image juicer you're using frantically because you know you have to return it) cool down -- and (b) too painful for a face-to-face, you are welcome to send a trusted friend, a disinter-ested man with a van, or your secretary supplied with garbage bags, packing tape, and bubble wrap (occupies exes for hours!).

⚡ Your stuff

Anecdote. A very excellent old boyfriend of mine arrived to pick me up for the movies. As I skipped gaily down the stoop outside the Studio Apartment of Justice, tickled whenever I get to ride instead of fly, I noticed that something seemed funny about his very nice car. Aha! *His hubcaps were gone.*

Yes, he explained matter-of-factly, they'd just been stolen. Like any good daughter of Breakup Mom, I freaked.

> **BG:** OHMYGODDIDYOUCALLTHEPOLICETOREPORTIT-
> DOYOUTHINKYOUCANGETTHEMBACKAREYOU-
> OKAY?
>
> **BOY:** Breakup Girl. *They're just hubcaps.*
>
> **BG:** Oh.
> Right.
> (Pause)
> WELLISITSAFETODRIVE? ISONEOFTHEWHEELS-
> GOINGTOCOMEFLYINGOFF? (Etc., etc.)

I know what you're thinking. First of all: "Of course it's safe to drive, you dummy; hubcaps are basically cosmetic."

And also: "I know where you're going with this, BG, and I want to let you know, my favorite tube of MAC Viva Glam / framed 1975 Cincinnati Reds National League Championship pennant is not just some . . . hubcap!"

Fine. Whatever. I am talking about an *attitude*. Point being: Yes, your ex "should" return your stuff. Manners dictate. But breakups are not always quite so neat as "should." A few CDs here and there, a fave sweater — sometimes these are the win-some / lose-some-stuff spoils of love. Sometimes, rather than scheduling an icky handoff, it's worth cutting your material losses. They're just hubcaps.

Sometimes, however, there's something else — say, your ex — holding you / your stuff back.

Dear Breakup Girl,
    I dated a guy who kept telling me, "I think you're set-

tling," which is code for, "I want to sleep with other people." So the calls dwindled, but when it came time to get my
stuff back, he kept stalling.

Now he's involved with someone else and won't return my
calls or even leave me a box outside. Why? Should I bang on
his door at four A.M.?
　　　—Fishgirl

Dear Fishgirl,
　　Are all his boxes and stamps at *your* house? Or perhaps
he's using your stuff as props? (Earrings in couch crevices
and peppermint lotion on the nightstand represent the concept that whomever he's with is "settling" for someone who's
not planning to settle down.)

Either that or he's just not dealing. I'm sure your ex is
complex and interesting in other ways, but this may not be a
conspiracy. People in general don't return *calls*, never mind
stuff. People in general don't send their travel buddies copies
of the Mazatlan '98 pictures like they said they would. He
probably just keeps saying to himself, "Yeah, gotta do that."

And/or, if you want me to get a little psychology on you,
he probably already thinks he's a bit on the irresponsible,
Bad Person side (witness his "settling" line. Even "lines"
can be telling). That heap of his ex's (your) Q-Tips and
Narnia Chronicles—not to mention messages—serves as hollowly satisfying "proof."

So what to do? Show up unannounced, and I guarantee you
New Girlfriend will be there. Not fair to her; unnecessary
headaches for you. So find a way to get him on the phone and
ask him nicely once and for all. Tell him you'll come to him,
whatever, whenever. If he can't deal with agreeing to be
home, alone, for five minutes, then the only thing that
should be settling is dust. On your stuff.
　　Love,
　　Breakup Girl

And sometimes, it's the stuff-leavers themselves who can't let go.

Dear Breakup Girl,
　　My ex and I broke up last year, but I have yet to get
my things out of his apartment. He told me he still has my
toothbrush. How should I get it all back?
　　　—Jaime

Dear Jaime,

Surely you've replaced the toothbrush by now. But BG does want to know what on earth he's doing with your old one. Has he bronzed it? Or has it become the "guest toothbrush"? Neither is good news.

In any case, here's what to do:

1. Note that it's been a *year*.

2. Confront whatever it is that's keeping you from picking up the phone and telling him nicely that you're coming over to get your stuff (minus the toothbrush). What is it: fear that you'll start liking him again? Resistance to saying the final, material goodbye? Laziness? You tell me.

3. Pick up the phone and tell him nicely that you're coming over to get your stuff (minus the toothbrush).

Love,
Breakup Girl

CURATING A BROKEN HEART

S / he doesn't need it back; you don't need it around; hate to waste; what to do? Perhaps the Schlesinger Library at Radcliffe College will take your, um, dated photos and letters and other mementos off your hands. Seriously. As a museum rep once said in a letter to the Cambridge *Tab*: "[We're] a women's history library with extensive manuscript collections documenting women's political movements and issues . . . but also families, girls, friendship, courtship, and other aspects of private life. So if [you] haven't recycled [your] letters and journals . . . and want a place to park them where [you] won't stumble upon them unless [you] mean to, my colleagues or I would be glad to talk to [you]. We don't take everything, but we are interested in ordinary folks and how they live their lives."

Jaimes of the world: Give it up or get it back. Either way, you're one step closer to over it.

⚡ Your Ex's Stuff

Breakup Girl's return policy: If your ex asks, you must return. You can buy stamps online now, so no excuses.

> First, do no harm.

Nothing destructive, okay? (See the chapter on revenge, page 65.) Even if you mean well (e.g., cryogenically preserving your ex's Air Terra Humaras).

> Do no heave-ho.

Toss that tired cliché about tossing your ex's stuff out the window. What's the point? Then it's on your front walk.

> Do know yourself.

If you want to return the loot of your own accord, be my guest (as long as it's not part of a breakup-triggered plan to give up your wordly possessions and join the Franciscans). But be nice. No fair leaving open boxes on his / her doorstep during monsoon season; also, under these circumstances, "charitable dona- tions" are . . . not. If you're magnanimous, s/he'll be less inclined to hound you if you "forget" something.

⚡ A Few Words About Gray-Area Goodies

If Preppy had one thing going for it, it was all that monogramming. When sorting time came, you knew exactly what was whose. But even that didn't help with all the in-between stuff: the gifts, sentimental / intellectual property, everything jointly owned (including, verily, the joint itself).

Taking the "co" out of co-owning

If you've got to divvy up a houseful of stuff that's always been "ours" — Beanie Baby collections, deeds and assets, teenagers — you are going to have to enlist the help of a disinterested third party with the wisdom of Solomon and, perhaps, the accreditation of the state bar.

This prospect does make the situation much messier, of course, but it is one of those burn-that-bridge-when-you-get-there kind of things. If you're contemplating a break, but this mountain of STUFF is in your way, go ahead on your own and make a list of your co-things with suggestions for how to divide without conquering. The idea here is not to be sly; get a head start on the practical and you may be able to sidestep at least some of the emotions that the who-gets-the-Mac thing will stir up.

Re-/de-gifting

Promise me you won't freak if s/he gives your gifts back or reclaims his/hers. I'm telling you, it's all part of the hurting and smarting and purging and healing and cleaning and dealing and protecting and sweeping. (Also, if your ex de-gifts, promise me you won't re-gift it to the next squeeze.) (For more about the Ghost of Christmas Presents, see "The Holidays," page 222.)

> "I feel like I need to be a free bird, no strings, do what I want . . . have time to myself (which I get NONE of, since we live together) -- I just really feel trapped. On top of all of this we have shared a LOT of expenses, including the computer I am sending this to you from."
> -- HELPLESS

GETTING YOUR STUFF BACK!

Recovered Memory Syndrome

Sometimes, you want to get back stuff you never actually had in the first place. That's not supposed to be a metaphor. Instead it's the:

PREDICAMENT of the CHAPTER!

Stray Cheese

Dear Breakup Girl,

My boyfriend and I broke up five weeks ago, after a year. I was in love, and it was pretty painful to be "too serious" with an otherwise wonderful, lovable guy who would every now and then begin talking about his fantasy around-the-world-solo adventure, complete with sex and the exotic, unknown foreign woman. You can see how that might bother me.

Now I miss him like hell. We had a few weeks of sorting out stuff and a couple tearful phone calls and meetings. I haven't talked to him for two weeks and I'm trying to keep it up. I figure that feelings of outrage and nausea when I think about him going on a date are a good sign that I'm not ready to "be friends."

Here's my question: photos. The pictures we took over the course of what was mostly a wonderful year together were with his camera. He has them all.

I am debating writing him and asking him to make and send me some prints. But I don't trust myself that this isn't some way for my id to sneak past my ego and reinitiate contact with the boy. Emotionally I think I want that, but I know it will just make me a weepy mess at this moment. I am not at all over him. But I want some of those photographs. It's like I've lost a record of this entire year of my life. What should I do?

—Emily

Dear Emily,

Yeah, I can see how his travel fantasies might bother you. And thus why, more than ever, you'd want photos of the journey you two *did* take. Sure, maybe it's an in for your id ...but who knows, it could also help with the healing. So why not write a terse but polite letter with your request—no drama!—and include a SASE? Maybe just ask for some negatives and tell him you'll make the copies, then return? Only a little work for him, limited contact for you. And if he doesn't respond, well then, ick. But you can't bug him again. So if you can't put together a photo essay of that year, write an ESSAYessay about it. Then put it away.

Love,

Breakup Girl

THE ORIGIN OF EX LUTHOR

...BY LEAPS AND REBOUNDS

In *Webster's* dictionary, *rebound* — as in "stocks rebounded quickly from Monday's decline" — means recovery. The connotation being that you, or the Dow Jones Industrial Average, have already made a healthy comeback. But in Breakup Girl's dictionary, *rebound* — as in "Steve rebounded quickly from Monday's breakup" — is, ostensibly, *a means to that end* (i.e., Steve has a date/hookup on, say, Tuesday). The rebound doesn't mean you're "over it"; it's part of the process. In the face of loneliness, rejection, and free time, rebounds are your basic fix. They scratch the itch, make us feel wanted and noticed; they remind us that we've still got it going on. They are: Chicken Soup for the Loins.

At least that's the idea.

Now, Breakup Girl is not going to get all preachy about whether the act of rebounding is Good or Evil. I would, however, like to offer my empirical observation that in the context of relationships, the word *rebound* is most frequently used in sentences such as, "Well, it was *supposed* to be just a rebound, but . . ." or, "S/he didn't tell me s/he was on the rebound!"

In other words: It's rarely that simple.

⚡ Who and Where: Rebounds 101

Remember that right after a breakup, anyone who is not your ex looks good. (Specifically, anyone looks better than the one who's saying, "I'm breaking up with you.") Take as a given that you are wearing Rebound Goggles.

Which means: Your judgment may be impaired. Which is why you might write a letter like this:

Dear Breakup Girl,
    I just broke up with my beau of eight years; now I am FIERCELY attracted to a coworker. I have never asked a guy out. Should I start now?
    —Hopeless

Dear Hopeless,
    Let me guess: Is it Bob from Accounting...or *Joe from Rebound?* See, right now, *everyone's* going to look good—especially the beaux-to-be who are the worst ideas. Be particularly circumspect about stirring up a solution that contains not one but two combustible ingredients (hint: one's work). My advice: Let Octavio from the Piercing Parlor be your rebound. *Then* see how good Joe looks in the company cafeteria.
    Love,
    Breakup Girl

So no, I don't recommend bringing your rebounds to the office (or, more to the point, taking them home). But going away couldn't hurt.

Dear Breakup Girl,
    Have you ever heard of a person's hair going gray due to a particularly crappy breakup? I did take the matter (the bottle) into my own hands, but could a good, solid rebound also reverse this process?
    —Silver Queen

Dear Silver Queen,
    I prescribe Grecian Formula. As in: 1 round-trip ticket to Crete + 1 great little dress = 1 man out of hair.
    Love,
    Breakup Girl

How:
Rebounds of Decency

One of the most common complications is the lopsided rebound, where one party's intentions do not match the other's (e.g., he's dusting off his mack;

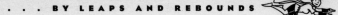

she's dusting off her hope chest). So let me send out a plea to the makers of the indispensable Japanese toy the Lovegety: no, not the one that dies if you ignore it, the one that picks up the signals of other Lovegetys with the same settings (e.g., "Let's meet!"). They've even got a setting for "KARAOKE," so why not "REBOUND"? This feature would match up like-minded people for We Both Know What This Is and Isn't liaisons. It's honest, efficient, and leaves little room for misunderstanding and hurt feelings. Just a thought.

In the meantime, we must be more primitive — and thus more circumspect. Two possible scenarios for me to get you out of:

When You're Rebounding, But They're Bonding

I know it's unrealistic to ask you to issue some sort of explicit preemptive "I WANT YOU TO KNOW THIS IS ONLY A REBOUND" disclaimer. (Though it might have a "Lovegety" effect if you happen to use it on the right person.) But please don't heap on indications to the contrary. When you're just looking to shack, don't play house. Don't take your Rebound to fancy dinners... at your parents'; make out with your Rebound in a divey bar. And keep in mind that if there is an exchange of gifts, you will be taxed.

Dear Breakup Girl,

When I was on the rebound, I got involved with a guy, let's call him Brandon. He's great, but I was fooling myself (and him?) when I thought I loved him. So, here is B telling me he loves me with all his soul, and here am I, finding that I...don't. So I broke up with him. He refused to be "friends" — though I really want to — and he hasn't returned my calls, not even about the silver pendant that I have had since birth and that I gave to him during our passionate little affair. Help!

—Porcelina

Dear Porcelina,

A sentimental silver pendant is not a rebound-appropriate party favor to begin with. While it is not Right for him to keep it — nor, for that matter, to toss it into Okefenokee Swamp, which is equally likely — it is Understandable. And the problem you've got now is that when you say, "I really, really would like to be friends...and by the way, do you hap-

pen to have that itty-bitty trinket lying around?" all he
will hear—understandably—is, "Cough up the necklace,
speck!" All you can do is buy some worry beads and wait it
out.
Love,
Breakup Girl

Still, if you promise me that you're sending only "Hello, I'm recently single" signals, well, there's only so much you can do.

Dear Breakup Girl,
I just ended an emotionally straining relationship and
wound up sleeping with this fun, nice, good-looking friend
of mine...but after, I felt really weird—so we had "the
talk." He says he's cool with being friends. I think the
world is grand.
But now IT LOOKS LIKE WE ARE A COUPLE. He buys me gifts
and finds reasons to come over. I mentioned to other friends
that I liked a certain look on a guy, and he did it: he dyed
his hair, made other changes too. (If I'd thought he was
really listening, I would have said, "Antonio Banderas.") I
thought "the talk" would have prevented this. What do I do?
—Potential Meanie

Dear PM,
Whoops! About his liking you more than you like him, and
also about your not saying Antonio Banderas. Anyway, YES,
you have to be responsible for his feelings. Or at least for
not deliberately/callously toying with them. But he is an
adult, and you have been quite clear. For him, it—everything: the shopping, the loitering, the hair dyeing—is a
calculated risk.
A lesson to be learned here, though, is that people say
yes to the Talk even when they're not planning/willing to
walk the walk. "Yes" might just be an "I'm saying yes just
to go along with this because I feel it's my only way to be
near you" substitute; believe your yes-person for the sake
of argument, but take it with a grain of Mrs. Dash.
So, PM, you've been honest with him, yes? Fine. *Now* be
honest about this: At what point does feeling good stop being
worth feeling bad?
Love,
Breakup Girl

Yes, you need to watch out for your reboundee's feelings. And, at the end of the day — but before you make that booty call — also for your own.

So, rebounders: Is this liaison more like a delightful, restorative bed-and-breakfast get-away...or does it make you feel as if you never went anywhere in the first place? As one Taylor-Belle wrote:

> Friends have told me that the best way to forget a guy is in the arms of another guy. Well, I have tried that. And no one else even compares to [my ex].

> "I don't under-
> stand this rebound
> thing. Maybe it
> works in some
> other universe
> where dates are
> easy to come by,
> but in my universe,
> I'm unlikely to get
> a date if I'm feel-
> ing depressed over
> a breakup."
> — B.

ACTION!

Right. Advocates of safe(r) sex warn that when you sleep with someone, you "sleep with every-one else s/he's ever slept with." Well, Breakup Girl would also like to warn you that — especially in a rebound situation — when you sleep with some-one, you sleep with everyone else *you've* ever slept with. Keep that in mind.

When You're the Reboundee

Sometimes, people do come right out and make their intentions (i.e., atten-tion span for you) clear, whether they mean to or not. Peaches writes:

> Last month, I met a man: lots in common, great sense of humor, easy to talk to. We go out on our first date, and in the middle of dinner, he starts telling me about his ex. She had called him the previous week, and he thinks they may be able to work things out. (I felt like Charlie Brown trying to make a field goal!)

(This is not only a big Rebound Flag, of course, but also bad date manners. What's Peaches supposed to say, "Who-hoo"!?) Failing such truth in adver-tising, how do you avoid winding up on the short-term end of a rebound you took to promise more?

First of all, if your suitor/suitette is "going through a divorce" — even if it is "amicable," *assume that you are a rebound.* (If s/he is "*going* to go through a divorce," assume that s/he is not only cheating but also lying.)

Just assume. Take it as a given. If you stick it out and things turn out differently, yay. But if you hear yourself saying things like, "No, Breakup Girl, *this* one will turn out different; you'll see," then I repeat, *assume that you are a rebound.*

Dear Breakup Girl,

    Last fall one of the professors in my department began making overtures: meals, e-mails, gifts. He was going through a divorce, but our "relationship" continued until it became apparent that I wouldn't break up with my long-distance boyfriend (horrible, I know).

    Over the summer he eloped to an exotic foreign destination—mere weeks after finalizing his divorce and mere months after ending our "relationship." I am hardly in a position to feel sorry for myself, but could you explain what I meant to him? Barely weeks into our "relationship" he was professing his love to me. Also, wouldn't it be polite for him to have contacted me regarding his new marriage?

    —Another Not-So-Bright Graduate Student

Dear Grad,

    Yes, it would have been polite. But what you had, Grad, were office hours with Professor Rebound. *Courtesies not included.* Now go work things out with your boyfriend.

    Love,
    Breakup Girl

Ending marriages — or, for that matter, any big-deal relationship — also give rise to the Friend-bound, or what I prefer to call the Zipless Rebound. Some signs:

I got a call from a man I've known almost ten years but hadn't heard from in at least two. He tells me he's filing for divorce, and would I like to go have pizza and a movie the next night? I got that giddy feeling and got all spiffed up. But when he answered the door of this flophouse, he was in sweats, the pizza was congealing, and the only pictures I saw were of his wife. He talked my ear off about her for two hours until I had to excuse myself.

(Pertinent note for rebounders: Reboundees don't *talk* you through the tough time, they just *get* you through it. Ideally. They are not the people you spill to. They are the people with whom you get to pretend nothing ever happened. You can't have it both ways.)

When Is a Rebound Not a Rebound?

Ricochet Rabbit asks an excellent question:

> A few months after the end of a major relationship, I met a VERY neat guy—and fell head over heels on the first date. It has been a nonstop snogfest for the past three months. *IS IT IMPOSSIBLE for THE ONE to show up in the Rebound Time Zone?* I feel normal, but are my emotions necessarily too screwed to make a rational choice?

Ah, the Rebound Zone. It is fixed neither in time nor space — nor is it surrounded by an anti–The One force field. While some people seem to be in perpetual rebound, invoking one *R* word just to avoid another *R* word, it's also possible to leap over the whole rebound thing altogether. See, people sometimes exit relationships with a never-clearer sense of what they require and what they can't abide the next time around; ergo, the next person who shows up will — almost necessarily — fit the bill because the freshly single person simply won't have it any other way.

So now that Ricochet's at least put herself on mini-alert — "Note to self: It's possible that my feelings for Snog Boy could be tinged somehow by my breakup with Major Guy (P.S. to self: Hello, when are *anyone's* feelings for Person X *not* tinged by Person X-1?)" — well, what else can she do? She should step away from the microscope and try to relax (hah). And enjoy (snog).

And what you should do in a similar situation is . . . take things a little slower than Ricochet. Give yourself a chance to ask yourself, "Would I be dating this person if I weren't not dating my ex?" See, when you're reeling from one person and falling for another all at once, you can get a bit dizzy. It's harder to think when your head's spinning. Also, when you're snogging.

Then again, Breakup Girl is less worried about someone who writes to say s/he's confused after a few weeks than she is about someone who writes to say s/he's sure.

'Cause listen, all you Rebound Rabbits out there: *Of course* your vision of the New One isn't always clear. Your last relationship may have left you with that "I should have known" feeling; now you're seized with "I should know now." Makes sense. But maybe you shouldn't know now. After several months, maybe. But after one or two? Nah. Some people can barely get it together to go on more than, like, a couple dates in as many months in the first place. You're asking a lot of yourself and your vital organs. It's thoughtful and conscientious to be asking these questions — and to not lead anyone on — but try try try try not to need all the answers now. Trust yourself. If it really is only a rebound, you're the one who'll bounce back.

PREBOUNDING

Occasionally, when a wrinkle occurs in Rebound Time, the rebound actually predates the breakup. This is known as the "prebound" (a clever term I first spotted in an article by Stephanie Dolgoff in the October 1997 *Self*). As Dr. Judith Sills, one of my fave experts, told that plucky reporter: A prebound "gives you hope while you're distancing yourself and reminds you that the person you're with is not the last date on earth. Also, there's always a push-pull in letting go. When you find someone else attractive, the part of you that wants to let go has someone to let go of, and the part of you that wants to attach has someone to attach to." Yes, indeed. Just remember that as far as your partner is concerned, the only difference between prebounding and cheating is that with prebounding, you break up before it becomes a pattern. Phew?

BECCA'S PRE-BINDI

"I was the bassist in the pit band of a show; my boyfriend was the musical director. After the last show we went to a lame party (never celebrate anything in a house with paneling), where he tells me he's back with his old girlfriend. Who, by the way, happened to be at the show and the party (easily discernible by her bindi). (We are all Americans in our thirties.) It's his prerogative to date a raving bindi loony; I object to the fact that they'd been dating -- behind my back -- for six weeks, and he just HAPPENED to tell me the night of the last show. I guess that way he never had to find a replacement bassist." -- BECCA

THREE-BOUNDING

To all you third parties who are huffy because your ex has started seeing someone else in no time flat -- like Greg, who wrote, "I'm not sure she's worth chasing if it was that easy to get over me" -- hey, listen, seeing someone else has nothing to do with whether s / he is over you. Consider that you are the odd point on the rebound triangle, or that you are in, if you will, a "threebound" situation. It may be not so much their way of getting *over* you as their way of getting *through* the breakup. Don't run out and find someone, anyone, for yourself just to make your lives parallel.

PREDICAMENT of the CHAPTER!

The Hunter and the Haunted

Dear Breakup Girl,

Six days after a lousy breakup, I meet the sweetest guy on the planet. He cooks dinner, gives foot massages, and washes my car. I cannot imagine this guy playing games or being deceitful. He's brilliant and the sex is amazing and I'm learning about all kinds of things like respect, communication, expression of feelings.

Three weeks later, my ex shows up to tell me it's me he wants and can we please try again. I list the eighteen things I want changed and he says okay.

I can't see shutting the door on a year of #1 because I've had three awesome weeks with #2, who is fab but IS a Republican and a Baptist, and a hunter, for God's sake. So I am going away with my ex to see if he can behave. Naturally the new guy is hurt and angry, though I've pointed out that without closure on #1 I'm not going much of anywhere anyway. So I'm about to take off to a resort with my ex and I can't seem to get happy about it. I miss #2. I feel like whichever way I turn I am screwing something up. I need to see how I really feel about #1, but losing #2 is breaking my heart.

—Julee

Dear Julee,

I think you need a dose of perspective about guy #2. For which I need to use a word that may be scarier than *Republican*, *Baptist*, and *hunter* combined. Ready?

Rebound.

I'm not saying that just because he showed up during the Rebound Time Zone (six days later!) he can't be a real boyfriend in camouflage. But things seem to have moved fast in three weeks. Which could be because you're true soul mates or some such, or it could be because he was in the right place, massaging the right feet, at the right time.

If I were you, I'd go ahead and give the, uh, Democrat a chance. You've got more invested there. See how he does— not on one getaway, but over time—with the eighteen(!)

things (maybe the ten most importantest ones, Miss Julee?).
    Love,
    Breakup Girl

Dear Breakup Girl,
    My boyfriend just broke up with me...Now I am so angry
at boys that I want to date girls! Is this because I am angry
or because I have always been gay!? I am thinking about asking a gay friend of mine out on a date.
    —Confused

Dear Confused,
    If girls dated girls every time they were angry at boys,
then lesbians would have been on the cover of *Newsweek* way
sooner. But seriously, people who say gay people are gay
because they hate the opposite sex are people who hate gay
people.
    About this chickywicky: Do you want to ask a girl out
because you're sad about boys, do you want to ask a girl out
period, or do you want to ask *this girl* out? Think about it
...until you're less angry. No one—girl *or* boy—really wants
to be just a rebound.
    Meanwhile, hang out with people who interest, delight,
and support you. You need friends now, not dates (meaning
that also, it's not the best time to date your friends).
    Love,
    Breakup Girl

Dear Breakup Girl,
    If a girl suddenly tells you that (a) she broke up with
her boyfriend, (b) you have the same sign as he does, and
(c) apart from that, however, you're nothing like him, what
does this mean? She likes you? Yes, no, maybe?
    —Tiger Man

    Dear Tiger,
    She likes you. But wait until Rebound goes into retro-
grade.
    Love,
    Breakup Girl

Love Gone Back

RELAPSES VS. REUNIONS

You wouldn't believe how many letters I receive that go something like this:

> Dear Breakup Girl, I broke up with my boy/girlfriend three and a half hours ago and I really want her/him back.

Or this:

> Dear Breakup Girl, I broke up with my boy/girlfriend. We still sleep together and go on dates and visit each other's families for Christmas and live in the same apartment. I really want her/him back.

Or this:

> Dear BG, I broke up with my boy/girlfriend and since then I lost my job, my house burned down, all my close friends moved away, and *Melrose* was canceled. S/he told lies about and stole stuff from me, and we are completely incompatible. I really want her/him back.

People. One of the primary characteristics of a breakup is not wanting to break up. *But.*

Allow me to repeat this

MIXED FEELINGS AFTER A BREAKUP ARE NORMAL BREAKUP AFTERMATH, NOT NECESSARILY EVIDENCE AGAINST THE BREAKUP'S WISDOM.

Still, sometimes people hear these feelings as calls to action.

Hence: The Relapse.

As opposed to: The Reunion.

(Or, heaven forbid: sticking it out and, eventually, Moving On — see page 82 — which, as you'll soon see, does not preclude a reunion.)

Can you tell the difference? Let's watch.

• Do-Overs at a Glance •

	occurs when you have ...	time passed since breakup	what has happened in between: romantically	what has happened in between: in the rest of your life	defining activity of relapse/reunion itself
Relapse	Icky, lonely, breakuppy feelings.	In Breakup Time, an eternity; in Greenwich Mean Time, oh, between 10 minutes and 2 months.	"Nothing Compares 2 U" celibacy or rebounds with inferior beings (same thing).		Sex.
Reunion	Trusty, measured, grown-uppy feelings.	At least several months. Decades, however, are not unheard of.	A little of this (healthy relationships), a little of that (healthy singlehood).	Pretty much got my ducks in a row.	A reasoned, thoughtful, committed discussion about how/why things will be different this time. Then sex.

Allow me to elaborate.

⚡ Relapses

Breakup Girl understands why they happen . . .

Yes, indeed, breakups are Mixed Feelings City, and you're the mayor. One of those mediocre mayors who focuses only on the short term. Immediate problems plaguing the metropolis: loneliness, confusion, creaky plumbing. Quick, hard-to-resist fix: the relapse.

> Dear Breakup Girl,
>
> I recently parted ways with my boyfriend over a spaghetti dinner. Shortly after splitting, we met again and promptly hopped into bed. I believed that this encounter meant something, but when I called him to talk he was completely nonchalant. Was it wrong for me to expect more?
> — Tory

> Dear Tory,
>
> Ah, Classic Relapse. See, breakups can be right up there with oysters, figs, and *Red Shoe Diaries* in terms of their aphrodisiac qualities.
> The clarion call of the Relapse:
> "Wow, you look great without...commitment."
> So, a Relapse and a Reunion are two different animals. People: Safeguard your feelings — and don't toy with those of others. Break up, or don't; act accordingly. And if you are going to break up, you might as well be eating spaghetti at the time.
> Love,
> Breakup Girl

. . . but she doesn't necessarily recommend them

A relapse can be thrilling, furtive fun; sure can spice up that dreary stuff-retrieval trip to his/her apartment. And our buddy Tory, above, might even say that her case of mistaken identity was worth it. But I don't want you guys to get stuck in some sort of holding pattern that allows you neither to come back to earth nor to take off again.

> Dear Breakup Girl,
>
> Let's-call-him-Jack and I have been apart for six months

after dating for three years. Now I sort of have the hots
for someone else AND am enjoying being single. Thing is, Jack
and I have started sleeping together again. We are always
drunk when this happens, but the sex is hot—though he doesn't
always kiss me before or after, so it's not that romantic.
I know it's stupid to have sex with an ex, but what if it's
nice and you aren't nursing false hopes of reconciliation?
    —Back with Jack?

Dear Back with Jack?,
    I'll take your word for it about those hopes. And I will
allow that sex with an ex can offer fond, old-home-week satisfaction (or we-shouldn't-be-doing-this passion)—all without the hassle of, you know, meeting someone. Or getting to
know them. Fine.
    But my concern is that recycling this relationship will
hold you back from the next one—and, for that matter, from
your current phase of healthy, restorative singlehood. It's
the Sorta factor: You're sorta seeing someone who makes you
feel sorta good. And that—well, let's just say this: For
your strength, standards, or self-esteem... *don't do Jack*.
    Love,
    Breakup Girl

⚡ Reunions . . .

. . . on the other hand, are not about getting to the edge, realizing it's scary
and different and savage and lonely, and heading back full speed. Chart that
course and you'll be off to a honeymoon in Bermuda (the triangle part). No:
Reunions are about heading off around the world and coming back full circle — from an entirely new direction.

According to extensive research done by Nancy Kalish, Ph.D., a devel-
opmental psychologist at California State University and author of *Lost &
Found Lovers: Facts and Fantasies of Rekindled Romance,* the couples who
are most likely to succeed the second time around are those who, paradoxically, have basically gotten over each other before they get back together.
That way, it's most assured that they're not reuniting out of loneliness, nostalgia, craving for stability, or simply because breakups suck.

Can I have a do over?

Depends on the following factors:

■ The past

Why did you break up the first time? If the reasons were related more to ill-timed circumstances (s/he was transferred to Babelthuap) than to irreconcilable differences (s/he didn't like *Babe*), you've got a better shot the next time around. As Laura writes:

> I'm thirty-six, divorced (for over five years), and have been seeing a great guy for four months. But last week, a guy I'd fallen head over heels a year ago came back into my life. I really like the guy I'm seeing but have never felt that "magic" with him the way I did with Mr. Return.
>
> My plan is to spend time with Mr. Return on a nonsexual, "friends" basis to see if there's something there. I want to be fair to the guy I'm dating, as well as to my soul— after all, I so want to find my destiny, and believe that abiding love has that "magic."

Sounds like a plan. See, she's even built in a buffer — the nothing-but-friends phase (we'll see how long that lasts) — just to make sure that that "magic" isn't just grass-is-greener fairy dust.

■ The in-between stage

The more time that's passed — paradoxically, the further you've moved on — the healthier your comeback may be. (Breaking up on Monday and reuniting on Tuesday because you're afraid to watch *Baby Monitor: Sound of Fear* alone does not count.) Neither does this:

> If you do dump him, then realize it was a bad idea, how do you ask him back out without letting him think that he has you wrapped around his finger?

Here's how: Pick up the phone, dial all but one digit of his number, hang up the phone, and wait at least two weeks. *Then*, if you really, rationally think that you want another chance (and you have at least two friends who endorse this decision), you may actually call him and ask him out. Once. Casually. If he says no, let it go.

■ The present

Hi, how's your life? If you honestly feel that you have all your ducks in a row — except one really cute one — then you're best prepared to say, "I got you back, babe" (and best prepared to cope if Take 2 tanks). Or: Are you adrift, casting about for direction, coping with a loss or change? Or, say, in a lousy relationship? If so, you might be looking around — or back — for a familiar face, one that looks a lot like a knight / Xena in shining armor. Happened to Loisaida:

> I've been married for seven years (not happily), and about
> a year ago I met up with my high school boyfriend. It was
> like we never broke up. My husband can provide for me mate-
> rially but not emotionally—my ex, vice versa. How can I
> choose?

Yes, indeedy, when your present is less than lukewarm, the past — especially when high school hormones are involved — can feel pretty darn hot. And a [re]liaison to a past love can certainly appear to fill in blank spaces in your current attachment. If so, it's not so much a matter of choosing between the two as it is a matter of using the situation to decide whether you can more-than-tolerate — or, hey, improve — the status quo; try to treat your future with Person from the Past as a secondary, separate matter.

Also: If you hear yourself saying, "Everything would be fine if only s / he would come back," then everything won't. The magic words BG wants to hear are more like: "Life's great; having him / her back would be a super-duper bonus." They are not guaranteed to be Love Potion #9 for your reflame, but their true magic is this: If s / he says no, you'll still be fine. Right?

■ The third party

Loisaida's question raises one PS: Is either of you married or otherwise attached? According to Kalish, reunions — even those initiated innocently — are highly combustible. If you feel that you must make some sort of epic play for the love of your life, I can't stop you; higher-drama things have happened, but they were on *Falcon Crest,* and lots of feelings got hurt. So proceed with caution. Okay, Tommy?

> I am middle-aged and single. Recently I got a call from my
> first love, whom I last saw twenty years ago. She is seeking

a divorce. Our lives have changed, but we both still have a flame burning. Would it be a mistake to pursue this venture?

Yep, Tommy should tread on eggshells until her walking papers are good and filed in triplicate; then they can run toward each other in a field of daisies, in slow motion. (One word of caution: She may have realized that T's her true love — but there's also the chance that she's rebounding . . . backward.)

■ This letter: Could you have written it?

> My boyfriend and I split up because he was confused and I was too dependent on him for stability. Since we've broken up, <u>I've gained a lot of self-esteem that I used to leech off of him</u> and we've been spending some time together. <u>Although I don't NEED him, I still care about him and have fun with him</u>. He seems to enjoy himself too. <u>I've dated other men, but I'm just happier around my ex. When we're together, it's just relaxed and fun</u>. Now I'm wondering if perhaps we should give our relationship another chance. Do you think this is healthy?

Refer back to the underlined passages to see why Breakup Girl said yes.

Here's the bottom line, you guys: You are fine without this person. And you'd be even finer with him/her. (Unless he is Joseph Fiennes, in which case I regret to inform you that he's saving himself for me.)

Back to the Future: Where Do I Start?

Spare the fanfare. Yes, a spectacular gesture can come from a sincere place. But when you rent an intimate nook like Madison Square Garden and hire Boyz II Men and the Dixie Chicks for a come-back-to-me serenade, the message you deliver is, "Hey! I'm gonna knock your socks off so hard, you'll forget to ask me how the relationship will be different this time!" Style's fine, but be ready to provide substance too.

IMPORTANT BREAKUP GIRL MAXIM

THE REUNION PROCESS IS MORE THAN A MATTER OF "PLEASE BE KIND, REWIND."

If you want this to work — or if you want your re-intended to listen in the first place — you can't imply that the breakup was no more than a blooper and that all it will take to get it right is to go back and recite the same lines, walk through the same motions. This approach presents no evidence — or promise of — change, commitment, clue. Nostalgia won't carry the day either.

Dear Breakup Girl,

   I thought I was over my ex-girlfriend, until New Year's Eve. She wound up lying plastered on the bathroom floor, and I, the sucker, stayed up with her, got her to bed, etc. When she woke up we started kissing and talking about old times, and she told me she loved me. I never got clear on whether it was a platonic "I love you" or the dreaded *I love you* "I love you." Do I call her and see what's up, or do I just let it ride as a party fluke?
   —Braden

Dear Braden,

   I'll tell you what kind of "I love you" I think it was, if you promise (resolve?) not to hate me.
   It was a "Wow, this guy held my hair back and took care of me all night, which reminded me of the sweet and good times we did have, which—along with the Spumanti haze—made kissing each other seem like a really good idea at the moment, which again reminded me of the sweet and good times, which, finally, for old and good times'—and Auld Lang Syne's—sake, led me to say 'I love you,'" I love you.
   Still, you want to do a quick what's-up, fine. But be prepared, just in case, to call some different numbers for Valentine's Day.
   Love,
   Breakup Girl

And finally, if you feel you must save yourself for someone, fine. I understand. If you can't put down that torch, just please, please, please find a way for it not to cast a shadow on the rest of your life. In other words: *Save yourself first.*

Dear Breakup Girl,

   My boyfriend broke up with me two months ago, after two years. We still spend the weekends together sometimes and act as if we are going out, even sleep together. But if I ask him what's up, he asks me why I have to define everything. He said he needed to break up because he feels that the only thing left for us is marriage, which he's not ready for: We're both just out of college and starting new jobs. He has debts to pay off. He told a friend that if we were both twenty-eight and stable, he would marry me in a minute.

I can wait, but it seems like I'm doing it wrong. Should I leave things the way they are, stay friends, or have no contact? We are best friends and tell each other everything. He has never hurt me. I am desperate to know if we have a chance.

 —Alice

Dear Alice,

Bad news, he's truly not ready. Good news, he may be some day. Sounds like he genuinely loves you and, simultaneously, genuinely can't deal with making the maximum commitment right now. That's why as far as hopes go, yours may not be false. Still—very important—I think the way to play this one is not to think about What's Most Likely to Get Him to Come Around, but rather, What's Most Likely to Not Make Me Insane. You don't have to cut off contact, but neither should you just play house. That way, both of your heads will be clearer in the short run. Which bodes well for the long run.

 Love,

 Breakup Girl

PREDICAMENT of the CHAPTER!

Go Away! Come Back!

Dear Breakup Girl,

My boyfriend just broke up with me, but we are still planning to take our vacation together. I did ask him if he would rather not go, but he's excited about it, and I suspect we'll have a really good time as friends if only I can remain sensible.

Well, and fashionable.

My best friend and I decided that if I was going to have any chance at winning this guy back, I'd need a new wardrobe— so several shopping trips later I am a new grrl. The real problem is how to stay sane and also charming, gorgeous, glamorous, carefree...while I'm pining for him and sleeping in the next bedroom.

—Mia

Dear Mia,

Oh, vacation girl. It's almost like you got the consolation prize on a bizarre game show: "Our winner will receive ...this spectacular engagement ring! And as for you, Mia... well, to thank you for playing, we're going to send you... to fabulous Puerto Vallarta! But, Mia, you won't be alone on those fabulous beaches, because we're sending along...your ex-boyfriend!"

But here's the thing: Breakup Girl once told someone that nothing is less romantic than a romantic vacation with someone who's planning to dump you. Let me amend that here: Nothing is more romantic than a romantic vacation with someone who just dumped you. If you think you guys aren't totally going to hook up, you're nuts. Here's the word of caution: In this situation, *Puerto Vallarta is not reality*. Whatever sunset-and-margarita-influenced episodes and influences occur on vacay...well, they *might* be evidence of a reunion on that horizon, but they might not. You've been hurt once; I just don't want you to go through the pain of dashed hopes. This means: Go with my blessing, but please, please, please apply SPF 50 liberally to your heart.

Love,
Breakup Girl

Dear Breakup Girl,

Is it so much a relationship if we break up six times a year but make up seven times over?

—Yvonne

Dear Yvonne,

That's not a relationship, that's a math problem.

Love,
Breakup Girl

BACK ATCHA
THE QUESTION
OF REVENGE

From Mesopotamia to Melrose, from Judas Maccabeus to Judge Judy, the drive for revenge has been a primary force in human / Nielsen history. It is safe to say (though Breakup Girl's college professors might have demanded some elaboration) that since the dawn of civilization, all wars — with the possible exception of the Cola Wars — have been fought on the basis of, "No one does that to me and gets away with it!" or, put another way, "Nyah nyah!"

So when you write to Breakup Girl and ask, "Hammurabi dumped me via tablet! How can I get revenge?" you are participating in the grand course of earth-moving, life-changing, history-making human events.

Then again, you'll notice that said course has not always been so grand. War is, like, bad. (When Breakup Girl wears her favorite Corcoran paratrooper boots, she is being ironic. See Double Standards, page 161.) And revenge is often, like, tacky. BG will thus not Pentagon Paper any instructions for Oreo-ing cars, nor endorse any urban legends of vengeance like that one with the photos of the bride and the best man. Wait, come back. I'll explain. And I promise that the reward — if not the revenge — will be sweet.

When Getting Even Will Get You in Trouble with Breakup Girl

First of all, what's wrong with a little good old-fashioned revenge?

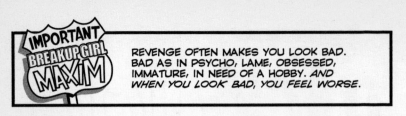

IMPORTANT BREAKUP GIRL MAXIM

REVENGE OFTEN MAKES YOU LOOK BAD. BAD AS IN PSYCHO, LAME, OBSESSED, IMMATURE, IN NEED OF A HOBBY. *AND WHEN YOU LOOK BAD, YOU FEEL WORSE.*

Indiscriminate revenge can flatter the oppressors. You are letting them know you're smarting, letting them see you sweat. Revenge — when reckless — is salt. In your wounds. And *you're* the one pouring.

But Breakup Girl does not mean to throw out the baby with the salt water. There is plenty right with *good* — emphasis added — old-fashioned (or, in many cases, high-tech) revenge. Such as: closure, justice, the last laugh, a great story. Which is exactly my point: Good revenge, while not a magic elixir, at least offers all of those possibilities.

So what *is* "good" revenge?

Revenge should not be about "getting even" — why would you want to be "even" with a scoundrel? Let us instead use the handy double entendre "getting *better*." That's *better* as in *feeling better* — and *better* as in feeling secure in the knowledge that *you are a Better Person than your unintended.* And so: *Stoop to nothing.* Instead, *raise the bar.* Living well is indeed the second-best revenge. But *moral superiority*, mesdames et messieurs, is number one. See, I'm not appealing directly to your sense of ethics, of right and wrong, of being good for its own sake. I am appealing to your ego, your packed schedule, your bank account, and — yes — your blood-thirst for vengeance. I am not telling you to maintain dignity and decorum because it's right; I am telling you to maintain dignity and decorum because it *works*.

Do not lose sight of the bottom line: Revenge is, after all, about YOU. Don't think for a second that you are going to Teach Them a Lesson or Make Them See the Error of Their Ways. I mean, you *might*, as a by-chance by-product of your plot, but it's too risky to *count* on it. I've said it before in different contexts: You can't make anyone do anything. And more importantly: Better People have better things to do.

Dear Breakup Girl,

    My boyfriend cheated on me and broke up with me for her. I had no clue. Now I just want to coolly humiliate him in front of his peers — just one calm remark that will make him

```
    look bad without making me look bad. What should I say?
        —Trying Not to Cry

    Dear Trying,
        One word.
        HIM: Uh, hey, how are you?
        YOU: Fine.
        Love,
        Breakup Girl
```

In that spirit, please take

⚡ Breakup Girl's RAT
(Revenge Aptitude Test)

When it comes to plotting revenge, BG recommends drawing up an elaborate blueprint, assembling all necessary materials (such as that bad Hell
Vortex guy on *Buffy*) — and then shelving the whole thing until/unless you
can answer yes to all questions in italics below. If you can: Plot on, dude. If
you truly can't: Remember that sometimes the mere act of going through the
motions, making the plans, and leaving it at that — plus marveling at your
own brilliance/self-restraint — does the trick.

1. *Does the alleged bad behavior actually merit revenge?* Or do I just
   feel hurt, lousy, wronged, restless? Hey, you guys: Being dumped is
   in and of itself not vengeworthy. But were there actual lies, calculated
   betrayals, veritable crimes and misdemeanors? Then we'll talk.

2. *Will this really scratch the itch?* Or just make it bleed?

3. Ask a friend: *"If I did [the revenge idea] to you, would it embarrass
   you?* Or would you be embarrassed for me?"

4. *Does the punishment I have in mind fit the crime?* Measure: level of
   magnitude, possibility of catching perpetrator at own game (e.g.,
   planting misinformation for a known snooper), opportunity to restore
   cosmic equilibrium, etc.

5. *Am I as cool as Salvia?* She writes:

```
    I fantasized about a can of orange paint spilled across his
    windshield. Going to his boss with evidence of him screwing
```

a student. Parking his schizophrenic mother on his doorstep. Instead, I went to Europe. Walked across Paris. Climbed the Duomo in Florence. Took an Italian lover. Lost forty pounds. Got my hair cut. Reclaimed my friends...and discovered that Golden Boy was never so golden in their eyes. Went to a party hosted by his boss; found out he wasn't invited. Took an American lover and stood in the sunlight while he admired me. Planned a Christmas party, and it was perfect. Planted spring bulbs. Heard from my hairdresser that he had seen me and had commented to her about how great, how really great, I looked. Got a promotion and a huge raise. Let other people know how much I care about them. The life I'm living is slowly squeezing out the hurt. It's a cliché, but it's the sweetest revenge.

⚡ Breakup Girl-Sanctioned Revenge:
Your Only Options

ReZENge

This is where you — brace yourselves — do NOTHING. (Variation: See sidebar, page 70.) Nothing in direct retaliation for the bad behavior, anyway. Trust me; this is an active response. Analogy: A friend of Breakup Girl's, when little, pitched a just-for-the-hell-of-it fit in the backseat. Friend's mom and dad did nothing. He screamed louder; still nothing. Finally, he balled his fists in unbearable frustration and demanded, "ISN'T ANYBODY LIS-TENING?" And stopped.

Brat: 0; Parents: 1.

I'm telling you: *Ignore the tantrum.* This is truly harsh, I promise. Nothing is more maddening to the fit-pitcher than the possibility that his/her bad behavior has had no effect.

Dear Breakup Girl,

When my boyfriend broke up with me, he called me every derogatory name in the book. When he finished his tirade I said, "Perhaps you should take me home." Haven't heard from him since. I thought I was taking the high road by leaving him in silence, never to speak to him again, but now I have an overwhelming urge to tell him what I really think of him. Am I allowed to mail him a hate letter, or does that falsely indicate that I care?

—Allie

Dear Allie,

    Mad props on not letting yourself get dragged into Derogatory Purgatory, where you're doomed to an eternity of "Are too!" "Am not!" Would that we all had such glacial self-restraint. But now, of course you have that urge to pipe up; you never did get your rebuttal in. At this point, though, you must run the Hate Letter Litmus Test (which also applies to hate calls). Ask yourself honestly: This stuff I want to say — *does the hate-ee REALLY need to hear it, or do I just need to SAY it?* In the latter case, say it to someone else — say, a trusty friend who's willing to stand in as a verbal punching bag. Or go ahead and write it, but give it to that friend for sending-prevention; proofread for decorum in a week. Then decide. Betcha it'll be a great read. For you.

    Love,
    Breakup Girl

In other words: People, with the possible exception of Hannibal Lecter and "Cathy," are fundamentally good. They know when they've done something bad. Their earthly purgatory is that they have to live with it. And being avenged, in a masochistic, "I deserve it" sort of way, can be oddly satisfying to them. Deny them this gift.

Dear Breakup Girl,

    Even though I'm wildly happy in my nine-month relationship, I'd like to take revenge on the rat who preceeded the Man of My Dreams. We met on a work trip, did the Deed a couple of times, and he asked me not to tell our mutual friends. Which was fine, till another of our mutual friends told me that she and he had been together for a while and he'd asked her to keep quiet. I spilled the beans and we had a good girl-power afternoon comparing notes. Then he denied to her that he and I had ever been more than friends, and they both froze me out. That kind of behavior cries out for teaching a lesson, don't you think?

    —Baffled

Dear Baffled,

    With all due respect, I am going to say the same thing to you that Breakup Mom says to Breakup Dog when she (Dog) tries to eat a rotting squirrel: "No. Drop it."

    Love,
    Breakup Girl

DO NOTHING . . . THAT S / HE KNOWS OF:
THE ART OF VICTIMLESS REVENGE

Dear Breakup Girl,

  My ex-girlfriend cheated on me, lied about it, hurt me, lied some more, and did every nasty thing in the book to me. One year later, though I was over her, the nagging desire for revenge persisted. So I installed Kai's Power Goo on my computer, pulled up a picture of her on my screen, and went to town. The warped, distorted, Edvard Munch-ish finished result can be viewed at: [BLACKED OUT BY BREAKUP GIRL CENSORS].

  Turns out that placing a hideously — and, I may add, totally unrecognizably — altered picture of her on the Internet was good enough for me...I didn't need to leave dead squid in her car, put Magic Shell on her windshield, or spread horrible rumors about her. Sometimes revenge is simple...
  — ND

This -- especially in contrast to ND's hypothetical alternatives -- is a good example of what I like to call Victimless Revenge: using the tools / technology at your disposal for Goo and not for evil. The distinction lies in (1) the fact that ND's work of art, while not flattering, is not cruel or violent, and (2) his implication that it was intended pretty much for his eyes only. Had he specifically asked me to, say, link to it from BreakupGirl.com, well, that would have been another story.

Kill with Coolness

Do something really cool; then *send word*. Of course, it *should* be enough that you are doing more than fine, but admittedly, your avengee needs to know this. Make sure the information gets to her / him. Are you listening, *Dawson's* crew? This is one of only two sets of circumstances under which you are allowed to rope a third party / messenger into your dirty work (for the other, see "Betty Currie-ing Favor," page 36).

Dear Breakup Girl,

    I want to get revenge at my ex-boyfriend because he broke up with me and then he told everybody some stuff about me that's totally untrue. Do you think I should ignore him or should I tell him that I don't accept that he's running around telling lies? Some of his friends are on my side,

which is good, but it would be better if he knew that too. What should I do?
—Matilda

Dear Matilda,

Letting him know that you don't appreciate his lying is not revenge, it's telling the truth. If you want to call him on it, be my guest. And if you do, remember that just because he doesn't act like he feels bad doesn't mean he doesn't.

As for the friends, you are allowed to play one Flaunting Card. If they're really on your side, maybe one of them will be willing to let the boy know that they don't appreciate his lying either. (Strictly speaking, this is not revenge either). But really, your best bet is to hold your head high and make it clear—just by being your bad, cool self—that whatever Rumormonger said is false. Ultimately, it's his street cred —not yours—that's most at stake.

Love,
Breakup Girl

> Breakup Girl, it warmed the cockles of my little heart to hear my ex say, "So you got a cat, you moved, is there anything else I should know . . . you got married, you have a kid, maybe?" When we were together he always criticized me for not being adventurous enough. Maybe I just didn't feel free to explore then. I had the typical post-breakup fantasies of his seeing me with a fabulous new guy. But I had no idea how good it would feel when he saw me with the fabulous new me.
> -- LIVING IT

Dear Breakup Girl,

I need to know how to get back at my ex. He's a big jerk and seems to think he's all that and more. I want to teach him a lesson he'll never forget. What should I do? (And yes, I have moved on to someone else whom I love.)
—Hope

Dear Hope,

You should move on to someone else whom you love.

Oh, wait, you did that.

Then you're all set.

Love,
Breakup Girl
P.S. But does he know that?

Derring-Dos

And yes, there's always room for the whimsical and witty. The kind of things that make your target say not, "Damn, s/he's really lost it over me," but rather, "Damn, s/he's clever!"

My fave example is from the world of work, and ooh, look, it's about me!

Wearing her reporter hat, BG once wrote an article about yummy salads in NYC restaurants. The following week, the food guy at a magazine that fancies itself a rival took it upon himself to write a mean, petty, personal article about how bad my article was. (Hi, it's about salad. Slow news day?)

My alter ego's response: Had one of the salads in question delivered to him at his office at lunchtime the next day, with a note (penned by a willing coconspirator at the revengealicious restaurant) that said, "Dear S., Eat me. Love, Lynn."

Brat: 0; BG: 1.

Oh, wait, then I wrote about it in a book.

Brat: 0; BG: 2.

But not a memoir.

Brat: 0; BG: 3.

PREDICAMENT
of the CHAPTER!

The Sorry Avenger

Dear Breakup Girl,

One month ago my girlfriend dumped me, and her reason why was that she didn't want a relationship at this point in her life. I could understand that, but when I was told that she'd started to date other guys, I flipped. I lied and told her I'd cheated on her—just to hurt her—and now all it's doing is hurting me more.

I'm not nuts—only with love. I can't tell her the truth because everyone that knows her thinks I cheated on her and she told me she can't trust anything I say to her anymore. Now that I screwed up I need to find some way to tell her that I was just lying to her about cheating on her. If you could in some way HELP me to find a way to solve my BIG problem. I've never wanted to hurt her this way; I just lost my head and I can't seem to find a way out of this mess. I don't usually ask for help, but this is huge. Tearfully,

   —K.

Dear K.,

   Oh, kiddo. Yes, coming clean will probably make a difference. No matter how gross and embarrassing it is, it's better than having this secret eat your brain.

   And what you don't realize is that you already know what to say. It might go something like: "I could understand when you told me you didn't want a relationship at that time in your life. But when I was told that you'd started to date other guys, I think I flipped. I lied and told you that I'd cheated on you—just to hurt you—but now all it's doing is hurting me more. I've never wanted to hurt you this way; I just lost my head. I'm really, really sorry."

   Breakup Girl cannot predict how your ex will react. Be prepared: She may be even madder; she may not forgive you; or worse, she may not even seem to care. Once you've come clean, all you can do is let any chips on her shoulder fall where they may.

   And after that annoyingly unsatisfying answer, let's move quickly along to why your story is so helpful. You make a better case than Breakup Girl ever could for why anything more than April Foolish lies are forbidden as revenge tactics.

   So: Let's quit lying, wreaking impulse revenge, and—hello, K.—apologizing for asking for help. We're rooting for you, K-Man. And thanks: We've looked at revenge from both sides now.

   Love,
   Breakup Girl

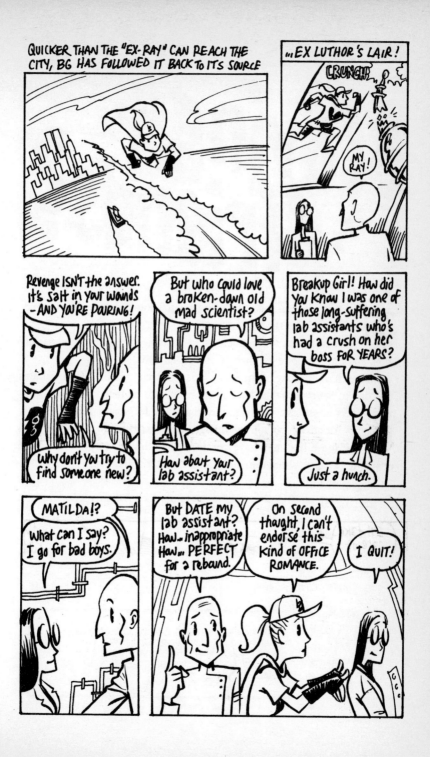

Staying Friends?

More often than not, "Let's be friends" signifies the end of a relationship, not the beginning.

Then again, look at Jerry and Elaine. They mananged to stay friends, and they're not even mature or well-adjusted.

Then again *again*, one of the many reasons Breakup Girl did not mourn the passing of *Seinfeld* is this: No longer are exes-to-be faced with the intimidating, even misleading, role model that was Jerry and Elaine's post-relationship friendship. Inspiring though their example may appear, BG believes that these two may have contributed to the prevailing fool's gold standard / imperative about remaining friends after a breakup.

But Breakup Girl!

Doesn't "staying friends" after a breakup mean that you're mature, enlightened, and civil? That you're good people? That you broke up *right?* (That you'll get back together?)

No, no, no. (*No.* And that's the one you really wanted me to say yes to, isn't it?)

Then what's "friends" for?

SOMETIMES OYSTERS (RELATIONSHIPS) HAVE PEARLS (POST-BREAKUP FRIENDSHIPS), AND SOMETIMES THEY DON'T. IF THEY DON'T, THAT DOESN'T MEAN YOU HAD A BAD OYSTER.

That is: Your ability to be friends with an ex is not a measure of your maturity or the value of the romantic relationship that went before. A post-breakup friendship, when it occurs, is a measure of a particular vibe — a two-way vibe — with a particular person under particular circumstances. Nothing more, nothing less.

⚡ With "Friends" Like This . . . ?!

Still, many of the "friendships" that folks perpetrate / connive / contrive / salvage / salivate over post-breakup are anything but. What you have may be friendship as . . .

A fix

Friendly calls, e-mails, etc. — hey, better than nothing. Or is it?

Dear Breakup Girl,

My ex wants us to be friends, but I'm torn over it. I can't imagine not seeing or speaking to him. It would be like cutting off a limb. But I'm finding myself still hanging on his calls and e-mails. If I don't hear from him for a week I get upset. I doubt there's much chance of a reunion, much as I might dream. Am I torturing myself unnecessarily? Staying friends: mature or masochistic?
   —Lilygirl

Dear Lilygirl,

Yep. Masochistic. This is not friendship, it's I Can't Believe He's Not My Boyfriend. Squeeze substitute.

Which is not necessarily the foundation for a friendship. Right now, keeping the lines of communication open means keeping the wounds open.

So ask your fix to respect that you need to cut off communication for

a little while. A "friend" should
understand that.
  Love,
  Breakup Girl

A proving ground

Staying friends, you think, will prove how kind, decorous, and grown-up you are.

And, if you are Susan's ex, how take-backable you are.

Dear Breakup Girl,
  My ex-fiancé and I seem to be having the most amicable breakup ever. He calls maybe twice a week and we talk for an hour or so. It is clear that he is trying to prove himself to me by doing all the things he should have done a long time ago and telling me about it and about his long-term plans.
  This was so much easier when I was righteously indignant with him! It's hard for us not to automatically hold hands or cuddle when we're in the same room, and when we hang up the phone he says, "Love you." I feel like a jerk not saying it back, and at the end of last night's conversation, I said it. How should we handle this?
  —Susan

Dear Susan,
  Cuddling, saying "Love you," and listening while (only) one of you shares is not under *friendship* in the BG dictionary. You're doing this because you love(d) this guy and want to be nice...but frankly, I'm not clear what either of you is getting out of it. You're proving what a great ex you are, he's proving what a great boyfriend he'd be—and you're both getting your USRDA of cuddling. Talk less, say less, drag things out less. The most amicable exes have nothing to prove.
  Love,
  Breakup Girl

> **THE FRIEND-LY MEDIUM**
>
> Post breakup, what we call a "friendship" is sometimes more like a peace treaty. Have you carved out whose territory is whose (as in: who gets the restaurant)? Yes. Are you civil to each other at parties? Yes. Do you make use of spies? Well, not that much, anymore. But are you really *friends*? Maybe not.
>
> And nothing's wrong with that. It's called being friend/y. Kosher-*style*. Dutchy-feely. And if it feels right to you, well, it's close enough.

Sometimes the mature thing is to say to yourself, "I don't need 'mature' let's-have-coffee-so-what's-new? summits to prove to ourselves how mature we both are about this whole thing." If that's really the only reason you're hanging, well: You drink enough coffee; you have enough friends.

What's left of a line

Sometimes "Let's stay friends" means nothing more than "Let's break up, but I don't hate you."

Dear Breakup Girl,

My ex and I decided to be friends, but every time I see him, he won't talk to—or look at—me at all.

Why would he agree to be friends, beg for forgiveness, and then act like a pig? He wrote this article for the student newspaper about a palm reader who told him he had a long love line, but "she didn't tell [him] when it would start." It seems as though he's out to get me or something.

Mind you, I feel fantastic, I look better than I've ever looked, and I have a lot of new hobbies and friends. But I don't have a decoder ring for his behavior, so I need your help, BG!

—Indifference Is the Coldest Emotion

Dear Indifference,

Nothing to decode. He is not being a "pig." He is being uncomfortable (one of the chief attributes of exes). And one of the chief attributes of the other ex is attempting to "decode" plain-as-day behavior.

About the article: He was fudging/finessing/obscuring the personal stuff for the sake of the story. Reporters do that. For good, not for evil. What, you would have preferred that he write about your breakup? I think not.

Meanwhile, you say you feel fantastic. Hair, hobbies, hangouts. Brava. All code for "Buh-bye!" And better than exercising your overactive post-breakup imagination. You've given yourself everything you need. So now give your ex your undivided...indifference.

Love,

Breakup Girl

"Safe" sex

"Safe," as in without all that dangerous "relationship" stuff. Guys, this is not a friendship, it is a relapse (see page 55). Do it if you must, but call it what it is.

From "More Than Friends" to More Than "Just"

But I'm not saying it can't happen. Why, some of my best friends are ... my exes. In fact, when these friendships do work, it's often because they find room to flourish when the "Should we break up?" question is finally resolved ("Yes") for the doubting, stressing partner. You know: *Phew*. Or because what you realized in the process of dating and de-mating was that you really were never more than friends in the first place.

Still, it's not going to happen overnight, especially if your new "friend" just happens to stay overnight. And even after ... a fortnight, say, don't expect this ex-turned-friend to be just like your others. You can have a friendship, yes — even a profound one — but it may always be a different flavor from the rest. Certain things only you two can talk about (dating each other); certain things you can't (dating other people). You'll have to sort it out as you go. How? Or, as Chris asks:

> One of the things my ex said in her "Can I talk to you?" talk was "We can still be friends." Not having had this work in the past, I don't know how — but I don't despise her the way I have other exes, and so far we're getting along well. What now?

Well, these new friendships have to be built on something other than "Wow, remember that incredible sunset in Capri ... buddy?" You already have a past and you can't change that, but there has to be some new fuel, some new context, for your new-and-different relationship. So here's the plan:

> "I have definitely found that the time to be friends is when you don't really care if you're friends or not. That sounds weird, but when all the feelings that drive you to be friends right after a breakup are gone (missing each other, residual attraction, etc.), then that's the time to try a friendship."
>
> —E. A.

1. At first, limit your interactions to occasional activities, such as movies, that don't require much communication.

That way you may be able to start practicing going through the motions of the friendship without putting undue pressure on the *e*motions.

2. Remember: It won't be the same. Don't expect it to — it isn't. So you might as well make it different: If you guys always went to foreign films, go see some kick-ass American blockbuster. If you always played mini golf, go see monster trucks.

3. But if it starts to feel (see above) like you're forcing a fit to just to prove something — or just to get a damn-s/he's-cool fix — then back off. You will miss your, um, friend, but you will also have an ex whom you don't despise. And you know what? That's actually plenty.

PREDICAMENT of the CHAPTER!

So *That's* What "Friends" Are For

Dear Breakup Girl,

   My ex was over moving my furniture the other night — I swear it was just a favor — and this guy that I've been dating on and off for a month and a half found out... and bailed. We were getting along so well... but now he says he "needs space." I don't understand — what should I do?

   — Patricia

Dear Patricia,

   First of all, I think moving heavy furniture is a very good thing for an ex to do. Second, I assume he wasn't, say, moving his stuff into your place. Finally, if guy #2 "needs space," why not send your ex over to move his furniture out?

   Seriously. If you really do have a just-movers relationship with your ex, then Dating Boy is overreacting — but I can see why he might have been intimidated. Furniture moving is not a delicate favor, but it is an intimate one. So give Mr. Space one clear, pressure-free phone call just to let him know that you see why that could have been weird and that you'd be happy to see him again if and when he'd like. And next time, do your own heavy lifting.

   Love,

   Breakup Girl

MOVING ON
FOR REAL

You guys have *no clue* what "moving on" (or "over it") actually means. If you knew, maybe you'd do it more often.

Or more likely — and even better — you'd realize *you already have.*

You think Over It, Moved On, and all those other closure terms mean that your ex has been totally "erased," Schwarzenegger-style, from your past.

No.

Here is a very important inspirational speech.

Does "over" him/her mean that we are indifferent? Does it mean we never think of him/her? Does it mean that our ex can tiptoe through our minds in the dark, silent, unnoticed, without knocking anything over? Hardly.

Here's what "over" means: Gone, yes. Forgotten, as if. Butterflies when we think of that person, maybe always. The difference is this: The itty-bitty "over" butterflies flit around and whisper, "Ooh, ooh, looky looky, there's that person who was a big part of my life...." "Oooh, ooh, I feel tingly and also sad."

That's all.

They are not icky moths that hang out and chew holes in stuff.

Here it is without all the lepidopterous mumbo jumbo: When we're over someone, we may still have feelings for/about him/her, but those feelings don't interfere with anything; they don't make us act on them. The feelings are just there. Of course they are. Our whole beings and minds are made up of patchworks of memories and networks of triggers. Everything, every moment, reminds you of something else. That's how we tick — it's just that some of those ticks sting. And this person is/was part of your life; at some level, s/he's hardwired in. So it's not about purging him/her fully, forever

and ever. It's about, little by little, being able to ignore, override — and one day not even notice — the bleeps.

And how do you do that? To some degree, you just decide to. Or at least to start. It's an act of will (your own, not your ex's, as you will see below). It's also a matter of defining your terms. . . .

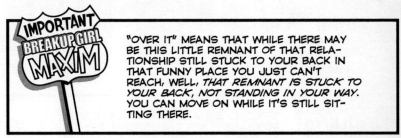

"OVER IT" MEANS THAT WHILE THERE MAY BE THIS LITTLE REMNANT OF THAT RELATIONSHIP STILL STUCK TO YOUR BACK IN THAT FUNNY PLACE YOU JUST CAN'T REACH, WELL, *THAT REMNANT IS STUCK TO YOUR BACK, NOT STANDING IN YOUR WAY.* YOU CAN MOVE ON WHILE IT'S STILL SITTING THERE.

In fact, you should. We do ourselves a disservice by lying around in traction waiting to feel 110 percent better. It's also called protecting yourself from getting hurt again. But at some point you have to acknowledge that we are all walking wounded. And that at some point you just have to get back out there, sling, eye patch, crutches, and all. And curl up with this book when you just don't feel like it.

SPECIAL BG MOVING-ON MAXIM 1
DON'T WORRY ABOUT GETTING OVER IT YET. JUST WORRY ABOUT GETTING THROUGH THIS TIME.

Dear Breakup Girl,

I've been in love with this man for four years. He's been unreliable, I've sworn never to see him, then he gets lovable, etc. Old story. Two nights ago he told me he's getting back with his ex.

I know: Get over him, move on. But I miss him. Everything I like to do reminds me of him (or her — every time I see a redhead now, I want to spit). And I'm so tired. I could take a class, I could go out, I could this, I could that, but it all feels like filling time until either he comes to his senses or I die in my apartment with my cat. Got any chicken soup for my soul?

—Christine

Dear Christine,

    You wrote this two nights after you got the news...versus four years of being in love. Right now it's not about getting over him, it's about getting through this time (and about looking only at black-and-white pictures of me). Go ahead and be tired, feel how you feel; allow things to be messy, difficult. A stiff upper lip now will only crack later. And eventually, when you're ready, we'll sign you up for that class. Maybe cooking.

    Love,

    Breakup Girl

SPECIAL BG MOVING-ON MAXIM 2
RESOLUTION IS A ONE-PERSON, DO-IT-YOURSELF JOB. OTHERWISE, YOU'D STILL BE IN A RELATIONSHIP.

As Ms. Scarlet wrote:

> I am desperately trying to reach closure, but I don't know how to do it without answers from him.

Again, again, again, as infuriating as this is, *answers from your ex are not where to look.* No one else, not even Breakup Girl, can finish your business for you. No fair having closure be contingent on a yet-to-be-had conversation or piece of information from you-know-who. No fair saying, "I can close the book on this relationship if and when I receive an itemized 'Why' list in triplicate." If you have specific questions, go ahead and pop them, but: The "answers" and your closure are unrelated. *Nothing your ex can say or do, short of coming back — and maybe even not that — will automatically tie things up with a magic bow.* Having resolution depend on a fantasy (which is, hello, what that is) is an excellent way to not achieve resolution. Which is an excellent way to have only blame, hurt, and gloom on your dance card.

And while you're at it, consider this: Isn't it possible that some "answer" from him/her could raise — even create — brand-new hey-wait-a-minute, you-felt-that-way, you-thought-I-did-what, how-come-you-didn't-bring-this-up-before? issues to resolve.

So make the answers up yourself.

Dear Breakup Girl,

My now-ex was going through a divorce when we started dating. A no-no, I know, but I'd waited two years after my own divorce, and *I* was ready.

Sure enough, he told me he needed more space than he'd realized. I didn't speak to him for months, until he called to tell me his divorce was final. He said he'd call me that night. Three months later, he hasn't called back.

I have tried to date people, but I haven't clicked with anyone. Will I ever be over him? I still do stupid things like check my voice mail, expecting something from him. Is this because we didn't really finish our business? Is he trying to put his life together so we can get back on track again?
—Tracie

Dear Tracie,

You're doing better than you think. Your heart and brain seem to be behaving normally; it's just that they're not always in sync. And the mail madness may indeed be related to the fact that you guys never did overtly seal the envelope and toss it in the dead-letter file.

Why didn't he call? What's he doing now? Who knows? You know how whacked your feelings and actions can be after a divorce. So guess what: You're going to have to decide *for* him. Give yourself the answers. Make it up. Invent your own plausible, noninsulting, nonblaming explanation for his vanishing act, and stick to it. And be patient with yourself. You may not get the mail you want right now, but you will get that click again.

Love,

Breakup Girl

At least read from this cue card: "Well, I don't have all my questions answered nor all the abject apologies I wanted, but heck, life is messy, and it's up to me and only me to find the wherewithal to move on." Which brings us to:

SPECIAL BG MOVING-ON MAXIM 3
DON'T WAIT FOR A FEELING. OVER IT IS AN ACT OF WILL.

As In Need of a Lobotomy wrote:

I went out with this girl for nine months and I was the happiest I've ever been. So here I am writing to Breakup Girl ONE YEAR after our breakup asking for someone to hit me on the head so I'll forget her. She's nice to me, but I wish she'd be mean. Why haven't I moved on?

Yes, indeed, wouldn't breakups be a cinch if they happened only with loathsome trolls? And if our hearts didn't act with minds of their own? Our minds don't help either: They expect that much-sought-after "moved-on" feeling to hit like a lightning bolt (or, in this case, a smack on the head).

However. While "moved on" is partly something that Just Happens as time passes (honest!), it is also partly a decision that you Just Make, no matter how you feel. In fact, you know that perky scientific factoid about how when you force your mouth into a smile, you trigger happy hormones? Sometimes forcing your bad self into a date just might send the right signals to the moving-on lobe of your brain. Even with movie prices being what they are, it's still a better deal than a lobotomy.

⚡ Other Obstacles to "Over It"

Charting your progress against your ex's

Dear Breakup Girl,

My boyfriend broke up with me three months ago. We remained close friends and are going to the prom. Then he drops the bomb that he is seeing someone and is that okay? I feel heartbroken because I didn't think he was moving on quite yet. If I am "supposed" to move on and am not, then does that mean that this love that I have fallen into is meant to be?
— Jolene

Dear Jolene,

Well, are you still going to the prom with him? 'Cause no, you're not. Not because you're punishing him—he's entitled to "move on," though it would be considerate of him to do it in Alaska . . . unless you live in Alaska, in which case, I don't know, Maine—but just because . . . it will suck.

More important, maddening as it is, it doesn't Mean Anything that he's seeing someone and you're not. Remember this

SEEING SOMEONE NEW AND HAVING MOVED
ON ARE UNRELATED. APPLES AND . . . BLUE.
SOME FOLKS SEE NEW PEOPLE *BEFORE*
THEY'VE MOVED ON; SOME PEOPLE FIND
THAT HAVING TRULY MOVED ON MEANS NOT
SEEING ANYONE AT THE MOMENT.

You know? So don't drive yourself nuts trying to chart your
"progress" against his. Short of moving to Alaska/Maine, do
what *you* need to do to move on.

Love,
Breakup Girl

Sleeping together

Dear Breakup Girl,
    The first time my ex and I saw each other after our
breakup, we had each lost about sixty pounds. He got a great
haircut that totally changed his look. We were both much happier as well. So we slept together.
    What I just wanted to say, and to pass on to your read-
ers, is this: The reason it's a bad idea to sleep with your
ex is NOT that you will despise yourself the next day. The
reason is that you will remember what it was about him/her
that you fell in love with in the first place (that smile!
that sense of humor!) and it will reopen old wounds you
thought were healed. You will basically go through all the
emotional work of breaking up all over again. That, as well
as resisting the siren song of possible reconciliation and
trying again. Don't do it! It's not worth it! Unless you're
the kind of person who also likes to hit him/herself over
the head with large heavy objects. Being over someone is a
precious, and precarious, thing that should hopefully last
forever. Even the greatest sex doesn't last that long.
    —A Somewhat Wiser Susan

Annoying your ex

Dear Breakup Girl,
    My boyfriend and I broke up about two weeks ago. I'm try-
ing to get over him, but I get urges to call him at work

(which I end up doing); he tells me to leave him alone, but I can't. What can I do to forget him or get over him?
   —Augustus

Dear Augustus,

People like to speculate about what it is that separates humans from the cheetahs and the chickadees. Is it the capacity to laugh? To measure time? To fork over four dollars for a mediocre macchiato? Here, as far as BG is concerned, is what makes us different from our animal neighbors: *We do stuff we know we'll regret.* Dare I say, in fact, *because* we'll regret it. Perhaps we've developed and enveloped ourselves in so many creature comforts that we can afford a self-fulfillingly self-destructive complex here and there. Keeps the gene pool interesting, I hear.

Augustus, I know you are smarting hard and I am so totally sorry. But the above paragraph and I are here to tell you that the thing that's driving you nuts—calling him at work even though you know both of you will hate you when you do—is the thing that makes you human. Self-flagellation, self-torture, ordering your bad self a hot fudge sundae with a side of guilt. He was your boyfriend, you miss him, you feel bad, you call him, you feel worse. Voilà. Impulse calls are totally normal...

...but not advisable. The way to get over him is to not call. Designate a patient friend to stand in for the doofus loser hose beast who dumped you. Next time you want to call the ex, call the friend and say what you were going to say. (Alternative: Write it down.)

Now I know this is like telling the dieter to keep carrot sticks at his desk so he won't eat M&Ms ("IF CARROTS TASTED LIKE M&MS, I WOULDN'T HAVE THIS PROBLEM!"). I know calling your friend is not hearing His voice. But your friend's voice will not say "Leave me alone." And, though you may not feel appreciably better when you hang up the phone with the friend, you will not feel bad. 'Cause right now you can kill the urge only by killing time. And each step away from the phone is another step closer to "over him."
   Love,
   Breakup Girl

Not having had the last word

Dear Breakup Girl,

My boyfriend and I have broken up five or six times over the past four years. After the last breakup we decided to be "friends" but started having four-hour cybersex sessions. Perhaps I can be forgiven for thinking that this was going to be the beginning of the NEXT phase of our relationship...until last week, when I flat-out asked him if he was seeing someone else and he said yes. When I said, "You've been having those conversations with ME and seeing someone else?" he told me to stop giving him my "self-righteous routine."

WHY CAN I NOT SEEM TO GET HIM OUT OF MY SYSTEM? Thanks for any insight you might have: Your Web site, Jonathan Kellerman books, and Häagen-Dazs Dulce de Leche ice cream are the only things keeping me going right now.

   — Perpetua

Dear Perpetua,

For my money, here's what you're stuck on: the fact that, after this final falling out, he didn't say those three little words. As in: "You are right." I know you've got four years of history stored up too, but this last "self-righteous" incident is sticking out on top of the pile. You are fuming. You want to fix it and you can't; you want to fix him and you can't. That, my dear, you're just going to

---

GETTING THE DIGITS

OVER WHOM?

• BG readers say the biggest obstacle to getting over someone is, well, still being in love with him / her.

• When asked how they knew they were over someone, most women responded: "Started dating someone who was not an Ex Substitute"; most men responded -- uh-oh -- "N/A. Yet."

• Most women said "Radio silence" tipped them off that their ex was over them. Fifteen percent of men and women said it was "Just a feeling I got from seeing the wedding invitation."

• NB! A statistically insignificant number of respondents said a "relapse" helped them move on!

• Also hardly a surprise: They say, "Cliché but true: TIME" is the biggest factor in getting over someone. Someday you people in the thick of it will check that answer off too.

• But how long? A majority -- 48 percent -- said "Half or less as long as the relationship lasted." Twenty percent, "reaching for Kleenex," checked "N/A."

have to ball your fists and accept. This is good news: You get to focus on that much more bite-size task (as opposed to figuring out if you're crazy, which you're not). And if one of those fists wants to hold an ice-cream scoop at first, be my guest; just don't drip on the keyboard.

Love,

Breakup Girl

P.S. "You are right."

PREDICAMENT of the CHAPTER!

How to Fall Out of Love

Dear Breakup Girl,

I have been in love with my girlfriend for four years. Unfortunately, she has decided she is no longer in love with me. We have lived together the entire time. She is my life. How in the heck am I supposed to fall out of love with her?

—Rich, Lost in Love

Oh, Rich,

You can't cause yourself to fall out of love as easily as you can cause yourself to fall out of, say, a hot-air balloon. What you can do is *allow* yourself to fall out of love. If she's really gone, don't fight it. If you hear yourself saying things like, "But Breakup Girl, no one will ever be like her!" stop. I know that's how you feel, but it's not, like, True with a capital *T*.

You can also create the circumstances that will, over time, help you allow yourself to fall out of love. If you're in the apartment you shared, get rid of her stuff. If you're in a new apartment...get rid of her stuff. Don't hang out with her friends. If her name was Monica, Rachel, or Phoebe, don't watch *Friends*. You see what I'm getting at?

And if she is/was your life, then you've got to refill that gap. If you guys never, say, cooked together, take a cooking class. Rent the movies she vetoed. Get a dog. Learn Italian. Go Rollerblading. And when you're ready to move on—which, granted, may take a while—go Rollerblading with the dog.

Love,

Breakup Girl

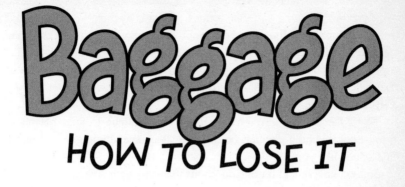

Baggage
HOW TO LOSE IT

Before I send you off on further dating travels / travails, I must stop and help you claim your baggage for what it is: a lot lighter than you think.

See, even though you may have declared yourselves "moved on" from A Certain Person, you guys are still packing and lugging around all sorts of heavy, bulky stuff. Saying, "Ooof, I had a breakup, now I have baaaaaggage" is pretty much a meaningless, last-millennium thing to say — like "insecure," "fear of commitment," etc. And also a great way to disengage and have more breakups. But listen, in a strictly statistical sense (and in a Bizarro world where people get married only once), all relationships but one come to an end. Many (conducted by people unacquainted with Breakup Girl) end badly. That is all sucky, but it is how things go. Breakups do not equal "baggage," you all. *Put. It. Down.*

Otherwise you'll sound like Jason:

```
I know I will heal through time and be a much stronger per-
son. I don't know if I will ever love again, but I will be
wise enough never to be hurt like this again.
```

Granted, our Jason was smarting from a harshisimo breakup that he felt he should have seen coming. We all use such standard, pain-based statements as our Strategic Defense Initiatives. But if you go around "protecting yourself from hurt" (as if!), you will also protect yourself from...*love*. *LIKElike,* even. Also, *fun.* Oh, and *life.*

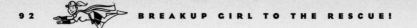

I want you guys to be like — I can't believe I'm about to say this — that gal in *Annie* who sings the verse of "NYC" that starts, "N...Y...C! Just got here this morning..." She strides forward, awestruck, thrilled, and nervous, drops her valises, and belts it out. She is about to enter a whole new megalopolis filled with pals and thugs, sailors and suitors, mystery, madness, energy, and people who will carry her luggage for her if she stays in the right place. Got that? *She drops her baggage — though it does stay by her side — to sing.*

That's the last *Annie* reference. But I will continue to mix metaphors throughout this brief chapter, because the "baggage" thing gets old really fast. Much like yours.

So. A couple quick, routine questions to ensure your safety:

⚡ Did You Pack Your Baggage Yourself?

Yes, you did.

> Dear Breakup Girl,
>   I have been played in all of my relationships. I have a new girlfriend who seems nice, but with my luck it will bomb. How can I be sure she won't play me like all the rest?
>   —Been Played

> Dear Played,
>   You *can* be sure she will play you "like all the rest." *Because that's the way you see relationships.*
>   What you are experiencing, Played, is *life*. What you, being human, are doing to make sense of it all, is calling it "my luck." You've issued the statement "I Am a Person Who Gets Played in Relationships." And so, in each relationship you get into, whatever its demise, you say to yourself, "There you go. I got played." Otherwise, you'd have to take responsibility, instead of blaming "all the rest." Scary. So how about issuing this statement: "I Am a Person Who Does His Best to Make Relationships Work." Now get in there and be a boyfriend, not a bull's-eye for the bomb.
>   Love,
>   Breakup Girl

Or, without mentioning *Annie*, we can set that statement to music.

Dear Breakup Girl,

I went out with a girl who cheated and lied. I forgave a lot until I finally threw her out.

I have "issues" with my dad leaving us when we were young, etc. I trusted her; she betrayed me. How do I deal with the baggage of the past and learn to trust new people in my life?

—El Gato

Dear El Gato,

Write on the blackboard a hundred times: "MY GIRLFRIENDS HAVE NOTHING TO DO WITH MY PAST. THEY WEREN'T THERE." Remind yourself that—on an easy-for-BG-to-say logical basis—Cheating Girl is unrelated to Splitting Dad. Two different people, two different situations; *you* are drawing and per-petuating the link.

Or: When Dad split, you decided, "Yikes! Can't trust peo-ple." This notion becomes the theme song you whistle through life...and as you choose girlfriends. Maybe you choose peo-ple whom you secretly know aren't Girl Scouts. Anyone else would clash with your theme song! See?

So what you need is a new theme. How about "Things have happened in my past that seem to follow a pattern...but they don't have to have any bearing on the next thing that hap-pens! It's all up to me! La la la!" Hey, at least BG didn't make you write it on the blackboard.

Love,
Breakup Girl

Is It a Big Heavy Bag That You're Hitting Yourself Over the Head with, *Three Stooges* Style?

Yes, it is.

Dear Breakup Girl,

Finally extricating myself from a horrible relationship. It's awful feeling like I've wasted so much time "working" on it. I feel guilty for letting elation and infatuation drown out the alarms. Now do I have to become cynical and build will in order to achieve a healthy relationship? Or will I punish the next guys for what I've been through? Seems like after I'm already sucked in I find out things that would have eliminated someone at the start, but by the time the

"bad stuff" is evident, I'm in love and want to make it work!
I dread the thought of going through this all over again.
   —Flip Flop

Dear Flip Flop,

   Boy, are you being hard on yourself. Should you have lis-
tened to the alarms and left the building? Maybe, but heck,
maybe they were false. Who knows, maybe all you heard was
the clang-clang of impending commitment. Have you wasted your
time? Maybe, but for everyone who does that there's someone
else who bails without trying, or who skips over
elation/infatuation and heads straight for Sturm und Drang.
Are you destined to build walls, exact punishment, root out
"bad stuff" too late? Good questions to ask, but they're
rhetorical. You've had a bunch of relationships, too short,
too long, too...whatever. Sounds to me like: life. Go have
one.

   Love,
   Breakup Girl

Relationships:
BEFORE

I have no intention of scooting you into a relationship as an end
in itself. Instead, I labor to Make the World Safe for Singles —
to help you shrug off the icky bridesmaid's dress / tacky
cumberbund of a feeling that single, as fun and free as it can be
these days, is still pre-attached, pre-married, Plan B.

The real problem with today's "Hooray for Singles"
atmosphere (which has its very own ozone hole right over my
parents' house), though, is that it makes us defend ourselves
on both sides of the aisle. We have to say both (a) "I went to
the opera alone, AND I'M REALLY OKAY WITH THAT,"
and (b) "I'd prefer not to die alone and childless, AND I'M
REALLY OKAY WITH THAT." But what on earth is wrong
with wanting a partner? This is why I'm also striving to make
the world Safe for Searching.

In fact, let's make it a search *party*.

DATING 101

BREAKUP GIRL's *Rules*

Things used to be so much simpler. Boy met girl at sock hop, girl waited by phone, boy took girl out for sundae, boy asked girl to go steady, boy asked girl to marry him (after checking with girl's dad), boy and girl settled down in Stepford.

Today, girl meets boy at Gender-Bender Nite at Click + Drag. Girl gets boy's beeper number. Girl hacks into FBI system to perform background check on boy. Girl wonders how long to wait before inviting boy to her home page. Girl meets boy's roommate. Girl likes roommate better. Girl asks roommate to marry her. Roommate's two mommies grant blessing.

In this Technicolor culture, where the politics of dating are one huge gray area, we crave the black-and-white code of hard-and-fast rules. No wonder books claiming to contain *the* rules have filled bestseller lists — many among them take us back to a nice, simple time when men were from Mars and women didn't seem to care. But in Breakup Girl's megalopolis, you'll be pleased to hear, the rules of dating are timeless. They do not involve politics; they do not involve planets. Instead:

IMPORTANT BREAKUP GIRL MAXIM

"THE RULES," LADIES AND GENTLEMEN, ARE MANNERS.

I don't mean complicated fork systems and all that stilted stuff. I mean respect, graciousness, civility: for other people *and* yourself. See, Hillary

Clinton consults Eleanor Roosevelt; BG consults Miss Manners (who, I hasten to add, is very much alive and well). Though the increasing popularity of yoga seems to have made New Yorkers a tad less snappish, I agree with the divine Miss M. that the decline of polite, dignified behavior has contributed to the decline of human relationships and society at large.

Reminds me of a passage from Patricia Wells's divine book *Divine Secrets of the Ya-Ya Sisterhood*. Daughter complains to Mom that she "doesn't know how to love." Her mom says: "Good God, child!…Do you think any of us know how to love?…Do you think anybody would ever do *anything* if they waited until they knew how to love?…*Forget love*. Try good manners."

Quit tripping yourself up over things like, "I just don't know how to do this dating thing! Aw, forget it." Or: "What would be the suave, irresistible, perfectly executed way to make my move?" Instead, ask yourself: What would be the polite/considerate/kind move to make?" (Should things go awry, don't ask yourself: "What bad behavior will love — or lack thereof — excuse right now?" Ask yourself: "What good manners will make this mess easier for everyone right now?") It's a start.

Think that sounds square? Think again (please). In a world dulled and chilled by haste and hate, trust me, manners are *hot*.

BREAKUP GIRL'S RULES OF DATING

1. Be nice.
2. Take "no" for an answer.
3. Whoever invited pays.
4. No dates at Hooters.

I'm telling you, if everyone followed these rules in all relationships (romantic and otherwise) there would be no war. Other than that, you will always give the best, most sincere impression if you always do what feels appropriate and comfortable for you (however "comfortable" it is to put your heart on your sleeve and your pride on the line). Date on, dudes.

⚡ OK, But Can You Talk Us Through Some of the Basics?

Right. We're off to a good start, but for me to leave you without specifics would be, well, rude. So here are answers to some frequently asked questions you may or may not want to ask more frequently.

1. How do I meet people?

> Dear Breakup Girl,
>   I wish I *were* writing you about a breakup, as that would presuppose having had a relationship. Where do I start?

To maximize your returns, you need to diversify your portfolio. Meaning: Don't just answer personals, don't just go to "events," don't just join groups/clubs, don't just ask friends to set you up, don't just sit home alone and watch *Point Break*, again. *Do a little of everything.*

Yes, this approach is partly pure math: increased probability. But it's not just BG telling you to Do More Stuff. Far be it from me, in fact. That's one of the copious ironies of *The Rules*'s global-domination strategy: The whole point, they say, is to live your life for Numero Uno and be so busy and fulfilled that you're not focusing unduly on men — and evidently the way you do that is by reading *The Rules*, keeping a The Rules journal, attending The Rules support groups, using The Rules calendars and notebooks and lipsticks (made none of that up) . . . no wonder you don't have time to return his call!

As Bridget Jones resolves in her diary: "Develop inner poise and authority and sense of self as woman of substance, complete without boyfriend, as best way to obtain boyfriend."

But you can't not at least get out there and try, with some degree of gonna-meet-someone deliberateness. Because doing *only* those "I'll concentrate on me," um, self-actualization projects will, arguably, bring you only virtual partners.

So when I say "Do a little of everything," maybe what I mean is "Do everything you do a little more." With a heightened sense of awareness. Whatever you do, you do 100 percent for you. Then tack on a bonus 10 percent wherein you look out for a mate for you. In other words, you are there at the museum to see the art, period (100 percent); also, who's that hottie by the Hopper (110 percent)?

That third eye is what will get you your first date.

It's also what spots one-step-removed opportunities. Did somebody say kayaking? I've always wanted to try that. You're going where? Yum, let's get a bunch of people together. Here, let me help you with that. I spy: a chance to branch.

This approach is what will set you squarely down on what BG calls the "Flirtation Continuum," where there is no longer a vast gulf in your life between Me Projects and Mystery S / He Projects; where you keep a general flirty, fizzy buzz going as an end in itself; where, thus, no one venture is the be-all — well, end-all — of your love life as you know it. It's a little zing, all the time. Keeping in mind, as always, the tenets of basic decorum (ruling out, say, being on the make at a wake), the whole world — not just SingleRama 2000 Happy Hour Madness — can become your . . . SingleRama 2000 Happy Hour Madness.

Getting yourself out is also a matter of getting the word out. Selectively.

> ## GETTING THE DIGITS
>
> ### USING THE DIGITS
>
> • Most BG readers say they wait one day between First Meeting and First Phone Call.
>
> • Where to meet? Most men and women, gay and straight, say it's hardest to work their mack at bars -- a majority say "happenstance" (random friends of friends, etc.) works best.
>
> • How long does it take to sense whether or not there's a future? Twenty-eight percent say three dates, 41 percent say three months, 26 percent say one marriage, and 14 percent say one spelling error.

Dear Breakup Girl,

At work I sit next to an attractive guy named Sam. I could go for him, but that's not the point. He just broke up with his girlfriend and has FOUR DATES this week—three of which are fix-ups from friends' parents. Ignore what this says about his reboundness. What does this say about his networking abilities versus mine? Is there some Jewish circle I'm not in on? What do you think about getting the word out?

    —Nice Girl

Dear Nice Girl,

Yeah, he's a good networker. Either that or some high-speed YentAlert went out, via bulk e-mail or phone tree, when Sam the JM became S.

> As for you, ask around. NOT VIA BULK E-MAIL OR PHONE
> TREE. Tell select friends (and parents of friends, I guess)
> you're looking. People who know you well. People who know
> other cool people. People, actually, who might know Sam.
> Love,
> Breakup Girl

Also: schedule, schmedule. Get creative. There's always a way.

> Dear Breakup Girl,
> My ladyfriend recently told me adios. I'm forty-three,
> work 2 a.m. to 9:30 a.m. My prospects are nil. I'm not a bar
> guy; I'm not aggressive. I like myself, think I'm a great
> catch. Give me some advice I can use.
> — Peter

> Dear Peter,
> Start a social group in your community called People with
> Weird Schedules and the People Who Love Them. There must be
> people in the same predicament who are dying to attend an
> *E.R.* Pancake Breakfast. Advertise in the paper, at the store,
> on the Web. And keep at it: I read about a group for tall
> folks in NYC whose first meeting had six people; now they
> rent convention halls. Good luck!
> Love,
> Breakup Girl

Someone wrote me from Chicago to say he did this. And it worked. More thinking outside the box = less sitting inside your house. (And, ideally, fewer dates with dolts who use jargon like "thinking outside the box.")

2. How do I ask someone out?

First of all, I'm glad the question is "how," not just "should." Please err on the side of popping the question. There are lots of folks out there — guys especially, given the climate of unfounded fear about crossing some actionable line — who do all sorts of e-maily, cally, friendy, huggy, back-rubby, "we should hang out"-y things without ever making an Actual Move. There's something to be said for working up to it, but at some point, that kind of flirting crosses the line into *flitting*. Which is what gnats do. So.

Related pep talk: *If you are pleasant and respectful* when you ask someone out, you will not scare them. You might not *interest* them (sorry), but, I repeat: *You will not scare them.* If on the off chance you do, it's because you triggered something (say, a memory of someone with that exact same freckle pattern, who scared them) that was beyond your control. But if you are nothing but nice, then that's how they'll take it. Even if you don't take them out.

So ask away — especially after reading pressure-reducing

IMPORTANT BREAKUP GIRL MAXIM

WHEN YOU ASK SOMEONE OUT, DO NOT "BE YOURSELF."

Pressure reducing? You'll see.

Dear Breakup Girl,
    There is this girl in my class who I want to go out with. We have common interests, but I can't seem to be able to ask the question. Tell me how to act, what to say, stuff like that. And if you're going to say, "Be yourself," don't bother because that won't do a thing.
    —Steve

Dear Steve,
    Oh, definitely don't be yourself. Do you think anyone is "themself" when they ask someone out? It's one of the most artificial, made-up, goofball things we do. I mean, what "ourselves" would say is, "I am totally hot for you and I dream of you all the time, and you'd be crazy to go out with me since you are, like, czar of the universe, but forget all that—will you marry me?" What we really say is, "Would you like to go see *Princess Mononoke*?"
    So what should your bad self do? Ask her an artificial, made-up, goofball question like, "Would you like to [do that common interest we have together] this weekend?" Then let this princess—or the next—get to know the real you.
    Love,
    Breakup Girl

License to not "be yourself" is not license to get someone else to do it, by the way. As Claire wrote:

I like this guy a lot. I tried to ask him out personally, but I chickened out and had someone else do it. He just says no or drops the subject or something.

Guys, guys, guys: STOP HAVING OTHER PEOPLE ASK PEOPLE OUT FOR YOU. Also, no notes. These procedures never work accurately or efficiently! I know they are standard forms of high school dating communication, but if you ask me, they should have gone out with the rotary phone. The kids on *Dawson's Creek* don't do dumb stuff like that! Then again, they're dating grown-ups. But still.

3. What am I doing wrong?

Probably not much, except thinking that you're doing something wrong.

> Dear Breakup Girl,
>   Now that I'm finally over my girlfriend, I've been interested in a few people. I talk to them, get to know them, even become friends, but when I'm about to ask the question, I find out that they're either dating someone else or otherwise unavailable (distance is the main thing, either me moving or them). Do I sense that they're unavailable and for some sick reason like that? Hard to believe—mostly I don't know that they're taken. Just today, I was talking to someone for an hour, ready to ask her out, when she mentioned that she's moving to France for a year. What the dilly?
>   —Corwin

> Dear Corwin,
>   Easy, killer. It's not necessarily "sick" to be

A DEBATE THAT'S GETTING REALLY OLD: SHOULD WOMEN MAKE THE FIRST MOVE?

Oh, for God's sake, do what you want. BUT. I will say that there's something to be said for waiting. Not because I think we should go back to the time when girls didn't ask guys out, or vote, etc. But because it's fun to get asked out! It's flattering! It's thrilling! Whee! And, more often than not, it's useful -- when he makes the first move, your preliminary guesswork is over: You know he's interested, or at least "curious" (one notch below "interested").

But the same goes both ways. If you want to be all you-go-girl about it, then go, girl. Ask him out. Once. He'll be flattered, relieved, yadda yadda yadda. If he's busy (or "busy"), you've at least made your point. Ball's in his court now. You don't have time to chase, cajole, or flatter. You've got to work on that bid for Congress.

attracted to unavailable women. Maybe you're just hot for babes who are NOT giving off the DATE ME DATE ME DATE ME MY MOTHER WILL PAY YOU vibe. Which is normal, if not advisable.

But if you really are getting to know these people, then what questions are you asking before *the* question? Obviously not questions with answers like, "I enjoy fly-fishing with my fiancé." *Ask things that will get you your data*, like, "What are you doing for the holiday weekend?"(answer will include "boyfriend," if applicable) or, "How long have you lived here?"(as in, "Three years, but I'm moving to France right after the World Cup"). See?

Also, if *you* keep moving, why are you working your mack on girls who aren't? Seems to me that you're not looking for unavailable women; you're looking for "proof" that you suck at the dating thing. That's the next thing you need to get over.

Love,
Breakup Girl

⚡ Advanced (Or Not) Dating Behavior: "Legal But Tacky"

Breakup Girl's rules allow for the important distinction "legal but tacky" (subtly different alternative: "tacky but legal"). Examples:

I. Illegal and tacky

Dear Breakup Girl,

I am a thirty-six-year-old woman who was seeing this guy, thirty, for about two months. I saw him Sunday and called him the following Tuesday evening, but he did not call back. I've called a few times to ask what's up, but nothing. I even saw him at a bar, but he ignored me. What happened?

— Janet

Dear Janet,

People! If you don't want to date someone anymore, muster the *huevos* to drop a dime. Trust me, it is uncomfortable, but it is in your best interest. When we get the call — which, after a couple months, need only be sweet and to the point — we get sad / huffy / wounded, etc. When we don't get the call, we get reason to believe that you're lame / immature / rude. *Which do you prefer?*

Love,
Breakup Girl

2. Tacky but legal

Dear Breakup Girl,

When my boyfriend and I broke up, he said we'd always be friends and that for the rest of the school year he wouldn't go out with anyone. We haven't talked since—and now he's dating one of my friends! What should I do? I want to be friends, but he broke a promise.

—Kayleigh

Dear Kayleigh,

The following is to inform you that, pursuant to your inquiry, Breakup Girl has consulted with her attorney vis-à-vis the enforcement of said "promise" (henceforth, "contract"). It appears that contracts are voidable if deemed to be unconscionably one-sided or if one of the parties agreed to said contract under duress. BG's attorney has also stated that "stupid contracts are unenforceable." Meaning: It was a dumb thing to promise—and to expect—to begin with. Hate to say it, but he was trying to be nice. His going out with your friend is tacky at worst—but legal.

Evaluate your potential friendship based on what he's like now, not on some dotted line he shouldn't have signed on in the first place.

Love,
Breakup Girl

3. Legal but tacky

Dear Breakup Girl,

Recently, my roommate broke the "roommate rule." I walked in to find him and my ex doing their thing in the living room. I don't wanna go home to more shenanigans. Do I have the right to kick him out? Are people allowed to date their roommates' exes? If so, how long should they wait before a couch-fest?

—Battered in Boulder

Dear Battered,

This behavior is technically legal, but Melrosically tacky. It is your right to ask them to take their business elsewhere. They should have thought of that. They should also have written a letter like the next one.

Love,
Breakup Girl

Dear Breakup Girl,

    I like one of my good friends. Problem is, he just broke up with his girlfriend, K., who is also a friend of mine. I know he's not over K., and it's not right to go out with a friend's ex, at least not yet. How long should I wait before asking him out?

    Jennifer

Dear Jennifer,

    Give it a couple of months. Not only out of respect for K., but also because you don't want to get jiggy with him until he has exited the rebound zone. If there really is something between you two, it'll last. At least you don't have to wait as long as Charles and Camilla.

    Love,

    Breakup Girl

PREDICAMENT of the CHAPTER!

Dating Comprehension

Dear Breakup Girl,

    I met a girl about three months ago at a singles function. She is really nice and we get along well. We've gone to a few functions together, but the signals are mixed; for example, she always seems to bring a friend along or suggest bringing a friend along. What do you suggest?

    —Wondering

Dear Wondering,

    Hate to say it, but "Would you mind if my friend came along?" is Dating Esperanto for "I like you, but I don't LIKElike you." But if other signals really are mixed—and *if* you feel like dealing—then sure, stick with the friend thing. If she changes her mind, she'll give you some other universal sign.

    Love,

    Breakup Girl

WHY?
don't I have a boy/girlfriend

A lot of us singletons make the mistake of thinking that finding someone is the hard part. And that once you do, you're set. We tend to forget that there is — ideally — a whole lifetime of Relationship Maintenance that follows. To put it another way (and to quote myself): Having a boy/girlfriend is like having a car with air-conditioning. It may be more comfortable at times, but there's a whole lot more stuff that can go wrong.

That is just one of several things I would like to point out to the many fine folks who write me to ask:

```
Dear Breakup Girl,
Why don't I have a boy/girlfriend?
```

And here's the problem: The folks who ask me that are fine folks. I mean, if they were saying:

```
Dear Breakup Girl,
    I invented the car alarm, my gums bleed when I'm nerv-
ous, and I am president of the International Jar-Jar Binks
Fan Club . . . why am I alone?
```

well, then we'd have a place to start.

Otherwise, it's hard for me to tell you precisely *why*. But I can give you some perspective about what might — or only seem to — be in your way.

Which is something everyone should have before they have a boy/girl-friend, anyway.

⚡ Why No *Ragazzo/a?**
No Rhyme or Reason

BG has made the acquaintance of plenty of people who were not conventionally good-looking or socially adept or, well, interesting — and they had boy/girlfriends. I mean, *really*. Losers have partners! How many parties have you gone to where you meet someone insufferable...and her boyfriend? How many alumni notes have you read where the most obnoxious guy in class is the first one married? Go freaking figure.

⚡ Having a Hottie for Hottie's Sake Is Cold Comfort

Boy/girlfriends, you guys, are not school supplies. (Grown-ups, just because I'm using school metaphors doesn't mean I'm not talking to you. And that's not just because I know you scope the cute notebooks and highlighters at Staples in August. High school, in a *Lord of the Flies* sort of way, is a metaphor for life.) The point here being: There's a lot of pressure — in culture (we'll get to that) and in real life (which, in a *Truman Show* sort of way, are not unrelated) — to "get" a boy/girlfriend. Having one "means" you are cool, attractive, popular, legit.

> Dear Breakup Girl,
>   I don't have a boyfriend. All my close friends do. I'm only sixteen and have kissed a few guys, but none really like me. All my friends are really pretty too, and I'm only average, so I think no guys want to settle for me. I do have low self-esteem. I'm fairly smart, but not a geek, and am in what is considered the cool group. I play in a band and have heaps of friends but can't seem to get a boyfriend. You'll probably say, You're fine the way you are, yada yada yada, but what should I do?
>   — Jayne

---

* Italian for "boy/girl" and "boy/girlfriend." Empirically, appears to be synonymous with "hottie."

Dear Jayne,

    The whole point of adolescence is to show how unique you are by being exactly like your friends, and there are all your friends with boyfriends. Plus, you've even kissed guys who haven't morphed into boyfriends. That taste of honey — with no real meal in the deal — can make you even more bitter. PLUS, yeah, it would be good if you could hook up your amp to your self-esteem.

    Which is why I'm going to say — don't freak — that you're actually not fine the way you are. Far as I can tell, you're talking about boyfriend for boyfriend's sake. I understand why, but it's not going to get you a good boyfriend. I mean, is there someone, anyone, you actually want to go out with? Someone in particular whom you feel something for?

    Then we'll talk. Or, ideally, then you two will talk. I know you're lonely; I know you're impatient. But the key is to remember that no matter how it feels, you do have a say, a stake, a choice — one that could include being alone, if there's no one around right now who does it for Miss Thing — in this matter. Get that tune in your head, and they will start to fall — not settle — for you.

    Love,
    Breakup Girl

I know this is really, really easy — if not totally obvious — for me to say, but if you look on a boy/girlfriend as your own personal Self-Worth-o-Matic, well, let's just say that's one of those gadgets with planned obsolescence.

⚡ *Dawson's Creek* Is Not Reality

Your first tip-off should be the guy in a rowboat wearing a sport jacket. Your second tip-off should be that the guy in a rowboat wearing a sport jacket went for months and months with no idea that Joey was in love with him. (Grown-ups: still talking to you too. Shut up, you totally watch it.)

    Movies and songs and TV fetishize love. Like, do the doctors on *General Hospital* actually doct? All we see and hear are people who yearn for it, who have it, who had it, who wear funny ties for it. All love, all the time. Which is kinda sorta how we feel deep down — and is what keeps BG in business — but maybe we'd have more grace under pressure and get something freaking done around here if everything in our culture weren't this big huge blinding yellow stickie in front of our face that says: "LOVE! GOT ANY

YET? HUH HUH HUH?" So yes, even Our Culture wants to know why you don't have a boy/girlfriend. But remember: You don't owe it an answer.

Dear Breakup Girl,

Well, here's yet another "I haven't had a boyfriend in __ years; am I pathetic?" letters. Except I'm nineteen and I have *never* had a real relationship. I am surrounded by dating / engaged / married friends, teen romance movies, and *Dawson's Creek*, where these younger people are far beyond my experience (I know it's just TV, but it's still depressing).

Okay. I was one of those driven, Straight-A-Activity-Girl overachievers in high school, and while that was handy in the scholarship department, it did not work wonders for my love life. It didn't bother me at the time, because I figured there was plenty of time for that Later.

Well, it's Later, and still no luck! I've seen my college friends — not to mention all those TV people — hook up while I stay single. Now I'm feeling lonely and wondering where I went wrong. Please help.

—Lonely

P.S. Am I pathetic???

Dear Lonely,

How you jump into the dating pool is: You jump into the dating pool. And as far as I know, that means: You jump into your life. Not *One Life to Live*. You already have friends, college, stuff going on. Those can be veritable boyfriend factories, if you let them. Go ahead and be Activity Girl again, but not the way you did in high school, where your main activity was Doing What I'm Good at to the Deliberate, If Subconscious, Exclusion of What I'm Afraid Of. And by the way — despite what you see all around you, which I know is galling — nineteen really isn't that old.

Love,

Breakup Girl

P.S. You are not pathetic. Asking "Am I pathetic?" more than once is getting there, though.

⚡ Shy Is Better than Loud

While I'm on the subject. Trust me.

Dear Breakup Girl,

I am seventeen years old and have NEVER had a girlfriend.
I am attracted to women and all but have never had a girl-
friend. It may be because I am shy when it comes to women.
What can I do about it?
—Andrew

Dear Andrew,
The guy on *South Park* who throws up when he talks to
girls, he's shy. Most other people are simply human. If walking up to a complete stranger and saying, "Wheredoyoubeen-
hereallmylifeoften?" is not your style, so be it. It's just
as well. So try to meet and hang out with people in situations where you already have a surer foothold, a more comfortable context. Thing is, though, when you LIKElike someone, you're *gonna* feel shy. It's part of the tingle. But take
heart, not flight: We actually think it's pretty cute.
Love,
Breakup Girl

⚡ Approachable Is Better than Stunning

Stunning makes certain people's knees weak, yes — that is, too weak to dare
walk over and start a conversation. Approachable — unlike "terrific," "great
personality!" and "such a pretty face!" — is totally a sincere, legit compli-
ment; it really means pleasant, inviting, attractive, someone I'd like to get to
know. Not just gaze at. (Also see page 122.)

Dear Breakup Girl,
I have been told many times that I look unapproachable.
I wear a lot of black (but my hair is blond); sometimes I
think that changing my look would secure me more dates, but
then I realize that I shouldn't have to change myself for
anyone. My question is not "What is wrong with me?" but "What
can I do (without totally changing myself) to make myself
more approachable?"
—Tara

Dear Tara,
First of all, changing your look in order to secure dates
will secure nothing. You might look good, objectively, at
first glance, but you won't feel right. And feeling right—
at second glance—is where first (and more) dates come from.
So let's make sure that how you put yourself together

now *does* come from your natural, most sincere happy-to-be-me — not confirmed-to-be-unapproachable — inner stylist. Do you see what I mean?

You shouldn't change yourself for anyone. But feel free to change if the way you've been wasn't true to yourself in the first place. When how you look — and act! don't let's forget that! — accurately reflects who you are, then boys who appreciate that won't just approach, they'll stampede.

Love,

Breakup Girl

⚡ Cheesy Bottom Line: It's About Chemistry

Barring certain nonnegotiable matters of personal hygiene, manners, and taste in superheroes, your appeal does not occur in a vacuum. Granted, certain things (okay, two) mean that certain people get noticed first. But as far as anything longer than one awkward, empty conversation is concerned, it's the Reese's effect: You could have perfectly good chocolate, but go figure, only certain people are going to trip over you with the peanut butter. (See, grown-ups? Talking to you. Teens will not remember those commercials.) I am talking about that elusive click. (NOT, may I remind you, that exclusive *clique* that requires a boy/girlfriend for entry.) So what to do? Well, remember that while much of that chemistry is just, like, out there...

⚡ ... Half of That Chemistry Comes from You

Which means: Don't shrink back, stung and defeated, into a spiny shell.

Dear Breakup Girl,

I want to be in a committed relationship so much and I never manage to even have a boyfriend or dates past one or two. What is wrong with me? I'm thirty, a little overweight, but I am sexy and probably more attractive than any woman who happens to be with someone I desire. Furthermore, I actually am very smart and very well-educated (abroad). My friend says I am an intellectual posing as a babe.

But everyone I am attracted to wants or is involved with someone else. The thought of being alone at Christmas is already starting to make me cry, and it's only August.

And by the way, I used to blame this feeling on where I

come from, which is a rural area. Since then, I have lived on two additional continents and in three countries, in each case looking for love (if I have to admit that). Obviously the problem is with me, and I am scared of always being alone or having to settle. Help.

—Scared and Loveless

Dear Scared,

If you're already thinking about Christmas, you're ahead of Hallmark, and that *is* scary.

Oh, and let's do away with the Intellectual versus Babe thing, shall we? It's a totally, like, false dichotomy.

Anyway. BG knows how frustrating and galling and unfair this whole enterprise can feel. But I also know that the only thing wrong with you is that you're convinced there's something wrong with you. Which, last time I checked, did not appear in *Cosmo*'s Top Ten Flirting Moves. Hence the following self-defeating phenomena:

1. *Psychology*. Consider this: *Humans would rather be lonely than wrong*. So once you decide it's hopeless, a part of you does shut down, quit trying, make sure that it stays that way. Case in point: There are attractive Taken people everywhere. Jane Perspective sees one, she thinks, "Drat!" and moves on. You see one, you think, "See? Again!" And while you're crying about another Christmas dust-biter, you don't notice the cute pizza guy. Your attitude shapes your reality. Seriously.

2. *Vibeology*. I am not accusing you of any overt tactical blunders. But I have this funny feeling that when you meet someone, there's this message running along the bottom of the screen saying, "THIS WILL NEVER WORK" or, "I KNOW WE JUST MET, BUT I CAN GET A GREAT COMPANION FARE FOR DECEMBER 23 IF WE PURCHASE BY MONDAY." Again, not Top Ten.

So just for the heck of it, try listening to your thoughts the next time you go out, the next time you see someone cute, the next time you talk to someone new. I will bet you that with a little practice, you might hear—and catch—yourself saying, "Here we go again. . . ." Then do something different. Like maybe actually having fun instead of giving up before word one.

Believe me, Scared, I'd hate to be wrong about this more than you would. Keep me posted.

Love,

Breakup Girl

So tamp down the angst and step out and go places and do things where the odds are higher that the chemistry/peanut butter/click person will be there too. And while you're playing those odds, have a little trust in fate. If you don't believe me, rent *Next Stop Wonderland*. Which also makes a powerful, lovely case for being alone, all to a balmy bossa nova beat. Rhyme/reason? No. Rhythm? Yes.

"Why Doesn't My *Daughter* Have a Boyfriend?"

Dear Breakup Girl,

I will soon be thirty. I have an exciting career, many hobbies, friends, and lots of other really cool, ultimate total stuff. I am happier than ever.

I do not have a boyfriend, a fiancé, a husband. My problem, BG?: I really couldn't care less.

My parents are doing that "You're getting up there . . ." routine. They've got their friends trying to push me out the door with their brothers, the mailman, and the local Blockbuster manager. They are saying things like, "Your standards are too high," "You don't want to be alone, do you?" and my favorite: "Aren't you concerned with starting a family?"

I have tried humor, sarcasm, yelling, and avoiding family occasions. So, BG, how would a superhero get 'em off her back?

   —Abigail

Dear Abigail,

Oh, I wouldn't get them off my back. I couldn't. That is: You can't. They are not going anywhere. You will not convince them of anything. They do/will not believe you. Mainly because much of this is not about you.

In this matter, your parents are being . . . *parents*. Which means they are worrying about their child and praying for — even enforcing, in their own "I'm cold; put on a sweater" way — her happiness. They are being as much Parents as you are being Cool Independent Single Woman. You are all just doing your jobs.

Oh, and also, THEY WANT GRANDCHILDREN. That biological grandfather clock is going *BONG-BONG*, big-time.

This suuuuuuucks, but you're going to have to smile and turn the other cheek. If you're as badass and secure and sure

as you say you are, it actually shouldn't be all that dif-
ficult.

    Love,

    Breakup Girl

PREDICAMENT of the CHAPTER!

A Masterpiece of Teen Angst

Dear Breakup Girl,

    I don't think that anyone in this whole entire universe could understand how I feel right now. You see, I'm four-teen, and there's this boy I'm so in love with. (We'll call him Z.) I've liked him ever since he moved here seven months ago. Then he started going out with this other girl, who I'm sorta friends with.

    Oh, Breakup Girl! My heart is so broken. I cry myself to sleep every single night. I'm the only one in my whole group of friends without a boyfriend. What's wrong with me? I can't be that bad! I swear, if those boys just gave me a CHANCE, I could be the best girlfriend. Nothing works. My heart is so big and loving, yet no one loves me. I'm so lonely.

    As for Z, well, I really can't get over this. When I asked him out in the beginning of the year, he said no because he didn't know me that well. But he didn't know the girl he's going out with now AT ALL! It's not fair. I truly LOVE him, with all my little shattered heart, I love him. I can hardly sleep, eat, or anything. I would do anything . . . anything for him to just love me. I know it sounds crazy, but we were meant to be. I saw them hug and I went bawling. It kills me.

    Please help me. I don't even love myself, all I do is pretend . . . pretend to be happy. I'm glad me and Z are friends, but I love him. I don't know what to do. . . . I wish I could just tell him, but then his girlfriend would be soo mad at me. I'm so nice—I swear, I could really love him . . . if I just got a chance—ya know?

    Why does no one give me a chance? Why should I have to be so lonely? What should I do? It's so hard to face him. I

just wish he could love me the way I love him.
    —Big Heart

Dear Heart,
    Oh oh oh oh!!!!!! You poor thing. Believe me, BG under-
stands. I think we all do. Right, everyone? We all have, or
have had, a Z in our lives. Or, more to the point, not in
our lives. Which SUCKS.
    But you can deal, and Breakup Girl will tell you how.
    1. I know you and Z are buds, but try and see if you can
avoid him for a while. Not in a huffy, uppity way; just don't
be around when / where he is. Seeing him—especially with Hell
Troll, I mean Her—right now is like (forgive the gross
image) picking the scab. Delaying the healing.
    2. Remind yourself that you're being a good friend and
a good person (Shut up, Breakup Girl, I want a BOYFRIEND! I
know, I know, bear with me). Not saying anything to him is
a good call. Tons of people write to me about how they went
ahead and blabbed their feelings to someone taken and are in
worse hell than they were before.
    3. Consider this: While you love Z more than Leonardo
himself, not having him is not the only thing that's bothering you. It's also that you're the lone wolverina while
all your friends have hotties on a leash. This also suuuuucks.
(And once again, believe me, BG understands.) But here's the
vicious circle that you're in: When you're blue about lack
of Z—and exhausted due to lack of ZZZZs—let's face it,
you're not at your big-hearted best. People can tell something's weighing you down. It's not you who's unappealing;
it's your current—and temporary—piney, bawly, hungry vibe.
So then no one asks you out; then you get bluer. And so on.
    So—and this is, like, the cheesiest thing BG has ever
said, but you started it—you DO have to love yourself first.
I swear. And guess what: You already do. You didn't write me
to say, "Boys don't like me because I'm a loser." You wrote
me to say, "My heart is big and loving . . . I could be the
best girlfriend . . . and yet no boy is interested?! WHASSUP
WITH THAT!??!?!" Stay fierce, not frantic, and they'll be
lining up, A through . . . well . . . Y.
    Love,
    Breakup Girl

THE CURSE
~ of the ~
NICE GUY

As little as we like to hear the word *friend* at the end of a relationship, it can be equally galling to hear it…as the reason not to have a relationship. Especially when we then go on to hear all about our intendeds' crushes, exploits, and other relationships. Which, of course, tank. And your sturdy shoulder is the first to know.

This, readers, is the curse of the Buddy. Of the Nice Guy. Of the Pal. Of the Friend-Boy, the Friend-Girl, the Kid Sister. Of, as Paul the Intern calls it, the Straight Gay Friend. (The term *teddy bear* should also be in here somewhere.) The curse knows no gender; it knows no limit to one relationship. It knows — it is — who you are.

Unless you talk to me. Who, as a hockey-playing, beer-enjoying superhero who will never, ever be willowy, knows exactly what you are going through.

In other words, *"There, there. I understand."* Ugh. See?

⚡ Who's Who in Buddies

Guys

■ The Original Loft Builder

Dear Breakup Girl,
    I have been trying to get to know these women in college. I did all the things a "nice guy" does. I helped move big stuff into their dorm rooms, set up computers and bed

lofts, what have you. That's how I am: When I like a woman, I try to help her out. Then I get to be . . . her best friend. I've tried not to be a "nice guy," but I just can't. It's instilled deep within me. What can I do to be the boyfriend, not the best friend/older brother/father/confidant?
    —Broken Heart Bob

Dear Broken Heart Bob,
    Of course you can't not be a nice guy. You *are* a nice guy, like it or not. And women do like it—even LIKElike it. The thing to do is to be a nice guy, not a Nice Guy. Be nice because you are, not because you're trying to. It's your character, not a campaign. And you've got a role in setting the tone, you know. The next time a girl piques your interest, ask her out *before* you fix her loft.
    And remember, some relationships do morph from platonic to romantic. A loft, after all, *is* a bed.
    Love,
    Breakup Girl

■ The Pastry Chef

Dear Breakup Girl,
    Women confuse me. My friend Lynore likes this guy named Stu . . . who broke a big date with her to go out with someone else. Lynore needed someone to lean on, and that someone was me. It started out, you know, hug hug hug. Then she started holding my hand, slipping her arm around me, and snuggling. *Then* she invited me to dinner at her house, and she BAKED ME A CAKE. All this, and she just wants to be my friend. But I'm falling for her. Every time she reaches for me, it's more painful to hold her. I tried baking chocolate-chip cookie bars for her; I gave them to her at school when they were still warm. She ate five but said "thank you" only once (while her friends all said they wanted to marry me).
    Meanwhile, "Tina" began speaking to me again after getting weirded out when I asked her out. I gave her a mint-chocolate cake with a note saying, "If I've done anything to mess up our friendship, please forgive me. Love, Brad." She hugged me and said she was my friend.
    But I still want to know: Why do girls bake cakes for and hold hands with guys they just want to be friends with?
    —Brad, the Platonic Shoulder Guy Friend

Dear Shoulder Guy,

Lynore wants to bake her cake and eat it too. You are her SnackWell's Boyfriend. You satisfy a craving—with 30 percent fewer issues and risks! And you thought you liked this handy, shouldery, huggy, cakey thing, so you kept getting your reduced-commitment fix. But now it's time for a gentle ultimatum, as in: "I'm glad I could be there for you, but now you're asking me for more than I can give as a friend. If you want to be friends, then let's do stuff friends do, like not hold hands, though I'm not ruling out the occasional Bundt cake. If you want to turn up the heat, just keep doing what you're doing." Otherwise, ask her to bake you something with a file in it, 'cause you need out.

By the way, Brad, baking cookies is building a loft. It is not making a move. The mint cake sealed what with Tina? *Friendship.* No *wonder* gals use you as a shoulder/pastry chef. Boys are allowed to bake for girls in only two situations: (1) when making a cute/ironic dessert for the otherwise romantic/manly meal you've just prepared for her (the elk you felled with your crossbow and braised in testosterone-infused oil), and (2) when you guys are already a couple and you do cute stuff like spell her name in chocolate chips on a cookie. Which you may not bring to school.

Still, I'm not convinced these women were going to come through for you, sugar high or no. Try elsewhere, less hard. Because I am convinced there's a gal out there eating raw cookie dough and waiting for a guy like you to call. And ask her out for chicken-fried steak.

Love,
Breakup Girl

■ Boy Soy

Dear Breakup Girl,

This gorgeous girl who graduated with me—and who dated all the "hot" guys—is at college in a different town. She wouldn't have given me the time of day last year, but out of the blue she e-mailed me to say hello. Our correspondence became truly witty and wonderful. Now we chat online every single night and talk every other.

One night she said she was having problems with her boyfriend and I had cheered her up. She went on to say, "If I were there right now, I'd kiss you."

Now she won't discuss it. She's dating another "hot" guy who's supposedly sweet, though she admits that he doesn't make her feel as good about herself as I do, but he's good-looking, and that's basically the only thing she says about him. What was she feeling then, and what is she feeling now?
—Carl

Dear Carl,

Her boyfriends are arm candy; you are Boy Soy. Yes, you have discovered her depth, but no, for whatever reason, she is not ready to give up Manimal for Mensch. I'm worried that when you feed off her attentions, you're consuming empty calories; this will take your time and drive you nuts. You might want to step away from the phone. If she wants to find you for real, she will.
Love,
Breakup Girl

Gals

■ The Girl Buddy

Dear Breakup Girl,

Whenever I meet someone cute and interesting, we end up buddies when I want more! How do I get past this without losing friends?
—Everyone's Buddy

Dear Everyone's Buddy,

Wouldn't it be nice to be intoxicatingly mysterious, to have men come up and say, "Friends, schmends, I must be your lover!" instead of "Buddy! Howaboutta gamea horse?"

But maybe, for some cosmic reason, you are the kind of person for whom serious relationships start as—and develop soundly from—friendship. If you trust that things will evolve when they "should," you'll be playing a mean game of horse with your devoted hubby while Miss Terious wishes she had more true friends.
Love,
Breakup Girl

■ The Kid Sister

Dear Breakup Girl,

One of my friend-boys might be going from KidSisCon 5 (strictly bud-o-rama) to possibly KidSisCon 3 (friends with potential). When I see him he looks glad to see me. When I ask him out, he accepts. Plus—hang onto your cape!—he has never asked me about another girl.

But I'm inexperienced at dealing with men when I'm not the advice chick or football buddy. How do I tell if he LIKElikes me? How do I not get hurt if he doesn't, or accept with grace if he does? How do I drill self-confidence into the illogical half of my brain, or train my logical half to become my inner Xena and shout it down?

—Everyone's Kid Sister

Dear EKS,

He's never asked about another girl? That *is* promising. So up and ask. Do your usual touch-football date, whatever, only in a slightly more romantic and date-y place. At the end, ask if he sees this as a friends thing or a more-than thing. If the latter: wheee! Enjoy the tingly, awkward moment; improvise. If he says "just," *lie*. Stand tall and say you weren't sure, you figured you'd check in. Then say bye. Once home, freak. Throw Nerf stuff, write to BG. Remind yourself that well, at least you know. The sting will fade.

Either way, you're ahead of the game, because as an experienced Buddy, you've dealt with men as Actual Humans, not just Pre-Boyfriends. That's all the inner Xena you need.

Love,

Breakup Girl

⚡ The Opposite of "Nice" Is Not "Jerk"

Dear Breakup Girl,

I've heard that my girlfriend wants to break up. Apparently she likes this "bad boy" loser. Drugs, sneaking out, drinking, doesn't say much, doesn't come to class much . . . Why do girls go for the bad guy?

—Joe

Dear Joe,

Most people assume that babes go for baddies out of some

sort of pathetic, zero-self-esteem, "Hurt me! Ignore me! You're right, drugs are more interesting than I am!" impulse. Well, okay, that's pretty accurate. But sometimes, it's also a misguided faux-noble mission to find the diamond in the roughneck. Or to make herself look good (though also dumb) by comparison.

Regardless, your job as the Good Guy is to investigate. Without using the Nice Guy term *check-in*, do a check-in. Is Girlfriend happy in the relationship? Take it from there. And don't worry. For every guy wondering why women go for bad boys, there's a woman wondering where all the good guys are. Be—stay—good.

Love,
Breakup Girl

⚡ There's Hope!

Dear Breakup Girl,

My ex and I were best friends for a year before we went out. He was completely in love with me the whole time, which sounds rude to say, but it's true. I did, admittedly, take advantage of that sometimes. But after a year, I finally gave in and said I would be his girlfriend—and though it didn't last as long as we'd hoped, it was the best six months of my life. So this goes out not only to "nice guys" for being such great friends—and to tell them to keep being great, 'cause it will pay off eventually—but also to encourage girls to give that "nice guy" a chance.

—Morgan

STOP! LOOKS. LISTEN.

I will always adore the Character Still Known as the Little Prince, from whom (well, from his pal the fox) we learn that *"On ne voit bien qu'avec le coeur. L'essentiel est invisible pour les yeux."* Which translates to: "It is only with the heart that one can see rightly; what is essential is invisible to the eye." (See, I was able to pay attention in Mme. Zombeck's class *and* pass notes with Juliet, whom you'll meet below.)

However. In the context of the topic I'm about to address, I now say to the fox: *"Mais non."*

⚡ Reality Check:
Let's Face It, Looks Do Matter...

Dear Breakup Girl,

    If a guy is interested in you, the only thing you find wrong with him is his looks, and on that basis you reject him, does that make you the most shallow person on Earth? Reassure me that you have to be attracted to someone, or else it wouldn't work...please?

    —Worried

Dear Worried,

    Yes, you have to be "attracted" to someone. Or at least feel potential stirrings. That said, can you honestly say that you rummaged through all of your hormones and neurons and other chemical apparati and came up with no gut-level attraction whatsoever? Or did you think, "Well, he's not the

world's biggest hottie; what will people think of me?" BG
doesn't know which. But you do.
    Love,
    Breakup Girl

Like it or not, we live in a culture that judges figure skaters' souls by the size of their thighs (shut up, waif-bots; who's doing the triple axels?) and male politicians' characters by their wives' (and interns') hair. And a culture where Neve Campbell has a job.

So yes, first — and later — impressions are filtered through Societal Standards, and they are all too often indelible. Boy, oh boy, do people get drawn to, stuck on, and blinded by Looks even when what's inside ain't so foxy. And yes, people make lame, obnoxious, ill-informed decisions about character (e.g., lazy) based on appearance (e.g., overweight). Which, alas, is also why the world does not look kindly/lustfully — at first glance — upon folks like Leery, who, frankly, is going to have a harder time with Step One (Being Noticed).

I'm a nineteen-year-old guy who has never had a girlfriend.
I admit, I'm a bit dorky. I'm a computer engineer at NJIT,
plus I'm short (5' 5") and skinny (115 pounds) and not good-
looking. But I'm a gentleman, caring, kind, intelligent, non-
drinker, nonsmoker. I'm sure I sound like an even bigger
loser now, but what can I do to get girls to notice or maybe
even like me?

Don't worry, Leery, we'll get back to you.

⚡ . . . So Don't Feel Bad If You Look After Your Own

Here's a letter from — full disclosure — BG's best friend from seventh grade, Juliet. She is the person Breakup Girl is going to marry "if it comes to that" (call it *Four Funerals* and a Wedding*).

Dear Breakup Girl,
    I'm getting my hair cut tomorrow. Do I trim it and keep
it at the current, face-framing, bobbish length—or do I go

---

* Our parents'

back to the ultrashort Winona do? (Note: My obsession with Winona's hair began WELL BEFORE she met Matt Damon. It's legit.)

As with any hair dilemma, this is not about hair—it's about life as a woman, femininity, following/resisting stereotypes, inner strength, etc. See, I love how short hair feels. But I worry: Do I have a striking enough face to carry it off? Do I need to be a modely waif? Will I look more butch than I really am, or like a housefrau with sensible hair? Do men like long hair better? In short, will I be cutting off my hair to spite my face?

And then the meta level: Why do I care so much what men think? Why am I worried about the ramifications of looking "unfeminine"? Why am I trapped by stereotypes even as I try to be a strong, freethinking woman?

Finally: WILL I RESOLVE ALL THESE ISSUES BY ELEVEN A.M. TOMORROW?

—Juliet

Juliet might, but Society won't. So, while I leave you in suspense about my actual response, let's discuss why Juliet, a regular Xena in the rest of her life, should get all Rules Girl* about hair and appearance? Hey, she's practical: She'd like to find her way to a life partner one of these days; what — given, oh, REALITY — is the shortest distance between two points?

And part of that reality is — despite all the feel-good stuff I will say here about the outer child of inner beauty — that there's still enough data out there telling us certain looks matter that, well, we worry. EVEN IF WE KNOW BETTER. It's like, "Just because I get all unconventional doesn't mean I magically change the conventions of those around me!...It doesn't mean I won't wind up strong, freethinking, true to Numero Uno...and *alone!*"

---

* "Do everything you possibly can to put your best face forward. If you have a bad nose, get a nose job; color gray hair; grow your hair long. Men prefer long hair, something to play with and caress. It doesn't matter what your hairdresser and friends think. You're certainly not trying to attract them! Let's face it, hairdressers are notorious for pushing exciting, short haircuts on their clients; trimming long hair is no fun for them. It doesn't matter that short hair is easier to wash and dry or that your hair is very thin. The point is, we're girls! We don't want to look like boys." — from *The Rules: Time-Tested Secrets for Capturing the Heart of Mr. Right* (Fein and Schneider, Warner Books, 1956, I mean 1996).

So if you've got looks angst wired in . . . well, how could you not? And in the largest metaphorical sense, we dress for success every day. What should I wear to meet his/her parents? Should I cut my hair for the interview? We are all, always, calculating, rummaging through our closets, changing our hair — and rarely with a second thought. Hey, you do what you gotta do, right? But when women do it in the Realm of Boy, we feel conflicted, guilty — even though there are a million reasons why it's normal and natural, almost like a reflex, for us to do so. So let's quit feeling bad about it. Women beating themselves up over What Strong Women Are Supposed to Be Like kind of defeats the purpose of Strong Women, doesn't it?

⚡ Then Again, Looks Don't Matter as Much as You Might Think

Remember, "societal" tastes don't hold true for every man/woman. (E.g., Juliet, I'm not convinced men like long hair better. Long hair, as far as they know, offers far more opportunity for (1) weird chemicals, appliances, and restraining devices in the bathroom and bureau area — and their corollary, (2) lateness.)

What we sense more deeply — are you listening, Leery? Juliet? — is the aura people emit, the thing we're talking about when we say, "There's something about him/her. . . ." Even computer boys like Leery should be sure not to underestimate the organic. As in chemistry. Point being, there's more to looks than meets the eye.

Impressions/attractions are frequently based on a lot of other je-ne-sais-quoi things: a gesture, a glow, a turn of phrase. Just as important, people get hooked on each other for a lot of lousy reasons that have nothing to do with looks. In other words, *looks are just one of a ton of things that addle our judgment.* Which is worse, getting together with someone only because their eyes and dimples make you melt, or getting together with someone only because, say, something about his/her personality satisfies some unmet need for a certain flavor of love/attention you didn't get from your parents? Let's all get over the self-righteous, facile notion that everything tangible and external ("looks") — and our attraction to it — is superficial, while our love for the inner whatever ("character," "soul," "what's inside") is pure.

Dear Breakup Girl,
    I am nineteen years old and have scoliosis and a cleft

palate. I can't find a girl who appreciates me for me and can look past appearance enough to have a real relationship. Help!
—Bobby

Dear Bobby,

Belleruth says, "It's too bad culture is driven to admire conventional appearance and reject all else. It takes extra work to maintain self-esteem in the face of shallow BS. The upside is that it really does build character and sensitivity to *not* be instantly fawned over for superficial reasons by superficial morons."

But Bobby, don't assume that any girl who goes out with you automatically "appreciates you for you" in some virtuous, essential way. *Who's to say that she's not just working her Nightingale complex on you?* I'm so not saying you're not likeable for the "right" reasons—just that those aren't always the reasons that folks, in their magnificent, twisted weirdness, glom onto.

"Fortunately," Belle adds, "you have options. Technology allows anyone to sidestep the appearance thing. Meeting people online and developing a rapport before meeting face-to-face allows for good things to happen to a guy like you. Not because you have anything to hide, but because it can uncomplicate the initial encounter. You could meet some pretty spectacular women this way, who may or may not be confronting similar challenges." Why not try my chat room?
Love,
Breakup Girl

⚡ So What to Do?

Who we are inside and how we look outside are on a continuum. It's not only about the genes we were blessed/cursed with; it's about the choices we make, how we carry and adorn ourselves, how we color in the butcher-paper outline we draw of our bodies. Which in itself is an, ahem, interface between how people relate to us — based on how we look — and how our personalities and characters are thus further molded.

But don't worry, I'm not about to chuck you on the chin and say, "Don't feel pretty? Just be yourself!" (the implication there generally being that "people will be so drawn to your personality that eventually they won't notice you're ugly"). What I mean is: When "*l'essentiel*" and the visible are in sync, that's when we look marvelous.

1. Look the Way That Feels Best

Which do should Ju do? The Winona. (Remember, this is the opposite of Hanson. Not About the Hair.) Not only because I believe her about the Damon factor (in any case, if that were the prevailing logic, she should get an Affleck — their relationship seems more stable). Because I will never forget seeing Juliet with her first Winona. I thought: "Where has that haircut been all your life?" Her eyes shone, she grinned, she glowed — thus making all of her questions irrelevant. Nothing to do with whether her face was "striking enough" or whether men would look at her or whether she was "too fat" (only humans, God bless 'em, wonder if their hair makes them look fat). She said it: She "loves how short hair feels." *It shows.* How you feel — who you are — and how you look are directly related. *That,* beyond societal conventions and ideals of beauty, yadda yadda yadda, is what makes you — even at first glance — attractive.

2. Make Your Life Look Good

You might feel good about your hair…what about your life?

Dear Breakup Girl,

I exercise, I have good hygiene, I dress well, wax my legs, do my hair. But I've got acne scars, crooked teeth, and the family curse of a huge butt. Not traits I can change without plastic surgery, and since I temp, I can't afford it.

It's hard getting passed over when you're with your friends, or finding that one of them invites you out so she can look better. It's hard to know that inside you're as beautiful as a supermodel, and a million times as smart, but no man comes near you because you are (in words I overheard once, from a grown man, no less) "a big bow-wow." Your advice?

—Miss "Great Personality"

Dear MGP,

Someone said that? Oy. Talk about scars.

Yes, you have been nonblessed with certain let's-face-it hindrances. It's harder to walk through life with your head held high when no one meets your gaze. And the reasons why they don't SUCK.

But what are you doing temping, Miss Million Times as

Smart? What is stopping you from upgrading your resumé and your income . . . and your sense of permanence and purpose in the world?

There's more than waxing and exercising to be done here. I get this funny feeling that at some level, you are passing *yourself* over. You are letting other people look better. You have sent yourself to the doghouse.

So. Do not hang out with people who bring you down. You are above that. Do not do a job you can do in your sleep. You are above that. Find one that matches your qualifications and stokes your ambitions. And that will help you pay, if you choose, for some non-frivolous dental/dermatological work (note: If you really want this, you're smart enough to do some research and make a payment plan, even without a new job). And maybe a Pilates class. (Though remember: Men generally do prefer McButt to McBeal. Right, guys?)

My guess is that you've been using your looks as an excuse to live your life sitting at someone else's desk. Now it's time to use your brains.

Love,
Breakup Girl

Oh, and what about Leery?

What he — and all Leerys — needs to do is figure out a way to *trust* that you can send a vibe as charming in person as you can on paper. If someone intrigues you, ask him/her out, because damnit, you're a caring, kind, smart person, and you know it. Or at least get yourself into situations where you — and your intended(s) — can get past the surface. Maybe, cornily enough, classes and clubs and community stuff, where you interact with folks on a regular, shared-interest basis. Where you give other people — most of whom, by the way, are also convinced they're "dorky," "not good-looking," etc. — the chance to see the self you like. It's the one they'll like too.

PREDICAMENT of the CHAPTER!

Cut Out This Knife Stuff

Dear Breakup Girl,

I am fifteen and have had only one boyfriend. I am thinking about getting plastic surgery so maybe I could get another one. Help!

—Sunkissed

Dear Sunkissed,

Oh, BG is so sad that you are even considering such a thing! I mean, if you were born with a birthmark that randomly happened to spell, "No, thanks, I'm already seeing someone," then I might look through my Rolodex under "Safe, nonsurgical laser removal." But we need to find some way to replace your self-esteem. First of all, it's not lame for you to have had only one boyfriend at age fifteen. Or, to put it another way, your friends who have had more are not necessarily cooler or happier—they just have a different set of problems. I'm also pretty certain that, well, if you've already decided that surgery's your only hope, you're not carrying yourself around school with a whole lot of security and confidence, are you? People can sense that. If you're trudging down the halls and hiding behind your notebooks, *that* is what's going to take you out of the running for homecoming queen. It's not attractive. And then no one asks you out, and then you trudge more.

So find something to do in or outside of school—a sport, a club, a volunteer project (no candy-striping in a cosmetic surgeon's office). Do it. This is not dumb "find a hobby!" advice [see sidebar]. The experience of activity and discovery *will affect how you look*. It will occupy you, give you confidence, a sense that you are someone behind your face. Even conventionally pretty girls don't always have that.

Love,
Breakup Girl

⚡ Why I'm Not Just Saying, "Get a Hobby and You'll Be Cute." Or, If I Am, Why I'm Right.

Everyone who's ever wondered "What's missing?" (from your face, your weekend, your soul) should read this response to Sunkissed from a been-there boy.

Dear Sunkissed,

    Recently I discovered the best lifestyle surgery: dancing! Dance classes are ideal for the single person, be it ballroom, country-western, swing, salsa, or tango. You, the single vixen, could be matched up with twenty fellas in the course of a night without ever feeling awkward, at least above the ankles. No matter people's skill, I have never seen anyone unattractive on a dance floor. People are so busy concentrating that they forget to be self-conscious. I haven't had so many crushes since junior high.

    If your town has no studio, you are now president of the local dance club. Enlist some friends and get an instructor or videos, and make your own scene. Tango, swing, two-step, or whatever. Even if all you have is girls, don't worry—once the guys figure out that's where the girls are, they will come.

    Make it your goal to be the hottest dancer in your whole school by fall. When it's time for that fall dance, march in and tell that DJ it don't mean a thing if it ain't got that swing, and then dance up a storm. Everyone else, still trapped in the generic two-foot sway-and-shuffle, will be in awe. And your dance card will fill up faster than the *Titanic* filled with water.

    If dancing isn't your thing, my main point still applies: Nothing is more enticing to a guy than a girl who kicks ass at something. Skateboarding, sculpture, chess, whatever— someone will dig you for it, and you will be too busy being Miss Kick-Ass to worry about your appearance, and therefore you will be utterly gorgeous.

    —Dancing Fool

⚡ But Weight! There's More

There are as many mixed messages about the weight issue as there are pills and programs and Camryn Manheims and "Feed Kate Moss" T-shirts. And

we ourselves send them, you know. How many of us say, "Eeeuw, how can Calista do that to herself!?" while thinking, ". . . and how can I do that to myself?" How many of us say, "I love me the way I am!" while thinking, "And I'd love me more if there were less!" How many of us have friends of all sizes — and weight maximums in our personal ads? Is that sincere preference, or programming? And even if it's the latter, so sue us, what are we supposed to do? Complicated, huh?

Dear Breakup Girl,

I'm seventeen and I'm a nice guy. I just can't seem to be dating or relationship material for anyone. I can get from flirting to a date but not from a date to a relationship, and that is killing me. I was hoping to use this year's homecoming as a chance to jump-start a relationship, but that backfired in my face miserably when I got yes for an answer twice and proceeded to get dumped the next day TWICE. I ended up going to homecoming with a group of friends, feeling like the biggest loser on the planet.

It seems that fate has cursed me with a big build (6'4", 240) and that seems to turn off lots of girls. I've already blown at least one relationship and I don't wanna do it again. Please help me out here.

—Lonely and Confused

Dear Lonely and Confused,

1. Often, as far as society is concerned, your size is the problem. BUT.

2. "Fixing" your size will not fix your life. In other words, people say, "If I lost weight, I wouldn't be lonely." Then they do, and only their wardrobe changes. They say, "I'm thin and I'm still lonely. I still suck." And gain it back.

So, L&C, there's no sense in, like, stooping. 'Cause you know what? *Nonbulky people write me with the exact same concerns.* No one morphs every flirtation into a relationship. No one knows how to "put it all together." No one loves getting hosed for homecoming and going with friends. But most people do forget to notice that (a) if they were with friends, they weren't the only dateless wonders, and (b) friends can be better, sturdier companions than a tipsy I-just-need-a-date dance partner. Lonely and losery for one night at homecoming is better than feeling like you have no friends to come home to.

You didn't "blow" a relationship, you *had* one. Don't make one big event into the "This is it!" be-all, end-all, start-all. So keep asking choice girls out, seeing where it goes. To the best of your ability, go on about your merry, messy, bulky way. Live as large as you are.

Love,
Breakup Girl

And hopefully, the Lonely and Confuseds of the world will find the In the Darks of the world.

Dear Breakup Girl,

What's a good way to tell my sweet, incredible boyfriend that I think he's beautiful and I adore his body even though he's fat, and I'd like the lights on once in a while (nudge nudge, wink wink)?
— In the Dark

Dear Dark,

"Sweet incredible boyfriend, I think you're beautiful and I adore your body. I love what we do in the dark, but I'd also love to try having the lights on once in a while. What do you think?"

If he's bashful, start with lots of candles (think: that scene in the latest *Romeo + Juliet*, except without the poison part).

See, big/beautiful people out there? Saying, "Here I am!" — not hiding — is hottest of all.

Love,
Breakup Girl

GETTING THE DIGITS

THE OTHER SIZE THAT MATTERS

• Both men and women prefer "trim" body type. But hey! Only two guys picked "bony." And for both sexes, "what-EVER" was the runner-up.

• True or false: "Overweight is a deal-breaker"? People who consider themselves trim and people who consider themselves heavy were likely to say "true."

• But hey! While women were more likely to say "true," men tied for "true" versus "false."

• Of BG readers who called themselves "heavier than I'd like," 36 percent said, "I actually believe that if my body were a different size, I'd be luckier in love."

• But wait, so did around 43 percent of the respondents who call themselves "pretty trim." Oy.

Office
Romance

I n today's gender-blending, team-playing, midnight-oil-burning workplaces, romance can be natural, even inevitable. Offices offer mates with common interests and similar schedules, plus a getting-to-know-you op that does not involve beer/darts. And heck, you know your intended has a job. Why, BG knows someone who met his now-wife at the office. "We live together and work together," he said to me. "We never see each other." Yep, love at work is a reality for us busy professionals. A very tricky one, as Jenn knows:

> I am totally attracted to this guy. He is funny, smart, and attractive. So what's the problem, right??? I *work* with him. Been there, done that . . . don't want to go back. While we're dating, can't focus on work. When we break up, can't focus on work.

Right. We also know that love doesn't always flourish under fluorescent lights. Workplace romance means putting your personal and professional interests on the same line — and in some unfortunate cases, that line could be unemployment. So, if you're having a cow about the prospect of dating someone you work with — well, you should be. Arguably, it's more complicated and issue ridden than dating someone you live with. But: You needn't have a bigger cow today than you would have had pre–Anita Hill, pre–Paula Jones, et al. (See sidebar.) That cow is one big red herring that's making us all more nervous around each other than necessary; the genders, despite

paranoia to the contrary, do mix way more smoothly than BG's metaphors. So let's all settle down and deal with workplace romance as a matter of dating dignity and professional conduct.

> **IMPORTANT BREAKUP GIRL MAXIM**
>
> FOR A LOVE-AT-WORK VENTURE TO BE WORTH THE RISK -- OF ALIENATING COWORKERS, DERAILING A FRIENDSHIP, BEING BANISHED TO THE "BAD" COPIER AFTER A LOUSY BREAKUP, OR WORSE -- YOU HAVE TO HAVE A PRETTY FIERCE HUNCH *THAT THINGS COULD REALLY, TRULY WORK OUT* WITH THE DILBERT OF YOUR DREAMS/GIRL FOREVER.

A hunch that comes from your gut, not from your fourth margarita at the "Office Olé!" fiesta, that is. Ask yourself: Which would you rather face, life *without* this person as partner, or the tricky — but worth it — business of working with him/her? Now ask yourself again. Because when it comes to office romance — at least in your department — you are allowed: one (1). Being pegged a cubicle hopper will not get you promoted. At least not for reasons you can be proud of.

⚡ The H Word

The only romances you may start at work are the ones that appear to be based on real attraction, respect, and promise — which are not a fertile growing medium for that other big scary risk: *harassment*.

That's why sexual harassment and workplace dating are, in BG's ideal world, *unrelated*. Some folks have been acting as if "sexual harassment" is some special code that women can yell whenever they don't feel like being complimented on their sweaters, one that magically transplants the offender to a seat in front of a cruel and castrating tribunal consisting of the female leads in *Thelma and Louise* and *9 to 5*. Um, no. There are legal standards — heavy-duty ones — that must be met in order to make a case for the class of *employment discrimination* (i.e., not kvetching) now defined as sexual harassment.

Do keep in mind, however, that women at work, whether pursuing or pursued, may — well, should — be a little more careful here than they might in a bar. Careful for different reasons, anyway. Even though workplace

romance is as old as the world's oldest profession, the days of women being suspected of sleeping their way to the middle are far from over. Arguably, women are the ones who — whether in reality or only somewhere in the back of their minds (or in the back of the supply closet) — still have to worry most about separating personal and professional, serious and stereotype. Keep that in mind, guys, when you're making your moves...or nursing your wounds. In some cases, it really *isn't* you. Got it?

The Coworker Crush: Making a Lateral Move

As office liaisons go, dating a "teammate" is usually the least complicated venture. Though don't be naive about stuff that could come up, such as competition for promotion; flirt with caution.

Everyone — including those of you whose cases I treat below — should also consider this: Office love does not have to be all-or-nothing. There's a case to be made for chaste professional flirtation (CPF, for future reference) that's consummated only in a positive, productive, "Let me impress you" energy and work ethic. And a little buzz that makes you psyched to go to work.

You're the Boss: How to Proceed

Perfect example of CPF: A looooong time ago (pre–Paul the Intern, I swear), when I had a McJob to support my hero habit, I lusted after a much younger lad I

BG'S TALKING POINTS FOR OFFICE ROMANCE:
Follow These Guidelines and Assumptions

1. **COMPANY CULTURE COUNTS.** Take note of the *unwritten* policy on office romance coded in frowns and nudges and raised eyebrows and tacit "Who-hoos!" I've heard of firms where office romance -- conducted with dignity -- is an accepted part of office life; others, are cold, Dilbertian / Orwellian hells where you can't even have a photo of your spouse on your desk. When in Rome, Inc., take your cues from the way romances have / haven't been conducted before.

2. **PROCEED WITH UTMOST CAUTION.** BG normally gets impatient with the indirect, hovering, "Let's wind up at the same party and see what happens" approach to asking someone out (or not). But in this context, yes, circle a bit more before you land.

3. **EVERYONE KNOWS.**

supervised. The attraction, he made clear, was mutual. Hanky-panky would nonetheless have been a lousy move. Still, our chemistry had its benefits: I strove to be the best boss in the world, and he was never, ever late.

If you *must* make a move, make it good. You're allowed only one.

Dear Breakup Girl,
    I am slowly going crazy for a younger woman whom I super-vise at work. I can hardly concentrate. She meets my gaze with quivering eyes, she does nice little things for me, and she even gave me a handwritten contemplative poem. But I don't want to come on to her and end up making this a dif-ficult place for her to be. Is all fair in love and work? Or is this strictly hands-off?
    —Jeremy

Dear Jeremy,
    The boss/subordinate thing—no matter how genuine and sincere your feelings—does indeed trip all sorts of wires: favoritism, cradle robbing, power struggles, you name it. So remember, the workplace is first and foremost a place of . . . work. You're going to have to decide which, hypothetically, interferes more with your performance: going out with her or not going out with her. If the sane, responsible adult inside you says, "It's worse this way; I need to make some sort of move," then you get one itty-bitty after-work-drink invita-tion with one honking, totally unromantic disclaimer: "I want you to know that your saying yes or no has NO effect on your employment status."
    Except it sorta does. If she, um, starts writing you love poems, then one of you has to contemplate switching jobs, even if just within the company. Sounds rad, but that's what the experts say.
    Finally, don't rule out the possibility of CPF [see above]. Not as poetic as pining, but at least your boss won't meet *your* quivering gaze with a pink slip.
    Love,
    Breakup Girl

⚡ Dating "Up" Without Messing Up

It's great to defy stereotype and like your boss. But what if you LIKElike your boss?

Dear Breakup Girl,

I'm a single guy in my midtwenties. I've been seeing this girl for several months, and everything's been fine until lately. See, she's my boss—midthirties, recently divorced.

Lately she's been wanting to get, er, frisky . . . at the office, during work. I'm afraid of getting busted, but also that if we break up, she'll trash my career. What should I do?

—Jake in Jacksonville

Dear Jake,

You're right; getting "frisky" will not get you on the short list for Employee of the Month. Neither will dumping your boss. Still: bail, bail, bail. Pray she doesn't retaliate. If you do wind up having to leave, well, let's just say that BG is not convinced you had wholesome, promising growth opportunities at Disclosure, Inc., to begin with. And remember that if you interview elsewhere, you'll have to tell them why you left your previous job. I'd fib.

Love,

Breakup Girl

But if you haven't "gotten frisky" yet, here's how to proceed. Or not.

Dear Breakup Girl,

I'm in my late thirties and have a serious case of the hots for my single, late-forties boss. In today's PC world, how can I let him know I'm interested?

—Sassy

Dear Sassy,

First, let your HR department know you're interested in the company's policy, if any, on "fraternization." Then do some reflecting on company culture: Have other people dated —cross rank—before? Were they feted, shunned, no-big-dealed? Are you on a teeny team where you'd upset the balance of power? Or would folks be glad and relieved that you two finally defused the obvious tension?

After all this, are you convinced that letting him know is a prudent, adult, necessary choice? In that case, your move cannot be as unrestrained, passionate, and magical as it might in the real world. It's dicey enough to say, "Um, it's totally no problem if you don't feel the same way, but

what do you think about taking our relationship to the next
level?" (shorthand: asking him out *once* for coffee or a
drink)—without hearing, "No, thanks," and then having to
show up for work the next day. Yikes!!!

Above all, Sassy, remember your own key word: *serious*.
This whole thing is. As hard as it is to find a guy when
you're in your late thirties, it's even harder to find a job.

Love,

Breakup Girl

⚡ The Mother of All Pink Slips

Talk about Casual Day. You break up with someone at work, and you are
going to have to be so way totally completely mellowly what-me-worry-ly
over it. Or at least able to act that way. (Pull this off and your waitering days
are over.) I don't care how heinously you were wronged; I don't care what
a troll your babe turned out to be. As important as it was to not bring your
romance to work, it is even more important to sweep your breakup off your
desk. Avoid, ignore, override. *This is your workplace.* Do not compound
your crisis by jeopardizing your job.

If that's not incentive enough, which Lord knows it should be, consider
that working well is the best revenge. Let your co-ex wonder, uncomfortably, how you can be so professional, so productive. That's the smart way
to let it smart.

Still, your life might even have to be, for a while, the Casual Day that
wouldn't die. Imagine having to overhear your ex get messages from your
replacement. Imagine not being able to bring your new squeeze on the company picnic for fear of being filed under "Moved On Too Soon." Imagine all
that, and then go back and decide if you really want to go through with this.

Dear Breakup Girl,

I went on three dates—one fairly passionate—with a
coworker, and then she says she wants to be friends. She gave
me no reason but the old "It's me, not you" line. I have to
pass by her office several times a day and feel very uncomfortable. How do I cope?

—BT

Dear BT,

I realize the vibe is oodgy—but it was three dates, not

three years. Basically, you're going to have to button up
your best "Weirdness? What Weirdness?" suit and stick it out.
And go find someone in a different line of work—say, someone with a home office.
    Love,
    Breakup Girl

Separate But Not Secret

I've heard of all manner of *Mission: Impossible* hijinks designed to keep
workplace couples secret: morning cab drop-offs on separate corners, code
words, umbrellas that emit pink smoke, that kind of thing. I will leave it to
you to determine the appropriate skulk factor. Does the Man frown on mix-
ing business and pleasure to begin with? Or do you just want to avoid the
"Did they disagree in the meeting because they fought last night?" spot-
light? Your call.

Do consider that past a point, shenanigans take too much effort and make
you look silly. One BG reader once spent twenty minutes hemming and
hawing before "outing" his relationship to his boss, whose response was
basically, "Duh."

Which is okay…as long as the reason folks are clued in is that you sometimes leave together after working late on a great report — or because you
ooze the undeniable chemistry required for this kind of thing in the first
place. *Not* because you misdirected saucy e-mail or whispered, "What about
my needs?" louder than you meant to. Okay? Whatever balancing acts you
do in your life overall, when you're at the office, work comes first.

PREDICAMENT of the CHAPTER!

Lose the Boss

Dear Breakup Girl,
    I hooked up with a superior, who then asked me on a
"date" to "discuss what had happened." Alcohol was involved
(again), so you can guess what happened (again). Flash for-

ward nine months: more drinks, another hookup. Then I find out he's been dating and basically living with someone else from the company for the last I-don't-know-how-many months. Meanwhile, we have become friends of a sort; he visits my office at least four times a day. He also invades my space to the point that his trousers are touching my arm. I want to tell him I'm not interested in a sexual relationship, but without any fallout that would alienate anyone. The entire office could find out. Help me with the right words.

    — LameOfficeGirl

Dear LameOfficeGirl,

    The fact that your situation is complicated makes it easier to exit. There are plenty of in-principle (non-personal) reasons for him to back off. All you need to say is something like, "You and I both know that there are a million reasons why your trousers shouldn't be touching my arm right now." What on earth is he entitled to be mad about? His only possible reasonable response: "You're right." (Or: "Left foot, green.") If he goes ballistic because of that, it would suck for you big time, but there would have been no way to predict or prevent it in the first place. Just try to stay (a) gracious, and (b) away from the gimlets.

    Love,

    Breakup Girl

GETTING THE DIGITS

I GAVE AT THE OFFICE

- BG readers are circumspect about office romance, most preferring to judge it on a "case by cubicle" basis.

- Twenty-one percent have been involved with a coworker in a "serious" way (18 percent "in my own mind").

- What helped it succeed? It's a virtual tie between "total openness" and "total secrecy"!

- Also neck and neck: Were two people in your office dating, what should their policy be? "Oh, please. They should just be open": 49 percent, versus "Work is work, and play is play": 51 percent.

- But should offices themselves have policies legislating / restricting romance? A clear majority say, "No. We're adults and should be treated as such."

cyber-romance

Studies show that approximately one bazillion people use the Internet to meet, greet, and (if things don't work out) delete. Surely you know that matchmaking/personals services, chat rooms (singleswithoutmakeup.com), and the like are veritable hotbeds of...hot beds. Being on the cybermake allows you to cast a wide net, to test the waters without risking that "shaved my legs for nothing" feeling and without judging/being judged on the relatively superficial. You know, *looks* (also see page 122). (OTHER superheroes would make a mean joke here, something about "On the Internet, nobody knows you're a dog.")

⚡ So, BG, You're Sure It's Not Lame?

Well, if you think it's lame to wait by the phone, try waiting by the computer. But inherently lame? No.

Dear Breakup Girl,
     I met someone online, but I have a problem with the stigma associated with cyberromances. Though it is not a romance yet, I hate saying how we met. I think I need to get over what others might think. Did I just answer myself?
     —Alex

Dear Alex,
     Yes. What they might think is: "Gotta try that."
     Love,
     Breakup Girl

So if you're looking online for an RLR (Real-Life Relationship), here is BG's Recommendation (less absolute than a Maxim): Use the Internet as a starting point. To meet people who could one day stand before you in flesh and blood, not font and bandwith. A relationship can be ignited — and enhanced — by Inter-action, but unless you can deal with the permavirtual ("Oh, I remember back when we started dating, I was sitting at my computer. Oh, and there was that time early on when I was…sitting at my computer…"), every effort should be made to move it to RL, PDQ.

If you do fall for a wholly virtual partner, ask yourself why. Why *would* you be attracted to someone so distant, impossible, epic, so . . . safe? Is it pure loneliness — s/he may be far away . . . but heck, s/he's *there?* Fair enough. Or…does s/he offer a great way not to have to bother with the icky dates and why-didn't-s/he-calls and other elements of actual — as opposed to virtual — romance? Breakup Girl hates to be a naysayer, but she also hates the thought of any of you staying in and typing on a weekend night. You don't need to "break up" with Internet Interest — just don't let him/her keep you from meeting someone who could actually knock on your door.

⚡ So Is Cyberlove Fundamentally Different from RLL (Real-Life Love)?

Well, yes and no.

> Dear Breakup Girl,
>
> I just spent $1,500 in air fare and hotel bills to visit a man I'd corresponded with by e-mail for seven months. We seemed well suited (we have identical graduate degrees) and were amazed at how naturally the relationship progressed.
>
> But from the moment I arrived, it was obvious that he was not really present or interested. I finally told him I felt like I was his mother's tennis partner's niece whom he had promised to show around town. He said he wasn't ready for a relationship, having been separated less than a year (which I knew). He implied that I had been amiss in thinking of this as more than friendship. (Yet he was the one who signed off "XOXO" and mentioned our "attraction," etc.)
>
> I'm feeling down, hurt, rejected, and even though I know better (I'm a psychologist!), I can't stop kicking myself for spending this money, time, and energy. I'm shocked by the disparity between what I thought we had and what happened when we met. Thoughts?
>
> — JH

Dear JH,

You know, I get tons of letters that say, "S/he isn't the person I thought s/he was!" . . . *from people who are talking about actual — not virtual — romances*. So: *I wonder if sometimes we point fingers at cyberspace for stuff that goes on — or would have happened anyway — in Real Life.*

We should be circumspect about any relationship in which the main activity is touch-typing. But JH, why kick yourself? If Degree Guy had written, "I am not ready for a RELATIONSHIPrelationship; if you visit I will treat you like my mother's tennis partner's niece," that would be one thing. But you took an adventurous, trusting, calculated risk. Some people don't even get that far.

Love,

Breakup Girl

When it comes to finding — and maintaining — a relationship, *cyberspace is a world no more ideal than any other*. When the first step is easier, the transition (if any) to IRL (In Real Life) is, arguably, harder. When the first step is easier, the transition to MIL (Madly in Love) is, arguably, that much easier. You don't know everything there is to know about this person, no, but that is exactly the point.

⚡ But Is Cyberlove Still, Like, "Real"?

Are your *feelings* about this e-pal real? Well, then, this thing is real. But cyber-only love is *not* real in a Velveteen Rabbity, flesh-and-fur sort of way. It just isn't — but that doesn't mean it's bad or pointless.

Dear Breakup Girl,

My boyfriend has all the key basics. He's kind, caring, giving, sensitive, mad about me. But he's moving far away. He wants me to follow, and I just might.

But I've started flirting with "Mike" via e-mail. He knows I have a boyfriend, and we've never met; it's a virtual/intellectual crush. But I get more butterflies from seeing Mike's e-mail in my in box than from seeing my boyfriend on my doorstep. We have some sort of brainiac connection that my boyfriend and I don't. Am I about to (a) sell myself short by settling, or (b) throw away the person who loves me most in the world for a false hope of something better?

—Akemi

Dear Akemi,

You realize, right, that this is not about deciding *between* Boyfriend and Mike?

First, Mike. I do not doubt your "brainiac" connection. But it's also easy to see why cyberlove could appear so clean, strong, and pure in the face of IRL hair-on-the-soap and cap-off-the-toothpaste love/cohabitation. You've got this chance—pressure, even—to take your relationship to the next level (across the country); no wonder you're hearing the floorboards creaking where it is now. And Mike's presence/correspondence may indeed give you insight into what might be in need of repair/replacement IRL.

Speaking of which. I can't help but notice something in —well, actually not in—your description of your relationship: It's a bit distant, passive, tepid. You lament the prospect of losing "the person who loves [you] most in the world," someone who's mad about you. *But why aren't you the subject of the verb* love *anywhere?* This, not Mike, gives me pause about your moving. Before you check your in box for butterflies, reread *your* letter. It—not Mike's missives—may have your answers.

Love,

Breakup Girl

⚡ Uh-oh. Does That Mean Cybersmut Is "Real" Cheating?

Sometimes definitions are beside the point. Take cyberporn. Let's say it morphs from a, um, hobby into a hindrance. Your partner's doing the porn thing solo and on the sly; your "needs" get left out; you — even with your bonus third dimension — feel inferior. If your partner is unwilling to hear these concerns and strike some balance, s/he may know how to download but not how to have a relationship. Cheating? Whatever. Problem? Yes.

Online *affairs* venture more into…well, Cheating Lite, maybe, but still.

Dear Breakup Girl,

My husband was spending ten to fourteen hours a day talking in chat rooms to other women who even sent him pictures. One day, I found him having cybersex. I found out who she was and told her how I felt. Then he had the nerve to tell me to apologize to her! Why should I owe anyone an apology? He says I am too jealous. I'm not thinking that he would ever run off with this person, but it just hurts that he spent so much time typing to her, and other women, and ignored me and his son. What do you think?

— Leah

Dear Leah,

Jealous, schmealous; he's your husband, damnit, and he is behaving badly! I don't care about cybersex being all "virtual" and anonymous and detached and all that. For him this may be out in cyberspace; for you, this is your life. On Earth. Call a counselor, even a lawyer. Plant your feet on the ground and demand some respect.

Love,

Breakup Girl

GETTING THE DIGITS

SICKOFTHE-BARSCENE.COM? • For all their evident Internet savvy -- and with the clear exception of the ultrasocial nexus that is the BreakupGirl.com message board -- BG readers don't tend to meet date types online. Only twelve percent of readers, gay / straight / bi, say they've found lasting relationships out in the ether.

So. Cyberaffairs lie somewhere between President Carter Affairs (lusting in your heart) and President Clinton Affairs (well, you know). And again, we can have all sorts of cyber-socio-neuro-psycho-philosophical discussions about the nature of virtual reality. But nothing on earth is more real than feelings. Especially hurt ones. So use the 'net to meet and greet, not to cheat. It's not "okay" just because your hourly rates are going to AOL, not a motel; use the Internet to bend the rules of punctuation, not the rules of honor and respect. (Also see page 187.)

PREDICAMENT of the CHAPTER!

Something Missing in Real Life

Dear Breakup Girl,

I met a woman online who seemed to have "the right stuff." We started chatting on the phone—and before I knew it, we were having phone sex. We decided to meet, and I made the offer that we wouldn't have just one date . . . we'd be friends no matter what. So we met at a neutral location and there she

was. Just like she described: 5' 4", black hair, busty. Except there was one thing she failed to mention. She has a rather extensive series of birth defects, as in: There were parts of her body missing. Big parts. Now, I'm not one to exclude people on their appearance or anything—really, I'm not—but after our meeting (fine but no sparks) she called the following day, no doubt hoping to make use of her cordless phone and another handheld electronic device . . . and I got this queasy feeling. I said I was busy (lie). She calls, and I'm afraid to confront her about why I'm blowing her off. Please help, Breakup Girl. I don't want to be the jerk I've become.
    —Queasy Rider

Dear Queasy,
    Ooooo-weee. Queasy, you're not a jerk. You're writing to Breakup Girl instead of teasing this gal at recess, right? In a society that overvalues, you know, limbs, you are allowed— if not conditioned—to be squeamish. Plus we are all still trying to sketch out that line between making an Issue out of someone's appearance and blithely pretending that something "different" isn't there (as in: "I don't even notice that you're black!"). Anyway, if you tell me there were no in-person sparks, well, I can't tell you to go make some.
    Also, you were surprised. No fair. I can see how she'd be scared to disclose—and risk meeting no one at all—but yeah, she should give due, if discreet, warning. Not only to ease others into something that may be distracting and jarring, but also for herself. Sure, people should be able to deal. But we don't. When she doesn't prewarn, she practically guarantees that people will go home and freak out and write to BG, or worse, blow her off awkwardly/rudely. She thus gets to be "right" that everyone is, oh, a bigoted jerk who can't see past what's missing, and also: lonely. *Everyone* does this kind of set-yourself-up-for-it thing in one way or another.
    As for you, Queasy, here's what our Belleruth suggests: "Tell her you weren't prepared for her unconventional looks and that it'll take some getting used to, as you had a different image of her in your head and now there's some internal reconciling to do . . . etc. That's at least more respectful and straightforward than disappearing. You can be lukewarm friends if you choose, but either way, if you're not interested, this is better." Keep your browser and your mind open and get back on that bike.
    Love,
    Breakup Girl

FROM FRIENDS TO MORE THAN

So you've got this great friend. You do everything together: shop, hang, talk, work out, talk about your lame love lives and NATO expansion. You know each other's families; you take care of each other's plants. You fend off friends' suggestions that you should be a couple, saying, "No way, that would be too weird!"

But then, somehow, you realize that what you really want to do together …is the one thing you haven't done together.

So you

(a) freak out, and

(b) make a chart.

PRO	CON
Friendship as sturdy foundation for Relationship	Friendship crumbles under weight of Relationship
Undeniable attraction, intense bond	Can't kiss friend: cooties!
Close-knit group of friends thinks we should be together	If something goes wrong, who gets the friends?
It's fate	I'm horny

Ugh. So what are you going to do? Especially 'cause you can't ask your, uh, friend for advice. Well, that's where I come in.

⚡ Diagnosis:
More Than Friends?

Here's what to ask yourself:

1. What flavor of friends are we?

Are you longtime pals from, like, before you were old enough to date? (Pro: the "Mr./Ms. Right There All Along" thing. Con: You've already bathed together.) Or are you more recent friends who, for whatever reason, have never had the chance to upgrade? There's no one right way to proceed in either case; I'm just trying to help you calibrate your feelings. In the latter scenario, for example, it's possible that you've become friends *because* you're attracted to one another — but you've been treading water for so long that no one dares take the plunge.

2. Is the crush enhancing the friendship — or interfering with it?

I can say with professional and personal certainty that men and women (or same-sex pals) can be "just friends." But that doesn't mean you haven't wondered "what if?" about practically everyone you know, and it doesn't mean you don't develop crushes from time to time (hey, just about anyone can start to look like the One when s/he is the One…Who Calls).

So: Does this crush *add* a flirty frisson to the friendship, or does it actually take something away — from both your rapport together and the rest of your life? Like, you really *don't* want to hear about his/her date. You can't enjoy the party when you're tracking your "friend's" whereabouts. And, as a result, you're lukewarm about the other hotties milling around. Dead end.

Once you've evaluated these questions for yourself, you can think about whether to:

GETTING THE DIGITS

A "FRIEND," INDEED

• Sixty-eight percent of BG readers have turned a friendship into a Relationship! (Eleven percent did that thing called "Friends who sleep together.")

• If you broke up, did you stay friends? Most say, "Yes, but it wasn't the same."

• How did the transition happen? Tie (37 percent) between "A mutual 'Let's see what happens' discussion" and "An 'I Can't Fight This Feeling Anymore' speech by one partner." (Runner-up: "An 'I Can't Fight This Feeling Anymore' collapse into bed.")

⚡ Do Something Or Just Deal?

If it still feels fun, I'd say take your time. No rash moves. Enjoy the crush while it lusts. I mean lasts. And that might be it: friendship plus. You get your good friend *and* all that tingly goodness. Ten percent more fruit juice. Yum.

```
Dear Breakup Girl,
     I have this friend who is a guy and yes, we really are
"just friends." Yet sometimes I develop this little crush on
him and can't help thinking how good a couple we'd make. But
I doubt we could go back to being friends if we went out and
then broke up. Also, I haven't any reason to believe he sees
me as anything other than a friend.
     Do you think I am anywhere near the right track with my
thoughts? I know I can live with the current situation and
be happy 94 percent of the time. Am I one of the people who
write to you and answer their own questions at the end of
their letters? <grin>
     —Maggie

Dear Maggie,
     Yep. <grin>
     Love,
     Breakup Girl
```

But if you're suffering, you're getting neither friendship nor good, fun fizz. Which is why you might want to take a chance, take a chance, take a chickachancechance (reference both to ABBA and to the teeth-chattering, stuttering fear that this prospect no doubt invokes). So now you get to figure out . . .

What to Say to Your "Friend"

> **How You Feel:** We would be perfect together. This is incontrovertible fact. I will die if we can't be together, and also if I mess this up. But hey, sport, no pressure.

> **What You Say:** Um. Hi. Um. Hi. Hi. Oh, I said that. Um. Okay. Hey, you know, I have to say, I'vealwayswonderedwhatit-

wouldbelikeifyouandIwereyouknow (sotto voce) morethanfriends.

What You Say (alternate): MMMMMWWWWWWHHHHH-PPPFFFTTTTTTT. (That is: sound of a big fat, brave kiss. The smooch surprise is a completely viable approach. But no matter how strongly you feel, I recommend that you bring this up without tongue.)

BG's point: Unless you take this last tack, I recommend that — no matter how strongly you truly feel — you bring this up as *A Conversation* about *A Possibility*. Keep decisions, demands, and death out of it. Way less scary, for both of you.

ALSO: If given the opportunity, find a way to squeeze in the point that while you couldn't *not* ask, it is also okay with you to remain friends. Unless it's not.

What Your "Friend" Might Say

1. Flat-out rejection
OWOWOWOW. Let's just get this one out of the way, 'cause IT COULD HAPPEN. Important: State that you duly accept the rejection and assert that you will not pursue or try to change his/her mind.

Still, if you feel like — for the next while, at least — your friendship would consist of proving how Down With and Over It you are, then you're welcome to take some time off. Or even — if you come to realize that your friendship was really running on hoping-for-more fumes in the first place — to let things fade.

2. "I need to think about it"
Hell's bells! Worse, perhaps, than Possibility 1. All you can do is: Take his/her word for it. Let him/her think. Don't try to earn or win or perform. Ask what s/he needs; provide it. (Note: See-how-it-feels nooky does not count.) Then proceed to Possibility 1, 3, or 4.

3. General/vague weirdness
No, this is worse. Here's what happened to Jenna:

. . . so a few days ago I told him I couldn't be around him anymore because I had feelings for him. He was stunned. It's been a week, and I haven't seen him. I miss him and now I just feel depressed. It's getting in the way of meeting new people. Now I'm wondering if I did the right thing.

Oh, I do know that our girlie did what felt right at the time. And now, yes, of course she misses him. It's almost as if she's going through a breakup with someone she didn't even get to go out with!

Still, weirdness doesn't mean they're not interested. It might just mean they're having weird feelings, one of which is, "Yikes, am I interested in a friend?" Might be worth looking into, gently. But if this seems to be turning into Possibility 1, then you need to lick your wounds, mourn, and smart for a while, and then get back out and try and meet new folks, no matter what. *That's* the right thing.

4. Cue love theme

Yesssss! (Also, *MMMMMWWW-WWWHHHHHHPPFFFTTTTTTT.*) For all the "cons" described above, many happy Harrys and Sallys do manage to keep their footing after making the leap from friends to lovers. In fact, they say that while the presence of friendship is what makes the transition rocky, it's also, ultimately, what pulls them through. Yay.

WHAT IF MY FRIEND IS THE -- ONLY -- ONE WHO WANTS MORE?

Dear Breakup Girl,
    One of my friends is in love with me, but I have no feelings for him. How can I tell him without losing his friendship?
    —Julianne

Dear Julianne,
    "Maybe I'm being presumptuous, but I have the hunch that you might like us to be more than friends. I'm sorry, but I don't feel the same. Which also means that I love our relationship as is, and I hope that still works for you too." If he can deal, make an effort to keep everything the way it was -- hanging out, talking, whatever you do together -- but turned down one notch. This will let him know you meant what you said, but it will also give him space to get over it. And don't get all Good Person and try to set him up with someone. He may not be ready . . . and you may find yourself oddly jealous.
    Love,
    Breakup Girl

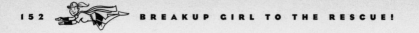
But wait. Don't run off without considering these . . .

Two Big Fat Friends-to-Lovers Caveats

1. You can't just add romance and stir.

It will not just be all the same stuff as before, plus kissing. I can't predict exactly what new issues and insights will come up between you; point is, don't be freaked when they do. No matter how comfortable you feel with each other, this IS new territory.

2. You are still taking a chance.

But when are you not?

Look, just like any other relationship that begins any other way, this may or may not work out. And if it does not, you may not be able to distill your old friendship back out, intact, from the fizzy new mixture. THIS DOES NOT MEAN YOU MADE A MISTAKE. Inspirational speech: Perhaps the friends-to-lovers evolution was natural, powerful, irresistible, even inevitable — just not, for whatever reason, permanent. Painful though the fallout may be, hey: better passionate messiness than tepid, prudent restraint and lingering what-ifs. Right?

PREDICAMENT of the CHAPTER!

No Frito-*Lay* Puns Here

Dear Breakup Girl,

I've been hanging out with this fellow for about five months now, and although we're officially just friends, I've had the hots for him for months. Recently, he's begun saying and doing little things that may indicate he now has similar feelings for me. Unfortunately, they are VERY little things, like tickling, mock fistfights, sexual innuendos, teasing, and joking about how he should put the moves on me when we go to the movies or that we should drive up into the hills and park, but never making good on these threats.

The other night we were on the couch watching a video when he took my feet and put them in his lap. I was congratulating myself on this huge display of affection when he leaned over and shoved a Frito up my nose! I might understand if he were, say, twelve, but he's twenty-seven! Another factor is that he's fairly shy and unsophisticated.

I am afraid to take the matter into my own hands and jump him; if I've misinterpreted his attentions, it would ruin our relationship. But I'm so frustrated right now that I'm kind of distant and bitchy around him, something that might jeopardize the relationship in the long run. Should I stick it out or stir things up?

—Frito Nose

Dear Frito Nose,

First of all, I laughed so hard about the Frito thing that milk came out *my* nose.

Good news: He likes you. Bad news: He is twelve. He is doing all the same things Timmy Osborne did when he liked me: you know, throw my Trapper Keeper in the mud, etc. *That was sixth grade.* You might think this Chip guy is cute and all, but remember: The person who is flirting with you in this manner is the same person that, if you date him, you will date. Okay, duh, but you know what I mean? What will you do for your anniversary, chew up crackers and try to whistle?

Harsh, maybe. But his being "shy and unsophisticated" isn't "another factor"; it's THE factor. I am really not trying to be mean. I just want to make sure he's someone with the maturity and forthrightness to come through for you beyond the flirting/snacking stage.

Still, okay. I've warned you, now I'll quit nay-saying. If you rilly have a good feeling about him as a full-fledged guy, I guess it would be safe to make an itty-bitty move. Maybe tickle his ear with a Bugle?

Love,

Breakup Girl

"TOO BUSY"
FOR A RELATIONSHIP?

 Many of the letters that Breakup Girl receives start off like this:

```
Dear Breakup Girl,
I have a question to ask you, if you're not too busy.
```

Emphasis mine. (If italicizing is important to me, I'll make time for it.) What do you guys mean, "too busy"? You are talking about Breakup Girl's job; the thought of being "too busy" to do it makes no sense. If I ever say I'm "too busy" to read your letters (not gonna happen!) that would be code for "I'm just not interested anymore" or, "David Duchovny is flying me to Fiji, and my laptop doesn't work there." In which case I'd come back and write a double-length column the following week, most of which would be dedicated to comforting Tea Leoni. Remember:

- ♥ We *all* have twenty-four hours today.
- ♥ The president has time to jog.*
- ♥ Argued another way: The president has time for at least one relationship.

My point: BG is, frankly, too busy to hear anyone else say they are "too busy for a relationship."

---

*Joke borrowed from comedian / friend Brian Frazer.

YOU EITHER WANT A RELATIONSHIP OR YOU DON'T. NO ONE IS "TOO BUSY FOR A RELATIONSHIP" S / HE REALLY WANTS.

I'll elaborate only briefly; we've all got stuff to do.

⚡ Too Busy . . . Wanting Out?

BG's dear friend Alberto used to work seven P.M. to two A.M. at a newspaper, with only Mondays and Tuesdays off. OF COURSE Alberto met the girl reporter of his dreams during this time. Who had the exact opposite schedule. I don't know how they did it — it wasn't easy, and it certainly wasn't magic — but they did, and they are still together. And now he has a better shift. You want it, you work at it, you work it out.

If you truly crave a relationship — with someone in particular or just... someone — and you truly are at a loss about how to carve out the time from, say, an all-consuming job, then that's your sign that something's gotta give.

Indeed, the job's usually the problem. Or the excuse. You guys always say stuff to me (and your exes) like, "I want to concentrate on my career right now and have no time for a serious relationship."

Well. My best friend and I have this joke where if someone asks one of us, "How's your love life?" we always say, "My CAREER is going GREAT!" We find this sidesplitting. Usually.

Anyway, if you really don't want a serious thing right now, that's fine — your call. But careers and relationships are *not* necessarily mutually exclusive. Why, look at John Tesh and Connie Selleca. Or the fabulously successful The Rules women (they get so much done because they've got their husbands around to run out for jewelry).

Also, I'm a little weary of noticing that it's only women who raise this concern. As Gloria Steinem once said, "I have yet to hear a man ask for advice on how to combine marriage and a career." Harrumph.

Here's the only scenario in which a "relationship" truly interferes with your work (other than career nonmoves like adult Xeroxing; see page 133): When you're messing around with someone you don't really care about because you're lonely and s/he's there, but then you lose sleep and feel emptier than before and get all spacey and blue at work. That's why, in a sense, it is actually the serious relationships that are most compatible with your meteoric rise up the ranks. Keep that in mind for when the one you do want comes along.

Which brings me to . . .

⚡ When You *Should* Be Too Busy for a Relationship

You *are* too busy for a nonrelationship.

Dear Breakup Girl,
     My boyfriend of about a year constantly disappoints me. He has a habit of calling me hours (even minutes) before we're supposed to go out and saying he'll be late or can- celing. I think I love him, but this behavior causes me to question that. I make time in my busy schedule (I am a law student) to see him, and I'm hurt by the constant disap- pointments. What should I do?
     —Marilyn

Dear Marilyn,
     BG looked at your Life-Runner, and you don't have time to make time for someone who won't make time for you.
     Love,
     Breakup Girl

And: If you're not in a relationship right now (but you'd like to be), you should not leave a hole in your life that spews time onto your hands. Have your life. A full, complete, busy one. One more time: Something worthwhile comes along, you'll work it out.

PREDICAMENT of the CHAPTER!

Less Busy Than Thou

Dear Breakup Girl,

I have a platonic/romantic relationship with my masseur, who's nearly twenty years older. We are remarkably compatible, except that he's jealous of my busy work and social life, saying that he gave all that up when he was a lawyer to pursue massaging—a more relaxing lifestyle. I've decided to see less of him, and at first he blamed me for my "change in priorities." Now he is chasing me, calling and paging me every day. I am ambivalent but torn. What is going on?

—Anastasia

Dear Anastasia,

First of all, *ambivalent* and *torn* are the same thing.

Second of all, *platonic* and *romantic* are not. Neither are "relaxing lifestyle" and "calling or paging every day." If Monsieur Masseur truly followed his dream and left the great American legal tradition for the Great American Back Rub, more power to him. But no fair for him to pass judgment on your lifestyle and get all less-busy-than-thou. He's clearly still defensive about his shift to life in the slower lane. Find someone else to get the knots out of your back while he works out the kinks in his life.

Love,
Breakup Girl

DOUBLE
STANDARDS

There are some situations in which Breakup Girl sticks firmly to her double standards:

♥ Good music. I conveniently forget that the Godfather of Soul is also the Mother of All Wife Beaters.

♥ Yum! I turn up my nose at milk-fed veal, but my bare hands have gleefully brought death and dismemberment to countless Maine lobsters.

♥ Statements, fashion and otherwise. War is bad, but my 82nd Airborne–surplus Corcoran paratrooper boots are good.

Basically, double standards occur when someone adheres both to a principle and to a big fat self-serving exception to that principle. And usually, the big fat self-serving exception means that someone (wives, lobsters, civilians) gets dealt a lousy hand. That's how BG describes it, but just to make this official, let's have a look at the definition of *double standard* in Breakup Girl's *American Heritage Dictionary* (a high school graduation gift from an ex-boyfriend who, like all of her high school boyfriends, is now married with children. See also, "Harsh").

> **double standard** *n* A set of principles permitting greater opportunity or liberty to one than to another, esp. the granting of greater sexual freedom to men than to women

So Steph's question is right on the money:

Why is it okay for dudes to flirt with all kinds of gals, but when a gal does it they think we're hooches?

Oh, because since the dawn of history there's been this idea that there's not enough room in Western civilization, in the Garden of Eden, or wherever, for both men and women to have sexual experience and power. Because, in a broad psychological / biological sense, it's a little nerve-racking to have no real way of knowing if you're the dad. Because the more sown your oats, the more alpha your malehood. Because…oh, BG could go on for hours. Those are just a few of the many reasons why it's "okay."

But it is NOT OKAY.

Why not? Well, first of all, it's just plain no fair.

And in the context of your actual relationships, realize that these boy/girl double standards are, deep down, all about (warning: *After-School Special* words ahead) insecurity and self-esteem. As in, "If she looks at another guy, she might not like me!" As in, "If I call him on his double standards, he might not like me!" (Or, more sinister, "Wow, he won't let me look at another guy — he must really like me!")

Point is, applying double standards to your own love life — and to others', which are none of your business — can get you into double trouble.

I'll talk to boys first, but girls, you are so not off the hook. Don't go away.

⚡ Boys/Men

How's this for self-defeating: The more double your standards, the more single you'll stay.

Dear Breakup Girl,

    I have been celibate for six years. One-night stands got old a long time ago (I've been sexually active since age sixteen), and the chance of AIDS is too great.

    Also, most all of the women I meet nowadays, in my age group (late twenties), quite often have morals lower than the average college jock. I can't imagine that type of woman one day becoming the "mother of my children." Should I lower my standards? Is wanting a reasonably attractive and intelligent woman, with morals, a sense of humor, and no baggage, too much to ask?

    —Hopeful

Dear Hopeful,

We should all have high standards. We all deserve to date Good People (who can be found in first class and steerage), and we all deserve to believe that we deserve to date Good People. "Settling" should be done only by the contents of cereal boxes.

Still, your standards need tweaking. The word *morals* makes BG nervous—not because "morals" are a bad thing, but because of how the term gets wielded. Normally, it's used not to hold oneself to standards, but to self-righteously denounce those whose allegedly fall short. Your letter, while well-intentioned, smacks of the latter. When you question the "morals" of the women you meet, I don't suppose you mean they're into kidnapping, insider trading, or building Wal-Marts in preserved wetlands. You say you can't imagine "that type of woman"—what, the type who likes sex?—becoming the mother of your children. That perception is what this type of superhero calls a Madonna/Whore Complex [see sidebar].

So if you want to marry a woman who shares your "morals"—*newfound morals, might I remind you, Mister Sexually Active Since Sixteen*—that's fine. And by all means maintain the "standards" that will make you happy. But BG suggests that you expand your notion of what and who would make a good mother. (Hint: not a virgin.)

Love,
Breakup Girl

BG STUDIES:
The Madonna/Whore Complex

That's Madonna as in Virgin, not Like A. Reams of scholarly papers have been written on this concept, but I'll define it briefly as the age-old Good Girl / Bad Girl, either-or double standard that doesn't give women a whole lot of breathing room.

There also seems to be a subcategory I'll call the Working Woman / Whore Complex (or, alternatively, the Professional / Oldest Profession complex). I got wise to it in a letter from PT, who wrote: "Although a career woman, she has made many bad decisions with past relationships, has been with lots of men, has a very promiscuous past."

Um, "career woman" and "bad decisions with past relationships" are unrelated. Speaking as a professional superhero.

Also: no fair expecting girls/women not to do or have done anything you would do or have done; you will work yourself up over something over which you have no control, cause needless problems, and drive your honey to write to me.

Dear Breakup Girl,

My yearlong relationship ended last week. I love him very much, but he cannot live with my past. When he was asking me some personal and unnecessary questions, I lied to him for fear of losing him, but then the truth came out: that I'd been with three other men before him. For five months, we have been trying to work through this, him accepting my past and the fact that I lied. Last week, he told me he couldn't stop thinking about my "mistakes" and that he wanted to see other people. How can I get him to accept the past and take me back?

—Discarded and Depressed

Dear Discarded,

Your "past," whether it contains zero men or the NBA, is not your boyfriend's to "accept" or reject.

This whole thing is a heady mix of

(a) a girl-virtue flashback to the Dark Ages, with a side of Madonna/Whore Complex [see sidebar] (he expected you to save yourself for him before you knew he existed? He dumped you because you'd seen people so that he could see other people?);

(b) a lame, cruel, easy-out excuse he's using to break up; and

(c) a serious ego shortage . . . for all parties involved.

We all get intimidated by our predecessors, yes. But your first warning sign—about your relationship and about your security in it—should have been the fact that you felt the need to lie about your past "for fear of losing him."

Geez, you know, I can't believe anyone's calling "three other men" a "past." People on *Knots Landing* have "pasts." You have a life. Now get on with it.

Love,

Breakup Girl

P.S. One more thing: No one should willfully misrepresent his/her past, but no one should feel the need to either. Hey, I think I'll sneak in an

**DON'T CREATE SOME FOOL'S GOLD STAN-
DARD OF FULL DISCLOSURE AND ASK EACH
OTHER MORE ABOUT THE PAST THAN YOU
REALLY WANT TO KNOW. THE ANSWER WILL
LIKELY BE: *MORE THAN YOU REALLY
WANTED TO KNOW.***

Girls/Women

Double standards work against you, but I don't see a lot of you working against them.

First of all, no fair letting boys/men treat you like milk-fed veal.

Dear Breakup Girl,

I've been going out with my boyfriend for five months; he's seventeen, I'm sixteen. Things were going well until I noticed how "friendly" he is with other girls. He says he loves me, and I truly know that he does, it's just that he cannot seem to stop "flirting" with other girls. He plays around with their hair and their clothes, and I don't think it is appropriate! He also gets jealous if I even receive e-mail from another guy. What should I do?
— Feeling Betrayed

Dear Betrayed,

Jealousy is weird. BG used to get fist-clenchingly jealous of her old boyfriend's crush on Benazir Bhutto, when in fact she knew she should have been impressed by his admiration of strong women and knowledge of current events. But did she make it, like, an issue? Of course not. Dumb, petty jealousies are a reflex of love; the idea is to laugh at and ignore them.

So if your boyfriend's like, "Oh, muffin, wanna hear something funny? I actually get jealous when that guy, who-ever he is, sends you those e-mails like 'MAKE $1,000'S RIGHT AT HOME' and that Neiman Marcus cookie recipe! Isn't that nuts? Ha, ha. I'm weird. Here, let me massage your feet!" that would be one thing. But if the vibe you get from your guy is more like, "Hey, you know, you need to quit reading e-mails from your platonic boy-friends so you can spend more

time watching me play with your friends' hair," well, that's
entirely another. In which case, what should you do with him
and his two standards? Three guesses.
    Love,
    Breakup Girl

Bad guy, yeah. But sometimes you gals are the bad guys. You complain about dudes who are "players," but you still hook up with them. You also call your sistahs *hooches, sluts,* and *hos* — when what you really mean is, "Damn, *I* wanted him!" or, "I hope I look cool in front of the guys when I agree with them." *You are not helping.*

Nor do I recommend that you use those bad terms...on your bad self.

Dear Breakup Girl,
    I am sleeping with two of my close guy friends. One of
them asked me about starting a public relationship with him
and I told him I wasn't interested, and from then on he has
been ignoring me. The other guy told me he loved me, and I
don't believe in love and don't want to experience it. Does
this make me a slut?
    —Clueless in Idaho

Dear Idaho,
    *Having sex outside of a "relationship" does not make you—
or anyone—a "slut."* But having sex with people who you know
want more of a relationship than you do, and then hurting
their feelings, does make you: lonely.
    Love,
    Breakup Girl

Dear Breakup Girl,
    I was riding on the bus with this guy back from a school
trip to Washington, D.C. He sat with me, we held hands, and
he tried to go up my shirt. His friends sat behind us and
were talking about what we were doing and they were teasing
him after the rest-room break. Now I'm afraid that he'll
betray me and that my whole reputation will go down the drain
as a whore. Why do the guys always blame the girls?
    —Alise

Dear Alise,

Washington, D.C. is a really, really good place to ask that question.

Love,

Breakup Girl

P.S. But seriously, you're right: It is totally no fair that his going up your shirt should (if it did) affect anyone's "reputation," let alone only yours and not his. Listen, sweetie, try your best to just stay above it all. And to have guys' hands stay above your shirt in public places. It's not your fault. I'm just saying.

So listen. Respect each other's — and your own — actions, choices, and dumb mistakes. If you think someone is doing something mean and lousy to you, get up offa that thing and call him/her on it. If you think someone is getting away with some bad behavior by flashing some fake "That's how men/women are supposed to be" license, call him/her on it. When it comes to standards, establish — and be brave enough to stick to (even if it means — gasp! — choosing to be single) — one set that works for you.

(You know, what I really mean is, Breakup Girl is allowed to have double standards and you're not.)

His and Hers
PREDICAMENTS of the CHAPTER!

Dear Breakup Girl,

I'm thirty-eight; she's twenty-four. I'm from a small town in the Midwest; she's from the big city. I thought she was this innocent thing; now I find out she used to work for an escort service.

When we make love, I have visions of other men doing the worst with her. I'm haunted by her past. Why can't I just let it go? Should I throw in the towel now and save us both the trouble?

—Kevin

Dear Kevin,

We all know that BG is not a big fan of what's known as the Madonna/Whore Complex. But don't we all secretly sort of wish our partners had been with no one before us (yet somehow were also nonclueless about being in a relationship)? Don't we all get a little "How dare you have dated them before you knew I existed"? Sure. And in your case, the "them" is a lot of guys. Who paid her. So.

Yes, the oldest profession is, "society"-wise, not the most respected. So yes, when it comes to her past, you've got a much bigger helping of ick. I understand. BUT. Lots of people have equally huge issues about the folks their partners actually, deeply loved. See? So it's up to you to tease out precisely why her past threatens your present and future together. If you feel that your girlfriends must be "pure," okay, but why? Do you feel as if you missed a chance to, like, retro-protect her? Are you bummed because you feel duped? Do you feel like just another john? You tell me. And remember, these feelings are all normal and allowed, but they have nothing to do with the real thing: Are you good and sweet to each other? Do you love and respect who each other is now? Can you talk honestly about all this stuff? If the answer to these questions is yes, make sure to explore the others. Searching your soul may temper your opinion of hers and may help those "visions" blur. Your discomfort with her past may not go away completely, but that doesn't mean you have to. Relationships, like women, are not either-or.

Love,

Breakup Girl

Dear Breakup Girl,

I am a thirty-year-old woman who is in a relationship. My problem is not the relationship but rather my past. I was an escort for three years. I left the business two years ago and have returned to grad school. My future is bright, but sometimes I'm afraid that my past will come back to haunt me, especially where relationships are concerned. I'm not ashamed of my prior occupation: I did it, I liked it, and it helped me to get to where I am now. But I'm aware that society (and men) frown on what I did. I'm afraid that if things progress with my boyfriend I will have to decide whether to tell him or not. If not him, then the next one. Should I keep

quiet and risk exposure or be honest up front and risk losing him?
    —Kristi

Dear Kristi,
    I'm not going to get Pollyanna on your ass: He might
freak. [See above.] I'm not saying freakage is right or
wrong; I'm just saying he might. Reality.
    Still, I think that you have to tell him (or whomever)
at some point. When? Well, on the one hand, there's Too Soon.
I do not think that this is a disclosure that need predate
involvement. But then there's Too Late—when any such reve-
lation could crash as a "How could you have kept this from
me?" shocker.
    So where's the point in between? It's where you've built
up enough trust to cushion the (potential) blow, but not so
much that the (potential) blow rends that same trust. On what
day that will fall, Kristi, I'm not sure. But I will tell
you this. I recommend that you date only guys whom you could
see telling, at some point, in the first place. I recommend
that you see that there is a middle ground here: that he
could be both thrown for a loop and able to deal. And I recommend that you get that dating you would be worth that.
    Love,
    Breakup Girl

"I'm Ashamed to Admit I'm Lonely!"
AND OTHER
TRUE CONFESSIONS
of Scandalous...Singles!

They're alone! Unattached!
Not normal!
There must be something wrong with them!

"No One Other Than a Wildly Unstable Lunatic Would Ever Want to Be Involved with Me!"

Dear Breakup Girl,

I travel about 85 percent of the time. I'll get three days' notice that I have to go to, say, Jerusalem for three months; I might wake up to find out I'm going to San Francisco for the day. It's hard to have a real relationship.

There is a woman whom I care about, but we drive each other nuts. When I'm in town we have a wild, irresponsible, torrid affair. Then we decide that the other is nuts, avoid each other, and then I leave town. This love/hate thing seems to be based on the fact that we're very similar, but we've gone separate ways in life. I'm a highly paid consultant; she's a stripper/full-time alcoholic. I collect exotic sports cars and condos in interesting places; she couch surfs and does methamphetamine and periodically tries to kill herself. I keep getting drawn back into her chaotic life, no matter how much I tell myself I need to walk away. Part of the reason, I'm sure, is that no one other than a wildly unstable lunatic would ever want to be involved with me. I'm successful but wildly eccentric. I look like a suit-and-tie

guy, but at heart (and on weekends) I'm a shaved-head-and-leather guy. Should I give up?
— Jason

Dear Jason,

I hate to tell you, but you're not as wildly eccentric as you think. Half those shaved-head-and-leather-on-weekends guys *are* suit-and-tie guys the rest of the time, like you. Half the relationships I hear about are love/hate, opposites-attract infinite loops. Half the jobs I hear about are unpredictable and heavy on the travel. Mine being one of them. So if you wanted BG to say, "Wow, you're weird, it's hopeless, don't bother settling down and committing to something stable, Breakup Girl gives you permission to mess around and complain about it for the rest of your life"—well, sorry.

So what DO you want, Jason? What is this thing you call a "real" relationship? Do you want in or out of the one you're in? Velveteen Rabbity, but true: It's real if you make it real. Like, I don't know, maybe you are a good match. Are you willing to take it on for real, help her quit doing unhealthy things? You have the means—do you have the will? If not, walk away and leave yourself open to something more stable (narrow it down to one condo?). If you really want this so-called real relationship, then I'm sure you're smart and successful enough to set up the circumstances that will allow you to build one.

Love,
Breakup Girl

"I'm Ashamed to Admit I'm Lonely!"

Dear Breakup Girl,

I've always been content with my life and myself, and I never thought I needed a man. Lately, though—I'm ashamed to admit it—I've started to feel lonely (I even shed a few tears a few hours ago). I have been without a man (a date, even!) for over a year. It's starting to get to me. I'm even starting to wonder what's wrong with me (and why the only interested people are the guy friends I want to keep that way). Some motivational words about hanging in there and having fun on my own are needed right now.
— Deborah

Dear Deborah,

Feeling lonely and feeling like you need a man are unrelated. A lot of people have a partner and are still lonely. Humans are social. They like companionship, not to mention reproduction (going through the motions, anyway). A partner —not, mind you, a savior, an answer, etc.—is a lovely thing to want.

If you feel bad (for the wrong reasons) about wanting to be with someone (for the right ones), you won't just get out there and do the voodoo that you do. Which you do do, because people do like you. Just because you don't LIKElike them doesn't mean it doesn't count. I know it's ironic (in the Alanis Morisette sense; like, it sucks).

But take their feelings as votes of confidence, not as winks at your inner spinster.

Love,
Breakup Girl

"Lumped with a LOSER!"

Dear Breakup Girl,

After a big breakup, I moved to a new city where I knew *nobody*. Now I'm *definitely* over him and looking to get on with the romance thing. Problem is, all my new friends are couples. On New Year's Eve we're going out to dinner, and I am the only one without a partner. The real problem is that the dinner is one of those medieval ones where you have to feed each other. What am I going to do? I don't want to be lumped with some single loser at another table. This is the first time that my singleness is really bothering me. I want to go out with my friends, but it could get awkward. What should I do?

—Desperately Single

Dear Desperately Single,

If it makes you feel any better, the thought of going to one of those medieval eateries even *with* a partner is one of Breakup Girl's worst nightmares. It might *seem* like a couples thing, but trust me, a raucous pageant of goose drumsticks, beer wenches, and live jousting will not give anyone the warm snugglies. The main reason people wind up feeding their partners may be that they'd rather not eat the food themselves.

Why not ask a trusted friend among the dinner crowd to invite a couple stag buddies? Not to fix you up; to take the pressure off. And don't automatically assume that other third wheels will be "single losers," because, uh, you're single and you're not a loser. I mean that! As a single woman in a new city, you're doing all the right things: finding friends before lovers, being a good sport . . . but drawing lines where you need to. Your love life will have a renaissance long before you reach middle age.

Love,

Breakup Girl

"PICKY!"

Dear Breakup Girl,

How can I stop myself from clinging to ridiculous fantasies about guys I hardly know and then feeling stupid when I find out, months later, that they are married, gay, or in need of a baby-sitter? Although my life is together otherwise, I seem to thrive on these pseudorelationships in which I don't actually know the guy but feel content and fulfilled just thinking about how gorgeous he is and how excited I am about seeing him next. Do I have fantasy relationships to protect myself from cruel reality? Also, it seems the more I know a guy, the more I see his imperfections — things like the way he chews his food or holds his pen. Why am I so picky about minor details when I have, in past relationships, managed to forgive massive personality flaws?

One big fat Hmmm . . .

—Clare

Dear Clare,

Hmmm, not so fat. Your only problem is that you think you have a problem. You've got some space in your life these days, and these fantasy guys are filler. Normal, normal, normal. Especially because if you do feel fulfilled in the rest of your life, these are not Calgon crushes. Still, if you want to waste a little less time: About the married/gay thing — um, find out first. If you're perspicacious enough to notice that someone's jaw cracks when he eats or that he writes that funny left-handed upside-down way, you're qualified to take a pretty good stab at his predominant lifestyle.

Also, excellent question about "minor details" versus

"massive flaws." It's totally fine to notice those details, even to let them annoy you. Just don't dismiss someone based on only them. Result-/payoff-wise, picky is the same as its spectrum opposite: indiscriminate. They're both ways of setting things up to tank. So be buoyed by crushes, be irked by "flaws"; just do your damnedest not to fixate on either at the expense of one big fat . . . IT.

Love,
Breakup Girl

"No One Will Want to Date Me Because of . . . My BABY!"

Dear Breakup Girl,
    I am an educated, attractive, fun-to-be-with, early-twenties woman with a seven-month-old son. I broke up with his father about two months ago and am ready to meet someone, but I am scared no one will want to date me because of my baby. Where would I meet a guy?
    —Single Mom

Dear Single,
    Yeah, it might be a little tricky. Anyone—male or female—who fantasizes about having all sorts of firsts with a soul mate might think, "No fair, s/he already got to do the kid thing with someone else." Or might never have thought about kids in the first place.
    Still, it can be done. I checked with my single-mom friend Rachel—who is getting remarried shortly!—and she says to be discreet (not cagey) at first. "I asked a guy to come into Toys 'R' Us with me, and I never heard from him again," she says.
    But she also pointed out that you do have a built-in screening process: It's not that a guy for whom a kid is a deal breaker is bad—but the ones who do stick around are, more than likely, way into you and not freaked about the dad thing.
    Where to meet? Well, at this point, Rachel's fourteen-year-old daughter piped up. "Parent-teacher conferences!" Not a bad idea. But I bet you'll find someone before your son is old enough to give advice.
    Love,
    Breakup Girl

"Is It Even Worth It After All the Horror Stories?"

Dear Breakup Girl,

I am an attractive, intelligent, successful, and talented young lady in my early twenties. I am also shy and so I never got into the whole dating/relationship scene.

1) Is it too late for me now, since everyone else has at least seven or eight years' more experience? Does my delay mean there is something inherently wrong with me?

2) Is it even worth it after all the horror stories I see in your advice columns?

—A Basket Case in CA

Dear Basket Case,

You do realize that the people with all this "experience" are the same people with all the "horror" stories. You'll be fine.

Love,

Breakup Girl

WHY IT'S OKAY FOR WOMEN TO NOT WANT TO BE SINGLE

The "the women's movement is wack" people -- and the people who love them -- are far too quick to point to women who feel lonely and say, "See, women SAY they're independent, but they really just want to get married."

Hello, why is this a contradiction? How come when men want to get married, they're settling down, but when women do, they're giving in? Couldn't it be about partnership? What's wrong with wanting someone to split the driving? Couldn't it be that we think we've got surplus excellence to share, thank you very much? So there.

That's a little less flip than Breakup Girl's usual quip: "I don't 'need a man,' I need an assistant." (Especially because I've got one.) (Guess which.)

Relationships: DURING

"Oh, God, I would *hate* to go back to dating!
It's so *hard!*" This is the I-felt-your-pain
proclamation of the safely coupled up.
It is also a big bluff.
Not that you folks want to go back to being
single. But the opposite of being single is hardly the
opposite of hard. For pairs, the only no-brainer,
really, is knowing whom to write in the "In case of
emergency" blank. Here's how to tackle the rest of
the totally worth-it work of being attached.

It Came From The Past

WHEN YOUR PARTNER'S EX

HAUNTS

YOU

Furniture moves. Doors slam shut and open again behind you. Memories hurl themselves across the room. Trust and closure drop off the edge and shatter.

They're heee-re.

In fact, maybe you only *thought* they were gone.

Gather 'round the campfire and scooch your sleeping bags close together.... Heard the one about the possessive ex who sucked the life out of your squeeze?

Or, even spookier, the one where the telltale jealous heartbeat you hear is actually... your own!?

EEEK!

How to ward off the curse? By keeping in mind these antislime precepts:

1. Our partners come with pasts, and sometimes those pasts come to parties. It happens.

2. People who have gone on to other relationships are allowed to be friends — like, actual, cordial FRIENDfriends — with their exes. Current squeezes pretty much have to hold their heads high and deal.

3. Current squeezes are, however, allowed to be upset if what's going on is not a cordial friendship but a leftover entanglement of feelings and manipulations. Or dates.

4. Exes must accept that current squeezes may hate them for no reason. And, unless someone makes that their business, it's not.

So let's get out our flashlights and rev up the Ecto-mobile!

⚡ Past as Poltergeist

Sometimes your squeeze's restless ex truly is an interfering poltergeist who loves to dig up clunky knickknacks and toss them between you. What's the best way to move from Amityville to Pleasantville?

By first making the essential distinction between your partner's past and your present business. Even if your partner's ex is behaving like a (as many of you seem to put it) psycho hose beast, it's not your place to stand between the two of them. It is your place to say, in tacky-but-tried-and-true couples-therapy speak, "When you get into these lingering things with your ex, *I feel . . .*" It's a delicate distinction, but how your ex handles PHB is his or her beeswax; how PHB's presence affects you is *your* beeswax, as in "your," plural. (And if you run into this person, you *do* have to be nice. You just do. Be briefly cordial; if you can't stand it, go powder your nose or check your wiper fluid. Do not say, for example, "Oh! You're the psycho hose beast I wrote to Breakup Girl about! How delightful to finally attach the face to the name!")

Sometimes these ghouls, like vampires, must actually be invited in. Maybe Cornelius's girlfriend never even asked hers to leave.

Dear Breakup Girl,

    My girlfriend had just broken up with her boyfriend—a dysfunctional relationship—when I started seeing her.

    Our relationship is dynamite, except that she keeps bringing up her ex. Every once in a while she gets all weepy and says that if he would come back to her then the pain she has will go away. I'm going insane. What should I do? Will this end? Her obsession with the breakup aftermath is becoming mine. Help!

    —Cornelius

Dear Cornelius,

    If you have indeed quoted your girlfriend accurately, what she has is not Basic Breakup Blues—which time does muffle—but rather: Major Unresolved Issues. The aftermath of a twisted relationship might as well be AP Calculus.

    And the thing that worries me most about Her Weepiness is this: *her use of the dreaded fantasyland "if . . . then"*

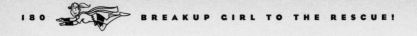
function that turns humans into saints and relationships into rescue missions.

So now, whatever issue was still lodged in her life at the time is now lodged in yours too. A dynamite relationship? Perhaps. But there's also a land mine buried here somewhere. Replace the blinders with protective goggles and do what you need to do to defuse it.

Love,
Breakup Girl

Your Own Demons

Or is the real mischief-maker a cobwebbed-corner-dwelling gremlin called ...*your insecurity?* Basic retrojealousy (as in, "How dare you date her/him when you didn't know I existed?" or, more reasonably, "How tough an act am I following here? And how'm I doing so far?") is totally normal in these situations. Even if (a) the present relationship is healthy, and (b) the exes involved currently loathe each other. So expect that gremlin to show up, yes — but that doesn't mean you have to listen to it.

Dear Breakup Girl

My boyfriend's old girlfriend is a basket case who often needs "rescuing"; they talk a few times a week. I trust that he doesn't want to be with her romantically, but he's never introduced us and I resent that they are perpetuating this relationship. He claims he's never been as close to anyone as he is to me and that he loves me and respects me deeply. Am I being stupid for not putting my foot down?
—Jealous

Dear Jealous,

New girlfriends and old girlfriends, especially when each has a case of jealousy and "basket," respectively, go together like oil and water. You *want* to meet her? Why? So you can see *The English Patient* and go out for pink drinks and bond? So you can smile nicely and be the stable, nonsingle one? I can think of way more productive things to do with your life, such as learning to make the perfect vinaigrette.

So maybe your guy is, well, nice. And he feels like he's got to do his ex-boyfriend time and let Basketta vent every "once in a while," even if he's brushing his teeth and playing Tomb Raider while she rants.

Well? Is he, you know, nice? *To you?* You use the word
claims about his feelings. Is that his behavior talking—as
in, his actions *when he's with you* truly do not illustrate
his words—or is it your insecurity? That's what you need to
figure out. Because yes, in the narrowest legal interpreta-
tion, you may ask that he cut off contact with her. But if
you do put your foot down about it, that may also be exactly
where you'll shoot yourself.
Love,
Breakup Girl

⚡ When the Poltergeist Is . . . You

When we break up, we *say* things like, "I want you to find the person who
will make you truly happy." Yuh. But what we really mean is, "I am the
only person who knows how to do that. I just don't feel like doing it right
now." So when our exes find new potential Happy-Makers, we freak a little. We feel the need to know and express the notion that "Well, my ex
may have moved on, but we had Something Really Special That No One
Else Can Ever Understand. Much less match." This impulse is what may
drive us to lurk — as, supposedly, a benevolent spirit — in our ex's new
relationship.

Dear Breakup Girl,
    My friend has been having trouble with his girlfriend.
Did I mention that he is my ex? Part of his problem with her
is the fact that she hates his hanging out with me, calling
me, and even (through a fluke) staying (on the floor) in my
room at school last weekend. We spend a good chunk of our
time discussing his problems with their situation. In fact,
he just called me sobbing because he was so frustrated with
her. I don't want to see his relationship end, but I personally think he would make a better bachelor than a
boyfriend right now. I have to be careful not to sound like
the "jealous ex," but believe me, we are much better off as
friends. Please help me help my friend.
    —Jessica

Dear Jessica,
    Imagine how you'd feel if you were having a rocky go of
it with your boyfriend and the person who talked (hoteled) him
through it was his ex. Now does this gal seem a bit less wacked?

Your involvement here is legal, but it's . . . *weird*. And it's not really working, is it? *Au contraire*. I think your job, as a friend, is to give Mattress Man once more your official opinion about bachelor versus boyfriend and then drop it. And rule the topic off-limits between you two. If he doesn't have other friends he can go to about this, well, that's a problem. AND if you two have nothing left to talk about, that too. Could be that you are/were running on fondess fumes. So if you are committed to staying friends, find new activities and sources of interaction (not sleepovers). You'll make a better buddy than a therapist right now.

Love,

Breakup Girl

MONEY, HONEY

Though BG's metier offers rich spiritual rewards, cash flow — no matter its quantity — is a concern for any single superhero. And even though "two-income family" appears, in her own adult life, to be an entity much like "the unicorn," BG well knows that the issue of money can tax a relationship, no matter what bracket. Whether you're a two-Beamer couple, a two-slacker couple — or, Hamilton help us, a one-professional, one-potato couple, well, let's see if we can settle some accounts.

⚡ It's Not About the Money

In the biggest picture, money doesn't mean a thing. It's just the pieces of paper and metal that are legally established as an exchangeable equivalent for commodities. That's why the Mexican government can just up and say things like, "Hey, let's get rid of some zeros."

Yet experts cite finances as a top cause of friction in relationships. Why is money such a big deal? Well, remember: Money is, by definition, *a measure of value*. Also, your currency has a past. Taken together, these points mean that society infuses money with larger-than-paper meaning, and so do you. How were you raised? Wanting for nothing? Coveting everything? Was money talked about or taboo? Did it drive a widget between your parents? Is being better off than they a big thing for you (or for them)? For these or whatever other reasons, you made up your mind that money equals success or that money equals all evil or that money equals masculinity or that money equals the reason you do or don't date. That's also why the

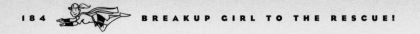

January/February 1999 issue of *Psychology Today* talks about people as Money Personalities (Planners, Dreamers, Hoarders, Spenders, Money Monks, Money Amassers, etc.) who — when they wind up as partners — clash. The color of money itself changes depending on how you choose to look at it, and in turn it shades your life and the love therein.

Dear Breakup Girl,

The guy I'd been dating for a year dumped me because — from what I seem to be hearing — I am more "together" than he is. I feel like his basic insecurities wouldn't let him date someone who had gotten her act together. I own a house and car, and make about $40,000 a year. I got here by going to college and dedicating myself to my career (I'm forty-seven). I try to contribute as much as I can when we are going out — sometimes I pay both of our ways, other times he pays, or we split.

Also: I'm an interior designer. My house looks like a magazine. I did most of the work myself because I couldn't afford tradesmen. I learned plumbing, electrical, painting — you name it. But these guys seem to be intimidated by my design!

Why do relationships have to be a contest? Why can't I date someone who makes less than I do? Why can't men accept me (and my income) and have a good time?
— Donna

Dear Donna,

With all due respect, you're not that rich. Forty thousand is just not enough to be the stuff of intimidating first dates involving helicopters, private islands, etc.

Thus the "intimidation" thing may be all in your head — or all in your actions and attitudes, not to mention your curtains. You are a do-it-yourselfer, Donna, which I admire. But I wonder whether, in relationships or on dates, you also work *around* the Tradesman in question. Whether he feels as if even when he pays all or half, it's because you've already done the math. Whether he feels as if there's not much left for him to do around there. Everyone, male and female, needs to know and feel that they are needed, handy, difference-making. Not just on a tour of someone else's fabulous, together showroom life.

So no, you do not have to date men of equal salary/

stature / whatever. But if you do not want to wander your big rooms alone, then you also do not have to date hapless guys for whom you feel like a stabilizing force and then say, "There he goes again" if they wind up feeling smaller than your sofa. You also should not have to define your own security by ta-da-ing it to others. That above all is something you do yourself.

Love,
Breakup Girl

⚡ So Don't Hide Money Issues Under the Mattress

Yes, bringing up money in a relationship is like opening Pandora's cash box (even in New York City, where people will discuss their rents with strangers but not their salaries with intimates). Relationship and financial experts concur, however, that putting things off will cost you even more. So try a little legal tenderness. When you talk about money, don't talk about money. Talk about in / dependence, support, partnership, gratification, plans, dreams. *Then* talk about the role that Washington, Lincoln, and Jackson play in all that, and take it from there.

Dear Breakup Girl,

My boyfriend and I are talking about moving to be in the same city. He's bound to Chicago for the next two years, and I'm in L.A. He has offered to help me move sooner by helping me financially. But I have always been a "pay my own way" girl and want to earn the money myself. There is a principle here I don't want to break. But it's excruciating to consider being apart for another year! What do you think?
— Languishing in L.A.

Dear Languishing,

If you're that serious about him — and about paying your way — then make a deal. Figure out about how much he's going to shell out and then make a "plan" for "paying" him back. Not that love and generosity should be quid pro quid (in England that's a pun); I'm saying this because it's bothering *you*. And you don't have to return the kindness in kind: Maybe you bake his favorite pie or tune up his transmission every week.

You two need to not only hammer out the nuts and bolts —

How much? When? Pumpkin?—but also at least to acknowledge some of the feelings and complications that could come up—What if you break up? Will you feel beholden to him? Would he want a refund? What kind of pie? etc. If you two can discuss these matters intelligently and reasonably in the first place, that bodes well.

Love,
Breakup Girl

Dear Breakup Girl,

My boyfriend always treats me to dinner, movies, and everything else. I'm getting tired of him paying for me, but I have no money since I'm a student. What can I do for him that is thoughtful and inexpensive so that he knows I really appreciate his generosity?

—Michelle

Dear Michelle,

Survey says: "COOKIES!"

Love,
Breakup Girl

⚡ Paying: The Way

Let me take this opportunity to reiterate an

IMPORTANT BREAKUP GIRL MAXIM

WHOEVER INVITED PAYS.

Don't you dare take out (a) a nice girl/boy, and then (b) a #2 pencil and a legal pad to calculate his/her share. TACKY (also see page 103). It's not about money; it's about manners. If you can't afford a particular venue, then go someplace within your means and be equally gracious there (as Paul the Intern would say, "Supersize that for the lady!").

the cheat sheet

*I*f there's any chapter in this book that could itself fill a book — if not an entire Time Life series — this is it. There's no evidence that people are cheating any more now than they did back when we pretended they didn't, but that's just it: We're *talking* about it more. As Joseph Hooper wrote in the April 29, 1999, *New York Times*, "Most experts think it is unlikely that infidelity is more popular today than it was in the 1950s and 1960s, when men often enjoyed the advantages of a sexual double standard, or in the swinging 70s, when open marriage had its vogue. But if psychologists and therapists have anything to say about it, we are entering a Golden Age of thinking about infidelity."

So what that GA means for BG is that — after doing some homework of my own — I have lots more to say to you guys about infidelity than "No!" "Bad!" or "Come on, everyone knew about President Kennedy!" Such as:

⚡ Cheating: Cause ... Versus Symptom

Used to be that infidelity (in a marriage, anyway) was taken to be a symptom of something rotten in Denmark / Stepford / wherever. But according to Dr. Shirley Glass — the mother of all infidelity experts, and of all NP-heaRtthrob radio personalities named Ira — affairs (especially men's) are often the *cause* of couple conflict. In other words, an affair — again, especially for men — is not necessarily a sign of an unhappy marriage. Fifty-six percent of the men Glass has surveyed who've had affairs said they were happily married (versus 34 percent of the women).

Whuh?

Well — truth-in-icky-stereotype alert!* — according to Glass, men *tend* to have sexual affairs (boinking over bonding) and women *tend* to have emotional affairs (bonding plus). In one of Glass's studies, 44 percent of cheatin' men said they'd had little or no emotional involvement, versus 11 percent of women who said the same. Which, Glass says, suggests that even some men who dig their partners don't turn down sex ops that present themselves.** (It's when an affair combines emotional and sexual involvement that the marriage is up the deepest creek.)

To be fair, you won't catch me casting any first beach pebbles on behalf of the gals:

Dear Breakup Girl,

    I cheated on my boyfriend, Rodney. I was at a beach party and I ended up kissing another guy (Joey) that I'd gone steady with before. I told Rodney, but he never gave me a chance to explain what happened. The truth is I cheated because I needed to know if it was Rodney I loved, or Joey. Even though I realized that I loved Rodney, he won't listen to the truth. How can I get the love of my life back?
    —Courtney

Dear Courtney,

    I'm pretty sure that you cheated on Rodney because you were at a beach party and ended up kissing another guy. Not because you had planned some chemistry experiment to find out whom you loved more.

    But. People don't love to hear things like, "I love you so much that when I cheated on you I didn't enjoy it!" You may have to drop it for now, punkin. I'm sorry. I know it doesn't feel this way now and that I am about to sound like your square aunt, but I promise there will be other fish at the beach. Catch them one at a time, okay?
    Love,
    Breakup Girl

---

* Please forgive the Mars/Venus factor here. But keep in mind that Dr. Glass does her clinical homework, and Dr. Gray works his magic unencumbered by actual research.

**Also: I assume — but do not know for sure — that these tendencies apply to men and women in same-sex relationships. You just get two of each, I'm thinking. But if you — unlike BG's G3 Supercomputer — can find anything else on this, let me know.

The fact that people like Courtney and, well, men cheat even when they're happy gives us a piece of hollowly good news: *that there's really no such thing as Cheating Prevention.*

> Dear Breakup Girl,
>
> I argued a lot with my girlfriend about this, but she assured me that the guys she hung out with were "friends." I put up with it until she finally cheated on me with one of them. Do you think it's too much to ask of a girlfriend to not have guy friends?
> —The Man
>
> Dear Man,
>
> *Don't you dare ask any girlfriend to not have guy friends.* Come on, Man, if a girlfriend asked you not to have any friend-girls, you'd call her a psycho jealous freak. I know you're smarting, but if someone's going to cheat, she's going to cheat, whether with a "friend" or not. Anyway, the best relationships—platonic and romantic—are those in which partners want and trust each other to have "other" lives, other friends. *That's* not too much to ask.
> Love,
> Breakup Girl

Even if you are hell to live with 24/7 (in which case you should work on that), *even then*, the decision to have an affair is *entirely your partner's.* So none of this "If only I'd made her favorite meat loaf more often . . ." Okay? Because remember: There are also people who are utterly miserable *and* utterly faithful. Go figure.

⚡ . . . And Effect

That cheating chestnut is pretty true: What sucks supremely about infidelity is the feeling of betrayal, the feeling that everything you set store by has sold out. And just to venture back into the Dr. Gray area: Turns out that — generally — men freak more when their wives boink someone else; women freak more when their husbands bond with someone else. (Not that either gender is really jazzed about any of this, of course.)

Speaking of freaking, let's hear a cautionary tale from a woman who signed herself, "If you met me you would never believe in a zillion years that I am . . . UNFAITHFUL."

I fell in love with a married coworker last year. Then my husband got transferred and we had to move far away. I was ready to leave my marriage for him, but he "doesn't believe in divorce." My thirtieth high school reunion is this summer, and here I sit, brokenhearted.

In these situations, everyone gets hurt, including the families who suffer the emotional absence. You have no one to turn to (it's a secret, remember?). Even if this person says s/he loves you, it's still untenable. You ask him/her to leave; imagine the rejection you feel upon hearing s/he cannot. I'm warning you: If you're married or if s/he is, stay away — do NOT break your heart like I have. Are you listening?

Eeeeuw. Enough said.

⚡ Rehabilitation: What It Takes

Yes, BG believes in rehabilitation. But it doesn't take what you might think it does.

I. The cheater

Your cheatee might want to know, "What did you see in [that psycho hose beast] that you didn't see in me?" Or, "What did you like about [Senator Packwood] better?" But that's not what Dr. Glass would ask you. She'd want to know: "What did you like better about *yourself*

> "I cheated on my boyfriend in college with an engaged boss. Seemed like such a good idea at the time . . . What I learned was this: I will never cheat on anyone again. Having to see the look on his face when I told him (he cornered / confronted me) made it all suddenly so not worth it."
> —BARRIE

in that other relationship? And [how] can we find that part of you in your primary relationship?" Yes, this is heady stuff. Think about it.

Also, microcheaters, see "What and Who Is and Isn't Cheating," page 198.

And (un)repentant serial cheaters, here is your challenge: Either get into a relationship that you'd rather die than screw up, or don't get into a relationship. OR: Aren't you dying to know why you're screwing up relationships you'd rather die than screw up? Talk to a professional so that maybe you can start to live.

2. The cheatee

Yeesh. Your task: First, hurt like hell.

> To me, the difference between boyfriends I have and have not cheated on is this: I have not cheated on the ones I really want to stay with.
>
> -- M&M

ROMANCE!

Dear Breakup Girl,

My husband has been having an affair for several months. He admitted to it only after I found a copy of a telltale e-mail message he sent using my address. He still sees her, sleeps with her, and buys her gifts, but comes home to sleep and change clothes. How do I get him out of the house? Divorce proceedings should begin next week, but until then, how do I put up with this? I have all her info—should I contact her? I don't know if her husband knows, but I wouldn't mind telling him. By the way, my spouse got her a $1,000 diamond necklace for Valentine's Day. (I found the receipt.) Any advice on how to get through the worst time of my life?

—Victoria

Dear Victoria,

Wowie zowie. I am SO sorry. A few things:

1. Not a good idea to contact her. Nor her husband. Clear temptation, but stay above tattling. Call a therapist instead. Helping you hurt, then heal, is a job for a professional.

2. He used your e-mail address? Either he hasn't figured out how to use AOL's "change screen name" feature or he wanted to get caught. Denmark was already rotting.

3. If he can afford diamonds, he can afford a hotel (in the Netherlands?). The only way you can start getting through this—and it's going to be a haul, emotionally and legally—is to clear your mind/home of virtual paper trails, QVC receipts, and lipstuck collars.

The rest: clichés. Seek out friends, family, Fabio-bedecked bodice rippers. Whatever works, dragging minute by dragging minute. At least getting heinous news and facing a horrific—but clear—task is, in some sense, easier on your constitution than being "If only he were a total jerk!"-type confused. Clean house; assemble allies; be strong.

Love,
Breakup Girl

Also, now that you know there is no such thing as cheating prevention: *whom should you not blame?*

Dear Breakup Girl,

   I found out a month before my wedding that my fiancé was having an affair. After soul-searching and couples counseling, I forgave him, and we rescheduled. But when I went to his house to pick him up to look at a reception site, I found him in bed with another woman. Now the wedding's off for good. My problem is that I want to move on, yet I feel I can never trust another man again. Suggestions? I don't want to spend the rest of my life alone because of what I let this jerk do to me.
   —Lindsey

Dear Lindsey,

   There's no grammatically graceful way to do this, but rewrite your last sentence so that it says that *you're* the jerk. NOT THAT YOU ARE. But this, bottom line, is how you feel. Never mind what he did: It's you—as far as you are concerned—who "let" him. So no wonder you don't feel like dating. Last time you did, you wound up feeling like an alone stupid jerk. See? Let yourself off the hook, and you won't have "let" him do anything.
   Love,
   Breakup Girl

GETTING THE DIGITS

THE MO-TELL

• Fifty-seven percent of men and 64 percent of women say they've cheated on a partner (figure includes "just a stupid blip that didn't mean anything" and "just some stupid blips that . . . now that I think about it, kind of add up").

• Most men and women err on the side of not fessing up ("Would have created more problems than it solved").

• More women than men -- though not a majority -- report "No remorse"!

• Most men and women report -- or hypothesize -- that their reaction to being cheated on was / would be to "cheat back." Oh, great.

Finally, yes, a trusty therapist could help, whether you wind up single or second-chancing (see below). Keep the following in mind as well: An excellent way not to have to do the tough work of reconstructing trust is to continue to seek out relationships with not-so-trusty people. Gong! I recommend you do it the hard way.

3. The couple

Worth a second try? Probably, even just in principle; if Lindsey hadn't given her ex chance #2,
she'd have written me to ask, "What if?"

And in practice? The cheater must Get It.
Demonstrating this includes temporary forfei-
ture of his/her right to say: "Quit glancing
sidelong at my beeper! Quit crying when we
take the only road out of town, past the no-tell
motel where we were caught! Quit microwaving my videotape of *From
Here to Eternity*!" Cheaters are also not allowed to say, "I DID A BAD
THING I KNOW I KNOW I'M THE WORST PERSON IN THE WORLD
I KNOW I KNOW I KNOW *NOW* CAN WE CHANGE THE SUBJECT
BECAUSE PHOEBE'S ABOUT TO FIND OUT ABOUT CHANDLER
AND MONICA?" You must sound — you must BE — truly contrite.

However. It takes two to grovel. The cheatee is also not allowed to (a)
want to make things work with someone whom s/he (b) refuses to forgive.
It is up to both of you to look down at the shared terrain of your relationship
— which is different from pointing fingers at one another — and see where
the faults and fissures lie. And figure out together — or apart — how to step
back onto solid ground.

Dear Breakup Girl,
    My boyfriend cheated on me, leading to a messy breakup.
Three months later, he called crying, saying how much he
loved me and how he messed up. . . . He wanted to get back
together. My feelings were still too raw, so I said it would
be best to take more time apart.
    Well, it's been nearly two years. We are good friends . . .
and lately I've been feeling as though I'd like to try things
out again. We've talked about why we broke up; the time apart
has made me realize I don't NEED him anymore but would LIKE
to have him back in my life on another level. He's been hint-
ing the same and has told me he'd never cheat again. Should
I give things a shot?
    —Time After Time

Dear Time After Time,
    You've done all the right things; you've said all the

right things — to each other and to me. Do I think you should give it another go? Time After Time, I do.

Love,
Breakup Girl

"Once a Cheater, Always a Cheater"?

Dear Breakup Girl,

Should I marry a man who is handsome, loving, vulnerable, tolerant, and in most ways very honest?

Should I marry a man who cheated in his two previous relationships — and on me, and lied about it?

He is all of those things. He regrets his mistakes and has promised I can trust him. I can't imagine waking up and not finding him at my side, not hearing his voice every day saying that he loves me, not being able to share our thoughts. We feel *right* together. But can a leopard change its spots? Can someone grow out of being sexually unreliable? Am I asking for disaster?

— Jackie

Dear Jackie,

First, a reminder: Cheating on you and lying about it are the same.

Second, reassurance: One can grow out of being sexually unreliable. A partnership can grow out of being betrayed. You stuck around; the others didn't. Does this mean you are dumb, in denial — or circumspect, committed, resilient? Either.

Other than that, even a superhero can't predict his behavior for sure. That's why, ultimately, this is more about you. You can't imagine not finding him, not hearing him. Gotcha. But can you imagine *not* waking up in a cold sweat, wondering if he's home? Can you imagine *not* wondering if you just asked, "One disaster, please!"?

I am not talking about moving forward with blind, deaf, mute trust. I'm talking about figuring out how to live and love your life — together — with this yuck in your past. He may well change his spots, but you'll also need to earn your stripes.

Love,
Breakup Girl

⚡ Tempted . . .

As Marjorie Ingall wrote in the April 1999 *Ms.*:

> I don't think lifetime monogamy is natural…as in bodies in motion tend to stay in motion. Yet part of the burden and joy of being human is that we can exert our will. We can say, "I'm attracted to someone else, but I've made a promise and will not act on that attraction." Lifetime commitment is a leap of faith. That's why it's so powerful.

So consider true temptation a "warning" heart attack. Not enough to kill you, but enough to make you pass on the Twinkies and rejigger your current lifestyle. Got that? *Pass on the Twinkies.* Instead, read the risk factors. Or, as Ingall writes, "If you are tempted to break whatever contract you have, hie your ass to couples therapy."

Still, hypochondria is unnecessary.

Dear Breakup Girl,

    I love my new husband a lot, but I still feel a need to go out, without him, with my friends. Well, in particular with one friend, who happens to be a man (a very gay man). The problem is that I feel that now that I'm married, it's not appropriate for me to be socializing without my husband—especially because in some ways I feel closer to this man than to my husband. On some level I feel like I'm cheating—am I feeling unnecessarily guilty?

    —Just Married

Dear Married,

    It is not weird for you to have a friend with whom you deal on a different (not higher, not lower) level from your husband. My concern is that you're concerned. Maybe you do have an itty-bitty, secret, fizzy end-in-itself crush on Gay Friend. No big. So are you "unnecessarily guilty?" Yes. Do you feel like your marriage is a delicate new sprout in need of constant care? Do you feel the same about your self-esteem? Do you feel like your husband's love has to be earned, incubated, protected, defended? Think about it. Actually, if I were you, I'd, um, ask your friend.

    Love,

    Breakup Girl

When You're the "Other"

Three words about their "other" relationship: *They're. Not. Leaving.*

Well, they might. I've heard tell of successful prebounds. (Page 52.) But assume they're not and plan accordingly. Meantime, do a little soul-searching: What don't you dig about the ones you can have? You tell me.

Speaking of your soul, I totally know that the sadness of losing/ missing someone bruises your heart. But guilt and lies and limbo eat your brain. And your spirit. And your limbs.

Dear Breakup Girl,

I'm in love with a man who is "separated" from his wife. It's been over a year and there's still no sign of their divorce papers. He stays there three nights a week for the sake of the kids and the others in "his" house, to which I've never been invited. Is it time for ultimatums? The sex is out of this world. Help . . .

— Bad Addiction

IF I'VE CHEATED, DO I HAVE TO TELL?

That's an excellent question to ask Breakup Girl. As in, not to ask the cheatee. As in, "Honey, just hypothetically, if I cheated, would you want me to tell you?"

BG's answer: *Not necessarily.* Here's a question for you: If you keep this secret, can you live with yourself? No? Good. *That's your punishment.*

See, sometimes -- like, when some one-too-many-gimlet thing happens that reallyreallyreallyreally won't happen again -- spilling your guts spills more blood than necessary. Sometimes people think what they're doing is sharing / expressing / confessing, when what they're really doing is unloading / dramatizing / self-martyring . . . *which is something you do for you singular, not for you plural.*

So you may be able to keep one flingamajig under your hat. Still, work/play on this assumption: YOU ALWAYS GET CAUGHT. Which, for some of you receipt-leaver-arounders and collar-lipstick-leaver-oners, may be the point.

Dear Addiction,

I'll *bet* the sex is out of this world! There's no aphrodisiac like estrangement! That goes for the sex he's having with you as well as the sex he's having . . . *three nights a week with his wife.*

This deal reminds me of that movie by David Lynch's daughter, *Boxing Helena*, where the guy cuts off Sherilyn Fenn's

limbs and stores her in a box for his pleasure (unless you're a Lynch, not a family film). Babe, the papers aren't coming and neither is your ultimatum. Grow some legs and walk away.
   Love,
   Breakup Girl

And if you're both the "other"?

Dear Breakup Girl,
   I have found a love that is perfect except we are both married. Her religious beliefs stop her from leaving him for me. I want her husband to know about this. I want the world to know about us. What do I do? She is my everything.
   — JC

Dear JC,
   Her marriage is your nemesis, but it is her business. No fair telling her husband. Or "telling the world," which is the same as telling her husband, unless he is aboard Space Station Mir. Do that, and you will lose her. Clearly, your wife has already lost you. Go deal with that first, okay?
   Love,
   Breakup Girl

What If You're the ...Fourth Party?

Dear Breakup Girl,
   If you know your friend's boyfriend or husband is cheating on her, is it your bound duty to inform her of this fact? In other cases, the cheatee felt angry and foolish that people knew before she did. But honestly, who am I to decide she ought to know? Is full disclosure always best?
   —Lilygirl

Dear Lilygirl,
   Belleruth says: "There's no hard-and-fast rule, but here's a diagnostic teaser: Float another to see how she feels about it. As in, 'I always wonder if I did the right thing when I didn't tell So-and-so about her cheating partner.' But if the thing blows over, best not to tell. It's generally best to err on the side of *not* doing. If confronted later, just say, 'I'm sorry, but I wasn't going to be the one to wreck the relationship by telling you, in case s/he

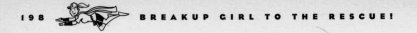
shaped up and it worked out.' Though if Cheater keeps at it,
that's another story." God, she's smart. Having Belleruth as
a friend in this situation would almost be worth having . . .
this situation.
        Love,
        Breakup Girl

⚡ What and Who Is and Isn't Cheating

1. Porn

Some slobbering over porn is not the same as cheating. (Now, if you were
to tell me that your honey had *written the musical score* for a porn flick,
we'd have a problem.) But if, as our Belleruth says, "a partner gets turned
on by the 'watching,' 'dirty,' or whatever factors, that's one thing ... but does
this person know how to have a relationship — sexual and otherwise — with
you? Or not? And is s / he keeping secrets? That is where the betrayal — if
it's there — will come in." So. Porn might not be a prosecutable infidelity ...
but that doesn't mean it's not a problem.

2. Cyberskulking

See page 144.

3. The unattached party

. . . is still an accessory.

Dear Breakup Girl,
        My friend just got married and has a newborn child. After
flirting for years, we finally did the deed, and now we can't
stop. Should I say, "Hello! You're married?!" or should I go
with the flow? I mean, I'm not the one cheating! Or am I?
        —Friendly Luva

Dear Friendly,
        "I'm not the one cheating!" Nice try, Luva. The "sound
of one person cheating" is a concept far too Zen for Breakup
Girl. If you're so "friendly," do no more deeds. Instead, help
the new mom find someone to talk to about postpartum blues.
        Love,
        Breakup Girl

PREDICAMENT of the CHAPTER!

"Can I Trust My Man with a *Party Girl*?"

Dear Breakup Girl,

I'm a waitress and I'm not sure what I want to do with my life. My boyfriend, on the other hand, recently had an opportunity to go to Austin and work on an independent film for six weeks. I thought our relationship could handle it.

But the star of the movie was Parker Posey. He hung out and did "guy stuff" with her. He said it didn't mean anything, but if I went shopping with her all afternoon, even that would mean something to me. Should I break up with him?

—Dina

Dear Dina,

Finally, a celebrity romance that *is* my business!

But what do you mean, "guy stuff"? Did they bond over WD-40 and play rotisserie baseball, or did they . . . hook up? Either way, you should take your concern down a notch. I AM NOT SAYING THAT "CHEATING IS OKAY AS LONG AS IT'S WITH A CELEBRITY." But if there's any case where a dumb-ass, I-couldn't-resist hookup *that has nothing to do with the quality or appeal of the cheated-on relationship* could happen, this is it. Let's face it, human frailty does include this unfortunate little phenomenon known, in vulgar terms, as star-you-know-what-ing (figuratively or literally, as the case may be).

So take action—talk, anyway—ONLY if this Parker thing starts to seep from Austin into reality. When he's back is he—and everything—the same? Does he treat you fine? But otherwise: Even though anyone in her right mind would be out-of-her-mind jealous of even innocent interaction, it doesn't help that you, basically, are the Clockwatcher at the House of Pancakes. He is a filmmaker; you are a waitress. He knows what he's doing; you don't. Boy does fancy Posey look even more threatening in this light!

"He worked behind the camera—she worked behind the counter. . . ." You may be at the "boy almost loses girl" part of the plot, but there may not be any reason why yours can't be a Hollywood—or indie—love story.

Love,
Breakup Girl

I've got a phone bill as big as my heart:
LONG-DISTANCE LOVE

The information age has made long-distance relationships (LDRs) both easier and more difficult. Used to be you had to wait months for the steamship to deliver one letter, or fight with your siblings to get the horse for the weekend. Now we've got the opposite problem:

"Why didn't you respond to my Instant Message instantly?!"

"If you loved me, you'd take the Concorde."

So yes. LDRs are hard. Built-in hard. Composite letter:

> My girl/boyfriend and I argue about phone bills, have trouble getting away to see each other because of work and expenses and feeling like we're blowing off our other friends, and then when we are together there's all this quality and quantity pressure for it to be GREAT . . . *Are we fundamentally incompatible?!?!?!*

Uh, not necessarily. But this thing *will* take some work. Go the distance by following these Road Rules.

⚡ Give Clear Directions

Do not assume that long-distance logistics — and the "meaning" that humans naturally attach to them — will just sort themselves out. What, roughly, is the plan? How often do you call, write, fax, e-mail, visit? Do you "see other people?" (See below.) Hammer this stuff out. For real. (Don't make me quote that too-oft-quoted scene from *Annie Hall* where each tells a therapist how often they have sex. He says: "Never! Three times a week, at most!" She says: "Constantly! Three times a week . . ." Make sure your maps use the same scale.)

⚡ Mind the Gap

Short-range couples say things like, "My partner and I enjoy three-legged races, tandem bicycles, and good old-fashioned holding hands." What about you? What is the backbone of your relationship?

> Dear Breakup Girl,
>
> My boyfriend lives in London and I live in L.A. The sep-arations are *really* hard on me. I feel really sad that he's not here to share every single little thing with me and vice versa.
>
> I know I have to be strong, but how? When I see him, how do I make him feel that he can't live without me? How do I get him to talk about his feelings about me? How do I alle-viate the pain of not having him near me?
> — Ina

> Dear Ina,
>
> Some people take to LDRs naturally. They like the built-in space and compartmentalization, the NOT having to nego-tiate daily life together. You are not one of those people. Sounds to me as if you are someone who likes and needs con-stant interaction and reassurance. Which are not common char-acteristics of LDRs.
>
> So of course the separations are hard on you, even though you L.A. folks probably get e-mail in your cars. That's why you do need to recast your expectations. Reality: It's not going to be the kind of relationship where you share every little thing. Even when you are actually together, because (1) then you want to do the big things — not, like, pick up your dry cleaning, and (2) at least in L.A. restaurants, the portions are too small to share.
>
> So. What can you two create to fill that space? Wishing you were together — and killing time while you're not — does not count. Counting the days till the reunion does not a relationship make. Instead, invent rituals and activities that are yours, that are special, that do help fill the time and space — watching *Seventh Heaven* with your phones cradled

on your respective shoulders? Sending creative care pack-
ages? Setting up an online "palace" where "Pooky" and
"Muffin" avatars can make out? You tell me. Get creative
about filling the space between you, as well as the space
around *you*, Ina. Make sure you've got stuff going on in your
life — school, work, whatever — that makes you feel secure,
skilled, capable, loved. Right nearby. I want you to look
across the ocean for romance, not reassurance.
    Love,
    Breakup Girl

⚡ Don't Stay Together for the . . . Frequent Flier Miles

That is, don't cling to a relationship just because it's there — to stick it out,
to make a point — because in that case, it's ... *not.*

⚡ "Seeing Other People" Is Weird

I'm not against the principle, especially if you're young, but you've got to
define your terms. If you're dating someone at home, is that person the
Main relationship, or the Auxiliary one? How much do you tell that person?
Plan ahead.

Dear Breakup Girl,
    My boyfriend's in Japan for the summer, and I live in
Seattle. We aren't supposed to be seeing other people. But
I've met someone and I don't know if I should tell my
boyfriend. It's just a summer thing — it's just hard to go
from being with someone every day to not seeing them for
three months. But if I tell him, I know he'd most likely
break up with me. What should I do?
    —Bridgett

Dear Bridgett,
    If you break up with Summer Thing now, like before I even
finish responding to you, then you don't have to tell your
boyfriend. Like, if you can safely say, "I know now that I
was a victim of Zima," then unloading your guilt on him will
cause more trouble and hurt than it's worth.
    Otherwise, Bridgett, of course it's hard not to see your
boyfriend for three months. It should be. And not that your

eye should never wander, not that you won't wonder "What
if . . . ?" — heck, couples do that when they're together. But
if you can't last *that* long without an extended roll in the
"Hey, it's summer" hay, then hey, I worry.
    Love,
    Breakup Girl

Above all, take good care of people's — and "other" people's — hearts, wherever they are.

⚡ Remember That Moving Is Not Magic

Close-range couples have problems too, just a different set ("Couldn't you go away more often?"). By the same token, relocating to be together — a bold move indeed — will not autoresolve all your problems. Except maybe the Concorde thing.

AGE
what's the difference?

A large age gap in a relationship is not by definition suspect, unless you are Anna Nicole Smith. Hey, my high school chorus–mate married Dennis Hopper, thirty years her senior, and when I see her in magazines at all those galas and premieres, she looks awfully happy. Sure, when there's a True Connection, this difference is downgraded to mere circumstance. And yes, Oedipus and Electra are allowed to play bit parts in your dynamic as a couple.

BUT. Lolita and Lolito are not.

AND. When the age gap is the main event, there's probably something going on there (insert admittedly facile pop-psych blame-the-parents theory) other than — dare I say in place of — actual, equal partnership.

⚡ Age Difference:
Paging Dr. Freud/Painting Dorian Gray

Is your age difference *an element* of the relationship or attraction, or is it *the* defining factor? Like, is the core draw that he is a George Michaelicious father figure? Or that she is super-Mrs. Robinsonic? *If you two were roughly the same age, would all the thrill be gone?*

See, if Mad had written to say, "I'm dating a man twenty years my junior and I've never been happier, more loved, more fulfilled, more balanced, more myself," I'd say, "And your problem is...???" However...

1. Here's to you, Mrs. Robinson

Dear Breakup Girl,

 I am not attracted to men my age or older. I am attracted to younger men, in their thirties, sometimes younger. If I care about them a lot, I will end up spending money on them, but I am being used. I am starting to hate myself for not being younger, though I do look good for my age, thank God. Do you think this will pass, or that there are men who will actually feel something for me?

 —Mad

Dear Mad,

 Why aren't you hot for your peers? 'Cause they're . . . old? . . . like you? Do you see your reflection in them? When you, in your dotage, dote on younger men, does it make you feel like Girlfriend's still got it?

 Or does it? You say you're "attracted" to these younguns, but . . . it doesn't sound like you're having much fun. Sounds like you're picking up Pool Boy, paying for him, and then saying, "See, he's using me!" Hmm. Just because a nice boy says, "I accept your invitation to the Fancy Place!" doesn't mean he's using you. And just because he's young doesn't mean he can't afford stuff. These people are not children; they are plenty old enough to say, "Hey, babe, Chuck E. Cheese's is on me."

 So I don't care how old your dates are. Neither should you. Care about this: Does he love and respect you as an equal, no matter how much dinner costs? Will he pay the next time? Do you have fun together? Do you toss a million outfits on your floor when getting ready for your date? Do you feel like passing notes about him in class? Do you get tingly and giggly—dare I say *girlish*—when he calls? And *then* do you feel young? Good.

 Love,

 Breakup Girl

See? Sometimes it's not about the age difference in your relationship, it's about your relationship to your age.

Hey, I bet you Mad's motivations (young partner as anti-aging serum) are not so different from those of the Tony Randalls and Presidential Scandals of the world, but society and culture's notions of the gender-and-beauty matrix seem to make us — some of us — less suspicious of older bucks with younger babes. Which is, alas, something Darry needs to keep in mind.

2. Here's to you, Mrs . . . Doubtfire

Dear Breakup Girl,

I've been seeing a much younger man for about two years (he's twenty-eight and I am fifty-eight). We are crazy about each other, but I'm afraid I'm more of a mother figure to him than a lover. We haven't talked about "where we are" lately, but should I let him go, or make something more permanent? Would it be fair for someone my age to try to wed a young stud like him?

—Darry

Dear Darry,

"Fair," schmair. Even at twenty-eight, he's a grown-up who can make that call for himself. So I ask you this: Are you worried about the mother-figure thing in principle or in practice? Does your concern stem from a vague "Is this weird?" notion—or from some actual dynamic you guys have (e.g., when he was late, you took away his phone privileges)? Or is there some Freudoid episode in his past (say, loss of his mother) that might predispose him to seek out a substitute? One in your past that might predispose you to be that substitute?

Even if your concerns are on the level of decorum, not devotion, you still need to work them out before you put marriage moves on Stud Boy. This coupling is a tad controversial; if there is something ageless between you, you must be prepared to withstand the eyebrows it's going to raise.

Love,

Breakup Girl

3. Here's to you, Miss . . . Lewinsky

And finally, from Mother Figure to Mistress Figure . . .

Dear Breakup Girl,

I am an eighteen-year-old intelligent female. I wasn't so smart last year, though, when I fell for a teacher of mine. This sounds bad, but I liked the idea of trying to seduce him and become his "mistress."

Help me get over this. I'm in college now, so I don't
see him often, yet I'm still obsessing. Please help me have
a normal, happy, healthy relationship with someone my age.
— Applepicker

Dear Applepicker,

Questions from our Belleruth: How, exactly, is Mr. Don't
Stand So Close to Me interfering with your life now? Did you
two actually, like, get together? Do you not date guys your
own age? Did you ever? Why not? Have you idealized this guy
in particular, or is there something compelling for you about
toppling a male authority, leveling the playing field by
exercising the power of your sexuality?

And what are you *not* getting out of your college experience — intellectual challenge, positive platonic role mod-
els, friends? — that might be making it hard for you to exit
the hallowed halls of Mistress High?

Talk to someone there about improving your quality of
life on campus now; that's the first step toward giving up
old extracurriculars.

Love,

Breakup Girl

Age Difference Versus Life Difference

Age difference can also manifest itself as "cultural" difference. Like if you
remember where you were when they kicked Puck out of *Real World: San
Francisco* and s/he doesn't, you guys may not have a lot to talk about.

Seriously, I get lots of letters from partners — one pre twenty-five, one
post — experiencing a harsh culture clash. And rightly so. There's more of a
gap there than between, say, thirty and forty-one. Arguably, lots more of life
happens to you in your twenties. Not that your thirties are some sort of black
hole, but think about it: Twenties are college, your first job, maybe your first
apartment, whatever. You're still changing, sorting stuff out. In your thirties,
well, I hope to God you're still sorting some stuff out, because otherwise
you'd be really stiff and stuck and boring. But in your thirties you are, ideally, more...set. Your art is framed, not gummed; your noodles are soba, not
ramen. So if your partnership spans that gap, you're not going to be "going
through the same stuff at work." You're not going to have comparable numbers of learning and shaping experiences (including relationships) behind
you. You're not going to be "in the same place."

Dear Breakup Girl,

My partner is six years younger (I'm thirty). I am his first "long-term" partner: He has only just left home; he has never traveled, taken risks, gone hungry, made mistakes. I sometimes feel like his mother, helping and teaching him stuff. I want a MAN, not a BOY, damnit! Sometimes I feel like I'm settling; sometimes I think my expectations are too high. He treats me like a queen, adores me (too green to be cynical about women yet). Our sex life is suffering because of the way I feel. PLEASE help.

—Feeling Lost

Dear Feeling Lost,

Those are a key six years. Same generation, big gap. And there's a sense in which it feels nice to be the mommy, nice to be the queen, the teacher, the wise owl, the mentor, the resumé-tweaker, isn't there? Makes you feel: big. Smart. Needed. Like you learned something from leaving home, traveling, taking risks, going hungry, making mistakes. I understand. Thing is, once you become truly independent, you'll be able to feel that way all by yourself.

Love,
Breakup Girl

When "Age Difference" Is a Big Old Red Herring

Keep in mind that when

(a) there's an age difference in the relationship, and

(b) there's a problem in the relationship,

it does not necessarily mean that

(c) the age difference is the problem.

Dear Breakup Girl,

I've been dating a guy nine years younger for seven months. He doesn't know how old I am, and I'm scared to tell him, but I'm beginning to feel guilty because he has started to mention the forever-together word. I've already been married, had long-term relationships, and don't care about commitment anymore. Should I tell him my age?

—Julie

Dear Julie,

   This hasn't come up? As in, "Yeah, I remember when John
Glenn went into space. No, the *first* time." *What do you guys
talk about?* Well, you guys should talk, never mind about how
many times you've been twenty-nine. If he's making together-
forever noises and you're withholding basic facts—including
your lack of interest in commitment—there's a gap here
that's not measured in years. Act your age and get to the
bottom of it.

   Love,
   Breakup Girl

One final useful concept, courtesy of BG's friend Louise. Depending on
what you're looking for, it's not how old they are, it's how done they are.
Done as in cooked. Ready. Steady. As in: sense of self no longer runny.
Sense of purpose firm. Toxins (mostly) destroyed in heat of past moments.
The key: someone can be warmed through at twenty-five, frozen on the
inside at forty-five. So when in doubt, skip the math; *test for doneness.*

PREDICAMENT of the CHAPTER!

Why Lie?

Dear Breakup Girl,

   I met this guy in ICQ, didn't expect to have real feelings, but we do. I sent him a picture of another person—a
knockout—told him I was ten years younger than I am. He
wants to meet in person. WHAT SHOULD I DO?
   —Troubled in Oregon

Dear Troubled,

   Oops. You kind of do have to own up. And here's the
thing. If he's mad, I betcha it won't be because you're not
that X-10 knockout. It would be because the picture messed
around with his feelings. So in order to save face, you're
going to have to speak the thousand words that that picture

didn't: Tell him you sent it before those unexpected feel-ings became real. Now that the feelings are real, so too will you be.

While you're at it, ask yourself this: Why didn't you think the true you was young enough, cute enough, brave enough? Next time you meet an ICQT, don't send a snapshot until/unless you're psyched to send the real one.

Love,

Breakup Girl

THE FOLKS

Some of you worry about meeting the parents; some of you — struggling in parent-disapproved relationships — wish you could get that far. And perhaps still some of you, in occasional fits of pique, wish you'd never even met your own. No matter what, our family trees send runners into our relationships. Here's how to cultivate optimum rapport.

⚡ Meeting the Family: What Does It "Mean"?

Meeting the family is significant, but it doesn't signify the same thing for every family. Some people hang out with their folks a lot because they have a bitchin beach house and invite "new friends" over all the time, no big thing. For others, it's a regular Middle East peace conference. This — even more than timing — is key. If your intended appears overeager about, freaked out by, etc., your or his/her own invitation, remember — literally — where s/he is coming from. Or, if you don't know, ask. "Hey, whoa, this parent thing seems to be striking a chord. Wanna share?" You two should be able to have a reasonable discussion about what the whole thing means. If someone raised you right.

> Dear Breakup Girl,
>
> My ex took me to meet his family about two months after we started dating. I took this to mean that he felt pretty serious about me. I think his family did too. And yet, it seems to have meant very little. And now, on top of having broken up with the boy, I will probably never again see these people with

whom I camped, did Thanksgiving, exchanged holiday gifts, etc.

So, do I just avoid meeting another BF's family unless I think we're about to be engaged? What I can expect from a guy who takes me to meet his family? Can I expect that he'll come to meet my family (who live quite far away) when I ask? This boy's categorical refusal to come with me because it would "mean too much" for him to travel with me and meet my family helped catalyze our breakup.

—Emily

Dear Emily,

When you do meet the 'rents, you may presume that he'd rather not break up. But not that it will magically never happen. And if it does, alas, you don't retain visitation (camping, Thanksgiving, etc.) rights. You just don't.

About meeting yours: When the situation comes up, it's reasonable to ask how he'd feel about it and take it from there. A categorical refusal of what's basically quid pro quo is a big red flag. But—though I'm not defending him—*expecting* someone to travel a great distance to meet your family may be an excellent way to get someone not to come home with you.

Love,

Breakup Girl

⚡ When Parents Intervene:
Time to Grow Up, or Suck It Up?

Are parents annoying sometimes? Yes. Do they mess up sometimes? Uh-huh. But, you guys, don't assume that just because people are also parents, they are clueless. Especially those of you who are parents. Okay?

A parent's job is to be a parent. Which is hard. And in a Breakup Girl context, it's hard for parents to watch their babies walk through those dark doors to adulthood labeled "DATING," "MARRIAGE" — or (gasp) "PARENTS THEMSELVES," even. (Or, God forbid, none of the above.) So no wonder they freak out here and there. Yet some of them, at the other end of the spectrum, actually make some excellent calls.*

Dear Breakup Girl,

I've been going out with a guy for nine months . . . I care

---

*Full disclosure. I mean everything I say here, but there's also something to be said for banking goodwill. Let's just say that this response will go over better at home than BG's current hair color.

deeply about him, I love him, blah blah blah . . . but my parents hate him and want me to dump him. I can't even talk to him on the phone without dad launching into huge lectures and comparisons to evil figures in history.

My guy is mean to me sometimes, but we've been getting along better, even though I sometimes want to kill him . . . Should I break up with him, how can I do it without being mean, and what am I supposed to do since I still love him? And his clothes . . . I don't want to give them back!

—Vera

Dear Vera,

Granted, parents are not always fully clued in. The proper use of *phat* and *def*, for instance, is something they're not likely to master (frankly, it's just as well).

But in your case, well, your father is not being unreasonable. If he had said, "Young lady, you're not dating until you're thirty-five!" then we'd have a problem (or at least a situation akin to BG's, without the father part).

But you said yourself that this guy is "mean" to you. And "mean" *is never okay with Breakup Girl.*

So don't dis your parents just because they're your parents. Talk to your dad (putting your hand over the receiver and yelling, "Da-ad! I'm on the PHONE!" does not count). Find out what he means. What are his concerns?

If you want to make a decision about your situation as an adult, then discuss it with your parents as an adult.

Oh, and if you do break up and he wants his clothes back, you need to return them. I don't care how "dope" they are, young lady.

Love,

Breakup Girl

If a parent or in-law is purely meddlesome or irritating, try try try to act like the outdoor wood stain in those commercials. That is, instead of letting those Momilies (or whatever they are) sink in — and make you all defensive and "Here we go again" — let them bead up and roll off.

Also, remember, grown-ups (ahem) can agree to disagree. Talk. Give the folks a chance to see you and your relationships as complex and human too. I'm not promising that you're going to have some sort of Lifetime / Taster's Choice moment, but still. Just changing the dynamic here is an end in itself. And bonus, now that you're listening, maybe you will happen to hear a nugget of really great advice. You don't have to tell anyone you're taking it.

That's right. Sometimes the grown-up thing to do is to let parents parent. Especially, I might add, when you're all going to grow old together.

Dear Breakup Girl,

My boyfriend and I are getting married this fall. We decided to move in together to cut down on the costs of living separately, but it turns out his parents are very much against the idea before marriage. What is the polite way to tell my boyfriend's parents to leave us alone, and that we plan to move in together with or without their blessing? And should we just tell them to butt out, since they aren't helping to pay for any of the wedding?

—Unsure in Missouri

Dear Unsure,

For this one, Breakup Girl saw fit to consult Breakup Mom. And I have to say, on the record . . . (deep breath) . . . that *I think what my mother said is right*. To paraphrase:

Moving in together is a decision you make as adults; technically you shouldn't need parental blessing. And yes, it would be wise, nice, and practical to save a little money. BUT. It doesn't sound as if you're starving or freezing. *So consider what might be in your best interest as a couple that, like it or not, is going to be part of a larger family until, ostensibly, death do you part.*

Trust me, you want to be on good terms with them, starting now. Don't underestimate the importance of this. If you waited, you would sacrifice some cash and convenience, but you would also make an investment in some very key good graces. Remember, these are the people who are going to be your kids' grandparents. Though if things go at all sour with them, Breakup Mom may still be available.

Love,

Breakup Girl

PREDICAMENT of the CHAPTER!

The Mother of All In-Laws

Dear Breakup Girl,

At my boyfriend's cousin's graduation party, his mother proceeded (again) to tell everyone that I'm too quiet and that I don't like to come to family functions. She said I took a scholarship away from her son (I got one; he didn't). Then she talked about how if her son got married, it probably wouldn't be to me. John told me this is how his family is and I should realize that, but this treatment is really starting to upset me, especially since I just kind of smile and sit there like an idiot. Is there any hope for this relationship?

—Quiet Girl

Dear Quiet Girl,

Mama mia. For what it's worth, Maw's comments probably made the other people listening uncomfortable too; you probably came across as more of an innocent victim than a loser.

Anyway, when you love someone warts and all, his/her family may be one of those warts. Usually, you suck it up, figure out ways to work around the sticking points. BUT. While Mom has crossed the line, Boyfriend is content to toe it. He's not willing to step up and say, "Yo, Ma, lay off my girlfriend at family gatherings!"? Never mind her; *this* is what's really bugging me.

So look around your relationship. Does he back you up, take your side, root for you, care how you feel, in other areas? If everything else seems to be in place, then bring up the mom thing again and see if there's a way to . . . suck it up, figure out ways to work around the sticking points. If not, think seriously about how many more family gatherings you want to go to with this guy. 'Cause of the guy, not the family.

Love,

Breakup Girl

the holidays

Other than your own three-month, three-and-a-half-month, ninth Groundhog Day together, etc., anniversaries, which holidays have the biggest effect on your love-fests?

⚡ Labor Day

... You know, the official last day (1) to wear white shoes, and (2) of summer romance.

What *is* it about summer? I mean, there's no such thing as a "winter fling," unless you're Smilla. How come? Summer's just *different*. It's hot, you're not wearing much, it's light out till ten...hey, it's *summer*. The time of year when vegans say, "Aw, what's one cheeseburger?" When people who normally don't go to a movie unless *The New Yorker* likes it get all spineless from lying on their backs in Central Park all day and say, "What the hell, let's go see *Curly Sue IX: The Quickening*. Hey, it's *summer*."

In the summer, we just want to see *a* movie; likewise, in the summer, we just want to see...*someone*. Whatever! He's got air-conditioning!

But BG wants you to be as vigilant with people's feelings — yours included — as Breakup Mom wants you to be about cooking the pink parts of your hamburgers thoroughly. No monkey business like: "I'll let him/her *think* it's a summer thing, but after three months of my shoulder-baring tank tops and ass-kicking barbeque sauce, s/he'll stick around." Or this:

Dear Breakup Girl,
    We broke up three months ago, his idea. After the oblig-

atory period of avoiding each other (while he played and I
pined), we're becoming friends again. Now, he and and his
new girlfriend are having problems and he's turning to me to
advise and comfort him. Part of me hopes the way he's acting around me suggests more-than-friends interest; I know it
wouldn't take much to fall head over—again. But we're both
going to college in the fall. Do I allow myself dreams of a
summer fling (the girlfriend won't be around much longer),
or do I squash them?
    —Wary and Wondering

Dear Wary,
    No way should he be turning to you for advice on your
successor. Taaaa-cky, no fair. Forget the not-so-hot fix;
chill with your real friends before you leave. I will thus
echo your use of a word that summer's zealous overplanters
and their neighbors usually wind up with way too much of:
SQUASH.
    Love,
    Breakup Girl

In many cases, though, summer flings are fine with BG...as long as you
do your best to follow the rules of rebounds (see page 45). That is: as long
as you *both* sense that it's a "summer thing," as long as you're both on the
same page of the trashy beach book — and as long as you've got at least a
thin film of SPF 50 on your heart.

Just 'cause it's a summer thing doesn't mean you're not sad when it ends.
I mean, usually it's just a particular song or a favorite restaurant that reminds
you of a past love. But what if that reminder is, like, the *sun?* Sigh.

And what if you *do* want that summer thing to become a fall fashion?
Well, it can happen, but not all by itself. Think ahead about the fact that
your schedule and the rhythm of things will be different; they just will. So
plan for it. You know, like try sharing something other than . . . a towel.
Like, *talking.*

Finally, remember: Just as you *can* score long-term during the rebound
zone, you can also find someone winter-weight during the warmer months.

Dear Breakup Girl,
    I have this huge crush on a goofy poet I met at the commu-
nity garden this summer. Our conversations are going swim-

mingly, and I even convinced him to weed his carrots. Yesterday Looks were exchanged. I'm giddy in a way I haven't been in ages.

But I'm worried that I'm ignoring all sorts of danger signs. I mean, we've talked not only about tomatoes and bok choy, but also about the demise a year ago of his brief and disastrous marriage. I *do not* want to get caught in someone else's divorce trauma. But I don't often find kindred spirits in this way. How dumb would it be to get involved, BG? Am I truly smitten, or am I addled by some heady mix of the summer sun and organic fertilizer?

　　—Giddy in the Garden

Dear Giddy,

I can see why you're concerned, and it's good to be cautious. But if you think about it, for all intents and purposes, *everyone's* last relationship was a doozy. Seems to me like you both have lives and perspective, and frankly, this whole thing seems Beatrix Potter-level adorable. So unless there's something you're not telling me—like that he's growing BRUSSELS SPROUTS—I'd say you two oughtta steam your next batch of bok choy together.

　　Love,
　　Breakup Girl

Dear Breakup Girl,

In August my Spanish class went to Mexico, where I met a guy named George from Nebraska. (I'm from Oklahoma.) One night we sat overlooking the ocean and talking for an hour, holding hands with his arm around me. Then we went back to our rooms (midnight curfew).

The next day everyone was sure we'd formally hook up. But he got in a motorcycle accident and had to be flown to Cancun, and I never got to say good-bye or anything.

When I went home, I discovered that the guy I have a crush on in my karate class is still just as attractive and amazing as always . . . but I feel guilty for flirting because I'm not sure where George and I stand. I haven't been able to get in touch with him, but I'm also afraid to tell karate guy how I feel. Why can't my life be as simple as Sandy and Danny make it seem?

　　—Confused Over Summer Lovin'

Oh, Confused,

Special Breakup Girl Greased-Lightning Maxim: Simple as Sandy and Danny made things seem, SPANDEX IS NOT THE ANSWER. Now I know you think that you and George go together like rama-lama-lama, kadingy, kading-a-dong. You feel like you'll remember Mexico forever, as shoowop, shoowally, wally, yippity, boom-de-boom. And you think moonlit nights like that, well, chang-chang, changadee-chang-chibop, that's the way it should be, wahoo, yeah.

But here's what Breakup Girl thinks: "George went back to Nebraska in traction; that's where it ends. Go to karate and flirt with your friend."

Love,

Breakup Girl

⚡ Christmas and New Year's Eve

The holidays are a tough time of year whether or not there's a dependent Claus in your life. It's hard to be single at yuletide because for one thing, you have to hear your parents say things like, "Won't your friend be joining us this year?" and "Well, did you sit with anyone interesting on the train?" and "Are you sure you have a good dermatologist?" At this cozy, snuggly, lovey-glovey time, you may also hear your exes say, "Can I have a do over?" As John writes:

> I thought my girlfriend broke up with me last week; she said, "I'm not comfortable with the term 'boyfriend and girlfriend.'" I was really bummed, it being right before Christmas and all. Then when I called her to cancel plans for a holiday party, she said she still wanted to date. . . . What is going on?

What is going on, of course, is that girlfriend wants to have her fruitcake and eat it too; apparently the term she's *really* not comfortable with is "Alone for the holidays."

It's also hard to be in a couple at the holidays, because it's...expensive.

The Ghost of Christmas Presents

When this specter comes caroling, we all get a little naughty. As in, "She's really annoying and we're totally incompatible, but that enormous Sharper Image bag I found hidden in her closet has taught me that I need to be more patient and accepting." Or, "I don't really want to dump him right after Thanksgiving, but then again, think of the savings!" Or:

Dear Breakup Girl,

    I have been planning to break up with my boyfriend of two months but would rather wait until next year given the holidays, finals, etc. If I know that he bought me an expensive present, am I under any obligation to stay with him or to return the gift to him after we break up? Is the fact that the gift is something I lobbied for extensively in a previous relationship—but never got—material to this question at all?

    —Prancer

Dear Prancer,

    No, you are not obliged to stay with him just because he bought you, say, the Seattle Mariners. No, you are not obliged to return the gift (though if/when it comes to that, it would be proper to give him the option to take it back).

    But Prancer, you *are* obliged to consider, right now, *how you will feel* at the moment when you accept this pricey trinket knowing full well that you're going to bail on this boy on January 2. Plus: How do you happen to know that Son of Santa got you an expensive gift? An expensive gift . . . after only two months? Could it be that *you* made his list and checked it twice? There's something going on here that doesn't sound to BG like the true meaning of Christmas. Make your own list of priorities, check it twice—and do the nice thing.

    Love,

    Breakup Girl

Don't mix your shopping lists with your laundry lists, okay? And keep in mind the roasted chestnut that everyone (except malls and televisions) tries to remind you of this season: *It's not about the stuff.* So you should be willing to cut your squeeze some slack; to look for love in places other than under the tree.

Dear Breakup Girl,

    My boyfriend has no clue what to do as far as romance, gifts, and manners. I can't count on him; he puts no thought into gifts and gets me the cheapest thing he can find (he leaves the price tag on). What to do?

    —Carrie

Dear Carrie,

Some people can carry a tune, some people can't. Some people can cook, some people can't. Some people can make that funny shamrock shape with their tongues, some people can't. And some people can shop, some people can't. Buying the Right Gift is a high-pressure situation in which not all of us display grace.

So I would tell you to suck it up and ask him nicely to keep all receipts—*if* he shows his love and thoughts for you in other ways. But there's one clause that makes me worried about your anti-Santa: "I can't count on him." Are this guy's presents an aberration—or an indication that he's not exactly God's gift? Trust your gut, Carrie, and trust BG on this one: finding someone who finds his own way to come through for you, no matter what—well, you can't put a price tag on that.

Love,

Breakup Girl

What Should I Get for Someone I've Just Started Dating?

AT THE EARLY STAGE OF A RELATIONSHIP, YOUR PRESENTS SHOULD NOT BE COMMANDING.

DO: PICK UP A LITTLE SOMETHING SWEET, WARM, OR FUZZY -- CHOCOLATE, MITTENS, DICE -- THAT SAYS, "HEY THERE, I THINK YOU'RE KINDA SWEET, WARM, AND FUZZY." *DON'T:* REGALE HIM / HER WITH ANYTHING TIME-CONSUMING, GRAND, OR INTIMIDATING -- A TEN-COURSE DINNER, A ROMANTIC WEEKEND AWAY, A MORTGAGE -- ANYTHING THAT SAYS, *"SIT HERE, STAY HERE, SIGN HERE."* YOU GIVE THAT KIND OF CHRISTMAS GIFT, I GIVE YOUR RELATIONSHIP TWELVE DAYS.

⚡ The Holiday Breakup

Y'all, if it's waiting to happen, don't just — like Prancer — stay together for the chimney. 'Tis better to wish you were standing under the mistletoe with someone than to be standing under the mistletoe with someone and wishing you weren't. And if you must do the deed, also do your best to anticipate special holiday-related wrinkles:

Dear Breakup Girl,

My five-year relationship just ended. Every year before, we've always sent cards signed, "From Kathy and Peter." How can I tell people about us without making the whole card thing a big bummer?

—Just Kathy

Dear Kathy,

This card thing is a gift. A major part of breakup humbug is the "coming-out" process; but you have a major public-relations tool right at your fingertips: *bulk mail*. Sign your name only and they'll get the idea; believe me, they won't have a chance to follow up until, well, Valentine's Day.

Love,

Breakup Girl

P.S. Be sure to have sprucey, smelly yuletide potpourri on hand, as this year you will receive record numbers of those Christmas cards made out of photographs of your cute married friends with black labs and sleds. Which smell funny when burned.

Dear Breakup Girl,

My boyfriend still owes me a Christmas present. He says he loves me and that he just has to go over and pick it up, but it's been a while. He's on house arrest right now, so I understand that he can't go out, but actually, he's been out many times already. He could have at least gotten me a little something, right?

—Cristina

Dear Cristina,

Modern technology has brought us many ways to shop without leaving home: catalogs, QVC, e-commerce. Also, the invention of food has allowed boyfriends under house arrest to prepare dinner in their own homes, however primitive, for their girlfriends. This guy doesn't owe you a material item of a particular value; he does owe you a gesture that indicates your value to him. In that spirit, I recommend you find someone with a shopping list longer than his criminal record.

Love,

Breakup Girl

⚡ Valentine's Day:
An Inspirational Speech

I'll keep this brief, because to spend a lot of time on this topic would just be doing what They want us to do. Breakup Girl's investigations, you see, have revealed Valentine's Day to be a conspiracy larger than ever imagined, involving the likes of Microsoft, Viacom, and the New Haven cabal of Skull and Bones, not to mention that wily chamomile mastermind, Jewel. (You thought it was Hallmark? Hah. That's what they *want* you to think.)

Anyway, You-know-what's Day is fast approaching Christmas in terms of hype, commercialism, and metric tons of red felt items exchanged on the open market. This crass consumerism comes with a backlash: We yearn for "the true meaning of Christmas" in days long gone. You know, back when a child's face lit up at the sight of a single bright orange in his stocking; when love made George Bailey the richest man in town.

Likewise, who among us does not wax nostalgic for Valentine's Day the way it used to be? You know, back when saints-to-be were beheaded for performing marriages, and when — as part of V-Day's precursor, the fertility festival of Lupercalia — Romans sacrificed goats and dogs and ran through the streets whipping women with their skins. Oh, also: love and kindness and honor and sweetness. Without Mylar.

That said, if you think about it that way, shouldn't *every* day be Valentine's Day? Shouldn't you always follow the maxim "Everyone in the class should get one"? Don't you have enough to stress about the other 364 days without worrying about this one? Try, try, try not to let the doilies get you down; instead, try to figure out what biliously cute and thoughtful tidbits you can dole out to folks today, tomorrow, and all year round.

In that spirit, here's a shout-out to actual couples: For all the singletons' self-pitying ranting at this time of year, please know that you are loved and welcomed today and any day, no matter how cute you are. Everyone should remember that you guys are under just as much stress as the rest of us, just in a different — perhaps more complex — flavor. Singles worry, "Will I die alone?" period, while partners worry, "Will I die penniless given the skyrocketing cost of doing 'enough' for someone on Valentine's Day?" or "Will I die alone and penniless because of something I somehow 'messed up' on Valentine's Day but will never understand why?" And remember, of course, it's all what They want you to think.

ULTIMATUM FRISBEE
CUT OR CLEAR?

In the game of ultimate Frisbee, people who stay to the middle of the field and lead the charge instead of breaking long for the throw are handlers. As they do so, handlers might yell, "Cut or clear!" — which basically means "Get open for a pass or get out of the way!" In ultimate, this admonition is sometimes considered obvious and annoying. In life, however — that is, in ultimatums — we are often entitled to yell, "Get open to commitment or clear your things out of my drawer!"

But when? What's the middle ground between blind faith and brute force? How can you tell the difference between Not Ready Yet and Never Will Be? Will the act of pushing drive someone away?

Tough calls. And they're pretty much case by case. But I will tell you this . . . though you're not going to want to hear it. An ultimatum is not about getting someone to do something. It is not bouncing the ball into the other person's court — that is, out of your hands. It is not a tactic, not a strategy, not a plan. It is not setting a pick. An ultimatum is a statement of *your* purpose. It is, ultimately, your responsibility. Because, ultimately, your partner is going to do whatever s/he is going to do. *You* are the one who has to come through.

Dear Breakup Girl,

I have been with my fiancé for over eight years. We have been engaged and living together for about five years in a jointly purchased house. The problem is that we still don't have a wedding date. We have discussed this on numerous occa-

sions throughout the years, but we still remain engaged without a "date" to wed. He says that I am the one dragging my
feet. I am beginning to wonder if I should give him an ultimatum at this point, or should I just move on???
　　—Constant Confusion

Dear Constant,
　　Five years? FIVE YEARS? Sounds to me as if the cake he
wants to have and eat is anything but that Scary Forever Cake
with a plastic bride and groom on top. And under similar circumstances, I might say yeah, it's time for the U-word.
　　But I am worried that your ultimatum might sound something like this: "I am ready to give you an ultimatum now"
(Silence). You talk about a "date" as if it's this separate
third-party thing that just shows up, like getting your couch
delivered. It takes two, Constant. To set a date, and to not
set a date. You are both not doing it. One of you is saying, "I'm not gonna set it, you set it," and the other says,
"I'm not gonna set it, you set it," and then you push back
from the table and wait for Mikey to call the caterers.
　　Instead, have a REAL conversation about this. Like, with
a calendar. And a pen. If you can't even get him—OR YOUR-
SELF—to that point after a couple of tries, start talking
about who gets the house.
　　Love,
　　Breakup Girl

⚡ Is It Time?

If you're considering an ultimatum, break deep for a view of the whole field.
Do you want to settle down, like, in life, or do you want to settle down *with
this person*, no matter what?

I. Walking the Walk

Cameo writes:

> I can't seem to get my boyfriend of eight years to commit to
> our relationship (marriage). I'm not getting any younger (I'm
> twenty-eight), and I want babies!

Guess what: I tell the Cameos of the world (male and female) to *walk*.

Not walk as in, "I'm walking out if you don't commit! Look at me! Yoo-hoo! I'm walking! I am so walking…sort of near that door! Waaalking! Watch me go…!'"

I also don't mean walk out the door…and then walk by his/her house ten minutes later to see if s/he's committed yet.

I mean: *walk*. Or. Give a gentle-but-firm "I'm walking" deadline and stick to it either way.

Does Breakup Girl believe that a relationship don't mean a thing if it ain't got that ring? No. (See sidebar.) I'm going with what Cameo & Co. tell me: that marriage (and in this case, babies) is what they want, and that it may not, alas, be available in the current (eight-year!?) relationship. I am not advocating some sort of mass walkout. I am just saying that — again — if commitment is what you want, you've got to demonstrate it too…wherever it may leave you.

Bonus: Thing is — I hesitate to say this, because I am in NO way advocating game playing — when you walk, your ultimatee just might realize that s/he is that someone. In which case, I should add, you may walk — *carefully* — back.

2. Talking the Talk (or the Tile)

Consider this: What's it worth to you to be with her/him, period, no matter what your status? Can you live and love in this relationship *right here, right now, complete and whole as is* without holding your breath for something to happen?

In the December 1998 issue of *New Woman*, Dalma Heyn writes about her friend Jen, whose boyfriend kept talking about how scary closeness was.

> Yet there he was at [Jen's] place, doing the dishes, fixing the washing machine, loving [her] in the most obvious way. Instead of pointing out the discrepancy, Jen let him talk. [She'd] say, "Mmm, closeness *is* scary."…[She] didn't jump on him or insist that he commit. [She knew] he just had these residual fears to work through. While tiling the kitchen floor, he announced casually that these tiles were so durable they'd last as long as their marriage did. They were engaged before the grout dried.

Huh.

Think your partner might be a Tiler? If you really aren't sure, get on his / her case…as long as you're sure *you* are prepared to make the ultimate commitment. But in a sense, waiting can be as active as walking. If you actually think s / he will come around eventually, back off. Heyn makes an apt distinction: "Unless the [person] you're waiting out is behaving badly, not just skittishly, remind yourself that you can wait as long as [s / he] can. And that trusting the process, and [him / her], and yourself, will let you enjoy these unencumbered months (or, yes, years) of courtship. You'll have plenty of time to be married."

⚡ Space: Middle Ground or Final Frontier?

Ultimatums are an either-or that, while powerful, leave out a vast in-between. So now, a brief journey into a realm that has fascinated humankind since the very first person looked up into the sky and said,

> **WHY THIS IS NOT ABOUT WOMEN CAJOLING MEN TO COMMIT**
>
> 1. I'd give the same advice to a guy.
>
> 2. BG has no interest in promoting the stereotype that a girl's best friend is all a woman wants, needs, and hopes for. Can we please all try to get over the notion that a woman who wants to get married -- who wants babies, even -- is automatically caving in to some evil, oppressive, "man-dependent" tradition? How about considering the marriage urge -- and the act -- as a sign of maturity . . . bravery, even? Where's the conflict? Where's the compromise? Quit mumbling about this and realize that you have to be just as Xena to make marriage happen -- and work -- as you do to "make partner," so to speak, in the other realms of your life. (And if you look at it that way, *not* asking what's up is, as they say, throwing like a girl.)

"Hmmm…I wonder what's out there! Everything's okay here…but wow, there's so much more to explore! Bet where I am now would look real different when viewed from there — for all I know, this place might not even appear so…flat. Maybe somewhere there are even…other people!!! Wow, I'm starting to feel like I really need some…*SPACE*."

On the upside, getting some "space" in a relationship allows you — unlike actual space travel — to stretch your legs and breathe, and — like

> "My husband left me for some 'space.' Turns out he meant the space next to one of the executive assistants from his firm."
> — BLIND

actual space travel — to get a look at the big blue picture. In "space," you cannot hear each other scream; that may not be a bad thing. When it starts to feel as if your whole relationship is about dealing with your relationship (like, you can't just go and rent *Titanic* without one of you saying, "'You jump; I jump' — would you have done that for me?"), yet you sense that somewhere, your heart is still in it, a "space" age can be an effective means of stepping back and getting some perspective on what's really going on.

On the downside, sometimes people say, "I need space," when what they really mean is, "I need to break up with you, but I don't feel like it." That is, once someone has headed off into space, the forces of gravity cannot be counted on to bring him/her back.

Here's how to make sure "space" is the right stuff.

Space: If You're Going to Go There, Go There.

No limbo. No fair saying, "Hmm. Need space. Okay, we'll still sleep together; we just won't spoon."

Space Is an *Absence*. So How Do You Give It to Someone?

When one half of a couple needs "space," the other half should assume position at Ground Control. You have a say in the matter too; you're not weightless. Request — and demand stickage to, on both of your parts — some guidelines: What level of "space" is needed? Cold turkey? Weekly check-in calls? Seeing other people: how many? How much can you see? How much do you tell? (Tip: not much.) Plan before the flight.

Then back off. Tess wrote to say her boyfriend "needed space" due to "fear of commitment."

> He never mentioned the fear to me before then, so I gave him a book about fear of commitment and how to overcome it. I also kept saying, "I saw a pretty ring today...."

See why that might be counterproductive?

Instead — don't forget the space-time continuum! — set a deadline for checking back in: week, months, whatever. Say that if s/he plans on orbiting indefinitely, s/he shouldn't count on your crash pad. No fair leaving you floating around forever. You have a life to get on with, with or without this copilot.

Still, Space Is Not a Black Hole.

If it's going to make a difference, space should be treated as an active part of a relationship. It's not vacation; it's a view from a different vantage. Remember what astronauts always say: Sure, they learned stuff about gravity and moon rocks…but what they saw most clearly was how much they treasured life at home on Earth.

I Do... OR DO I?

Weddings give you the willies? Well, they should. The prospect of that major a commitment is bound to trip some major wires. Marriage, for all intents, purposes, and people who are not Anna Nicole Smith, is forever. And that's a mighty long time. In other words, YIKES.

So even a severe case of the jitters does not a jilter make. But there are doubts, and there are doubts. And then you wonder: Are these just cold feet, or boots that should be walking? Or some overlapping, vicious-circling, crazy-making combination of the two? And then you sink into the Second-Guessing My Feelings Spiral. And then you are such hell to live with that your squeeze kicks you out. Which doesn't help, because that, if anything, will make you sure. Also, single.

So how on earth do you "know"?

⚡ The Porch Test

Well. A friend of BG's (FOBG) was once paddling around a lake with Sturdy Canoe Boy (SCB). She was struggling with the classic "He's *great, but . . .*" quandary, while he, on the other hand, was ... *not*. As they passed in front of his family's rustic summer cabin, SCB said, "Wow, you know, I can totally picture us at a ripe old age, sitting on rocking chairs on that porch, looking out over this lake."

Guess what? FOBG could not.

The thought did not alarm or revolt her, but *she could not picture it.*

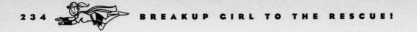

FOBG did not, mind you, have a lightning-bolt "It's over!" moment. But she noticed that thought, and she filed it away somewhere. And a few months later, when the time really came for her to either paddle or get off the lake, as it were, that thought presented itself as the clearest, most sincere, gut-level evidence that she should indeed bail.

So. I expect that those of you in the I Do / Do I? quandary will have — or have already had — one or more of these rocking-chair moments; your relationship will, when you least expect it, take the Porch Test. When it does, do not act impulsively. Just notice how you feel. That Just Know-ing feeling — as far as I know — isn't a magical, isolated, independent entity like that cartoon guy on Saturday morning TV who walked around inside you telling you how your stomach works. It's a composite of outside observations and decisions that you usually don't even realize you're making.

So think about it this way: Doubts are data. Quit worrying about the fact that you have them, or why, and just listen to them. Don't drive yourself crazy making lists of pros and cons: For a brief while, stop doing and thinking and deciding, and just pay attention. Take out your Life-at-a-Glance and set a date for setting a date. Give yourself some time. (If you're engaged in serious contemplation, you're not holding anyone hostage against his / her will. Your partner is a grown-up who can read the previous chapter if s / he wants to move things along.) A course of action will gradually present itself, like the crystals that form on a string dipped in sugar water.

Though as crystals go, I know, this one's rarely perfectly clear.

So, let's look a little more closely at:

⚡ Doubt Causers Versus Deal Breakers: What's the Difference?

Think carefully. Are you turning a fundamentally practical matter into a *Problem?*

> Dear Breakup Girl,
>   My boyfriend wants to marry me but doesn't have the financial means yet. He's planning on going to grad school part-time, but that would take five years — and a big chunk of "wedding savings." He also has a lot of other financial obligations.
>   Do I wait or move on? Who wants a five-year engagement? He's bringing in all this baggage before we've even begun.

Maybe Momma's right and I do have to marry for money rather than love. What do you think?
  — (Not a) Material Girl

Dear NMG,
  What exactly is your damage about his "baggage"? Is there something you're not telling me? Is the game he talks bigger than his checking account? Do you feel like he's looking for an out? Are you?
  Because, um, really poor people get married. Who said you had to have an enormous fairy-tale wedding (okay, besides Our Entire Culture), or that his being in the black is a prerequisite? If you really, truly do wanna tie the knot, have a small ceremony now and celebrate your five-year anniversary with the fairy-tale party.
  Love,
  Breakup Girl

And even if the Issues run deeper, well, if you can't discuss them to begin with, should you be discussing china patterns?

Dear Breakup Girl,
  I'm thirty-two, she's twenty-eight; we've been dating a little over a year. I had thought that we were progressing toward marriage. However, for the last several weeks, she has seemed unhappy. Neither of us has much interest in sex. Don't get me wrong: I think she is a great person. But at the same time, I don't want to waste her time and mine on a love that's grown cold. Is there hope to respark what we once had? If so, how?
  — Jim

Dear Jim,
  Time to pop the question. No, silly, not that question. This one: "Hey, muffin, is there something bothering you?" What worries me is not that you two are unhappy; it's that you have no clue why. Either you have to hone that thing we call Communication Skills, or you have to admit that your heart isn't in this. Is it? Perhaps passionate poetry just isn't your thing, but "Don't get me wrong, I think she is a great person," is what you say before you say, "However, I am a stronger candidate for school board." Not before you say "I do."
  Love,
  Breakup Girl

Which brings me to this

NO MERCY MARRIAGES.
THERE ARE FEW THINGS HARDER THAN
BREAKING UP. BUT MARRIAGE IS ONE OF
THEM.

Dear Breakup Girl,

   I am about to enter into a long and binding commitment to a wonderful woman. Problem is, I'm not certain if this is what I want . . . but it certainly is what she desires, and I cannot stand the thought of ever causing her pain. Any advice?
   —Wishing I Could Be Less Wishy-Washy

Dear Wishing/Wishy/Washy,

   Um, are you talking about GETTING MARRIED? Because if you can't say it—type it, even—in the privacy of your own computer to a superhero who has no clue who you are, then I hesitate to send you off to pronounce your vows in front of three hundred of your closest friends and an agent of the Lord.

   Now revisit the logic of your second sentence. *The acute sting and ache you will cause by leaving her is much less than the chronic pain you will cause her by staying with her against your will.*

   So if you do decide to leave, write me back. You might want to practice using the word *breakup* in the letter.
   Love,
   Breakup Girl

PREDICAMENT of the CHAPTER!

In Sugar and in Health

Dear Breakup Girl,

   My boyfriend and I live together in bliss. We're really good at working out problems, and he makes me feel (your words) like the "fresh and tasty thing I am." He's brought up marriage.

   But. He has dangerously bad habits. He smokes. He puts

sugar on pie. He goes through salt like, I don't know what goes through a lot of salt, but a lot. I cook for him; he doesn't eat it. He is fifty pounds overweight. I have NEVER seen him eat a vegetable. I talk to him about my concern often. He claims that he would rather die young than live a long life of tofu and squash. I can't make him see an in-between.

I want to spend the rest of my life with this man; I don't want to be a widow at forty. Should I stay? Is this a behavior problem or a deeply ingrained personality flaw?

—Worry Wart

Dear Worry Wart,

1. Sugar on pie? Ick/YUM.

2. Deer. Deer go through a lot of salt. Don't they have, like, salt licks? (And where can I get one?)

3. Your sweetie pie is a dear. That's why both BG and Belleruth caution you not to let this become an eternal power struggle. Belleruth says: "You can't push it, and nagging is feckless. It doesn't sound like it's worth getting rid of him over this, because it's a good relationship. However, you can tell him, just once and dead serious, how worried and upset you are. You can even do this in front of a couples counselor if you feel as if you can't make your point about this any-more. You can also cook for him in a way that is healthier than what he eats but satisfies his sweet/salt tooth too; you might wean him off his weird habits. Also: You could vaca-tion at a place like Canyon Ranch, which would show him you can eat well and deliciously too. Finally, as he gets older, he will be less and less able to get away with abusing his body. He'll get some symptoms that will shape him up."

We say marry the dude.

Love,

Breakup Girl and Belleruth

⚡ More Than "A Drawer":
Should We Live Together?

According to the U.S. Census Bureau, there were 500,000 couples living together in 1970; now there are more than 3.7 million. Slightly more than half of adults in their twenties and thirties have lived with a squeeze. Why such a dramatic rise? Factors may include economic necessity, relaxation of taboos, and increased desire to freak out parents.

But more important than the question of why couples love-shack is this: What happens when they do?

1. A Penn State study found that cohabiters are less enthusiastic about marriage than those who live with their parents. Before you say, "Duh, I'd marry the Grinch to get out of this basement!" allow me to finesse. Point is: living together actually *caused* couples to get less psyched about getting married. Before you say, "Duh, 'cause they realize they'd be marrying the Grinch!" let me further finesse. They don't get less psyched about each other; they get less psyched about *marrying* each other — and *more* psyched about keeping things the way they are.

2. A Bowling Green (Ohio) State University study found that moving in can get you down. Of the couples studied, "life satisfaction" was highest for married couples and next highest for couples who lived together two years or less (that is, until marriage or breakup). Whose "life satisfaction" was at rock bottom? *Long-term live-ins.* Huh. Sociologist Susan Brown attributes these blues to the wear and tear of, if you will, the relationship's permanent impermanence.

Now that I reread them, I see that putting these studies together in close quarters underscores their trivial differences. Ha, ha. Anyway, what we can distill from both of them is this: Living together does not necessarily work as a dress rehearsal for marriage. How come? For one thing, you've said "I do" only to the landlord, not to each other; there's always — *in theory* — a relatively easy out (unless you live in Manhattan, where the only way to get a good place is to marry a landlord). It's NOT the same.

But I'm not telling you not to live together, I'm just telling you not to do it as a dry run. Do it because you can't stand to go one minute in the morning without seeing each other. Do it because you're committed to each other, but not to the institution of marriage. Do it because your housemates have already turned your room into a study anyway. Okay?

Just a couple more things to note as you load up the U-Haul of love: (1) your cohabitation will make it approximately 89 percent more difficult for your friends to find worthwhile wedding presents, and (2) make no mistake: Even if you live in the same room, you will still e-mail each other.

The Birds, the Bees, and the UGLY

A young woman named Sasha wrote to say:

> I've been dating someone who is my best friend, my favorite person, a good and attentive lover, and a wonderful soul mate for me. I really, really love him and he has added so much to my life. My concern is that our sex life, although good, has never been particularly easy or anxiety free.

For all intents and purposes, that's — as they say — all she wrote. So never mind "Well, what exactly is the problem?" — my question is this: "Is anyone's sex life anxiety free?" Let's face it, no matter how nuts / comfortable we are about / with our bedfellow(s), sex is still the only enterprise that makes reasonable, sane people wonder things like, *"Does darkness make me look fat?"* Which is why it's time you and BG sit down and have a Talk. So here's an assortment of other frequently / uncomfortably asked questions.

First, let's go to the Teen Corner.

"When Two People Are in Love, They Lie Very Close Together . . ."

Okay, you all know that. And some of you even *know* it, in the biblical sense. Which Breakup Girl is not at all happy about.

Shout-out to all you high schoolers (and younger): It gives me the wow-times-have-changed willies not only to hear that you're having sex in the

GETTING THE DIGITS

THE SEX SPECS

• Nearly 60 percent of female BG readers had sex for the first time between the ages of fourteen and seventeen; among male readers, most -- 44 percent -- were between eighteen and twenty-one. (This is one of the rare times I'll say "Why can't a woman be more like a man?")

• Of those who haven't had sex (like, ever; not just that it's a distant memory), most -- men and women -- are waiting for "the right person." The second-most are waiting for "the right . . . *marriage*."

• How long do you wait before sleeping together? Forty percent wait three months, 28 percent wait three dates, and 11 percent wait three articles of clothing.

• Of readers in committed sexual relationships, most reported having sex as often as "reality" -- work, kids, exhaustion, surveys -- allows.

first place, but to hear the casual way you talk about it. When I was at Breakup High, we wondered how you made out without bumping noses. There was one girl in the senior class who was rumored to have had sex. *And I am not even that old.*

Even so, I KNOW I sound like a dumb old grown-up here, because there is no cool, down-with-the-kids way to say: DON'T DO IT or QUIT IT. But hey, most thirty-year-olds are way too young to be doing it too. We are *all* messing with fire. It's not about being Good or doing what is Right. It's this: *Do not underestimate how complicated sex makes things emotionally, not to mention how UNFUN sex is when things are that complicated.*

And oh, I want you to have fun. In fact, I want you to have sex. LATER. And specifically: with someone with whom you feel more than friendship, more than flirtation, more than just carried away. Like, A LOT more. With someone with whom you can have a big grown-up conversation about love and commitment and monogamy and latex (more about that later).

So I am not asking you to be a kid and (not) do it "because I said so"; I am asking you to be a grown-up and trust me on this one. Find someone who wants to go out with you because s/he gets: a cool girl/boyfriend. Not: "some." I don't mean to preach, you guys. I just don't want you not to know what you're missing.

With that, here's a brief ode to virginity.

Dear Breakup Girl,

I am a virgin, and it is getting in the way of my dating life. Boys like me, but every time one tries to get me into a relationship, I hesitate, because I don't like to kiss or make out. I just want to enjoy the person I'm dating for who they are and how they make me feel.

My best girl friend recommended that I ask my best guy friend—who has a girlfriend—to have sex with me so I know whether or not I like it and if it's something I want to save for marriage or experience sooner. I know it sounds crazy, but I would like to experience sex from someone I trust so greatly. I'm scared that if I don't have it now, I'll never have it, because I don't think I'll love or trust anyone as much as I do him. Should I rethink this experiencing biz? And how do I not let my virginity get in the way of dating?
— Still a Virgin

Dear Still,

We need to give Breakup Mom a moment to recover. In her day, "virginity" and "dating" did not so much interfere with one another. I'm just saying.

But now I will say NO! A thousand times NO! BG does NOT endorse this "experiencing biz"! For a million reasons, a big one being: *You don't want to.* You're not all that amped about kissing and you're talking about doing the nasty? Then again, you've already kissed logic good-bye: You're hav-

THE TRANSITIVE PROPERTY OF VIRGINITY

You wouldn't believe how many people write to say things like

My Special Friend doesn't call, ask me out, or remember my name. Still, I think we really have something. I mean, I lost my virginity to this person!

According to our wise Belleruth, the faulty logic at work here is this:

1. I would lose my virginity only in a really special relationship. And:
2. I lost my virginity in this relationship. Therefore:
3. *This must be a really special relationship.*

You see how that goes? True, you lose your virginity only once, and some people find that more sacred than others. But if you make other choices down the line, you can get treated well by someone special every day. I recommend you save yourself for the latter.

ing sex to find out if you want to stay a virgin? Hmm. And
finally: How delightful that you trust and love this
friend; how depressing that you think this is a one-in-
forever chance.

All of which says: You're not ready, you're confused,
and you're not secure and confident that you're a tasty babe
whom spiffy boys—sans girlfriends—will like no matter what
you do or don't put out. And the latter is the key to letting "virginity" and "dating" coexist peacefully and power-
fully.

Love,
Breakup Girl

⚡ Safe Sex / Testing I, 2, 3

Preachy, part deux: It also boggles my mind to hear about folks young and
not so — in nonmonogamous, non-baby-ready, non-test-prepped relationships — having sex without using eleven or twelve forms of protection. Yes,
even for one-night stands. Geez, especially for one-night stands. There's no
delicate, clever way to say this: Having sex without birth control / disease
barriers is just about the dumbest-ass thing you could possibly do.

Now, I know all of this stuff is terribly hard to talk about. Funny, isn't it,
that certain conversations can be more intimate and scary than certain…
positions. I know. But still. Heed this

THE ONLY PEOPLE YOU SHOULD BE HAVING
SEX WITH ARE THE PEOPLE YOU CAN TALK
WITH ABOUT HAVING SAFER SEX.

Ideally, you see, those two kinds of intimacy should go hand in hand. If
you don't feel comfortable piping up — about latex, getting tested for
HIV/STDs, whatever — with this person, that's a red flag. If he or she doesn't
feel comfortable piping back, that too; I don't recommend that you get that
close to someone that closed. This is an issue big enough (as in, life-and-
death) to press someone on — and, dare I say, lose someone over. As unro-
mantic as it may seem, taking these precautions is Just What You Do.

By the way, please get tested for STDs regularly even if you're not currently in a committed / sexual relationship. Like, every six months. Why?

Because that way you get used to it; diminishes the drama. Also, it's a card you can play whenever the situation next presents itself. As in: "Well, I was tested three months ago and I'm fine. What about you?")*

⚡ Freaked Out by a Fetish?

Transvestism, porn, stilettos, leather, S&M, Alf costumes — I've heard it all. Let me tell you, I'm a lot less shocked than the folks who discover these interests in their partners.

Are pursuits like these a "problem"? Depends on how intertwined they are with your relationship as a whole. WonderWear, for example, writes:

> I found out through a snoopfest that my husband of nine years is a transvestite . . . and has been for twenty-five years. It floored me and freaked me out. We have not had sex in two years, and it is getting hard to resist the urge to find someone else to have a relationship with. He says he can control it and won't do it anymore. . . . I doubt him. Our sex life prior to the discovery was infrequent at best . . . three to four times a year. I love him, but I am not in love with him or attracted to him anymore. . . . How long should I wait to feel something again? Or should I leave and give myself credit for trying?

See — never mind his fashion choices: Whatever the reason, they haven't had sex in two years; she's not attracted. Get to the bottom of that drawer. Belleruth says: "The biggest issue is the betrayal of trust — keeping that secret — and the sense of disorientation and upset at thinking you know someone and finding out you don't. It disturbs confidence and sense of self; you feel undone. His being a transvestite [everyone: insert here whichever "alternative" practice has freaked you out] doesn't mean he's a lousy husband, though, and it doesn't even make him less hetero. Hell — if you feel comfortable, dress him in your nightie and put on a leather jacket. Things could get interesting. In any case, I'd recommend couples counseling before you hit the road...unless you're looking for an excuse to find a new partner... and that's a different story altogether."

So is AR's:

---

*I'll spare you the sex-ed/HIV-awareness speech, but you also just do it even if you've done Everything But. Okay?

Dear Breakup Girl,

I just found out that my bright, adorable, talented, fun boyfriend is what some call a "sex addict." When we went over our sexual histories he CONVENIENTLY downplayed his fondness for porn, phone sex, chat rooms, etc., not to MENTION the fact that he'd also gone through a phase where he called escorts and visited booths in Times Square, etc. We've had many talks, and he's even started to attend SAA meetings. I practically feel sorry for him because—even when I'm grilling him for details that will just hurt me to hear—he's been contrite, giving, supportive, understanding; he says he was wrong and wants to forge a healthy relationship. But sometimes I feel "duped"; if I'd known about his habits when we started dating, I wouldn't have gotten serious—who would? Should I end it because there's no way I'll forgive him / deal with this side of him . . . or is this something that time, talking (thank GOD we are able to talk), or maybe (gulp) counseling can help?

—AR

Dear AR,

It's upsetting to discover he's kept secrets . . . especially secrets that seem to disgust—and, more importantly, dis—you. But do not throw out this babe with the bathwater from that seedy Times Square hotel! As Belleruth points out: "Guess he gets turned on by the idea of sex being anonymous, 'dirty,' whatever, and maybe he's got some split in his psyche with 'dirty' sex in one corner and 'love' sex in the other. But *it sounds like this guy knows how to have a relationship.* If in fact the kindness, sex, and intimacy are all terrific, *and* he's getting help for his excessive leaning into his fantasy life, why, that's grand."

So grit your teeth and do your bestest to stop grilling. Instead, Belle says, "Look to see if you aren't prudishly overreacting a tad. In fact, you might even want to tramp up your routine with a nice hooker outfit, just to indulge him." Might help him merge those corners. Even if that doesn't do it for you, I suggest you try to stop confusing this with low morals and disrespect. Doing that would be waaaaaaaay sexier than righteous indignation. Be strong. Together.

Love,

Breakup Girl

Above all, yes, talk. Even if it's not a turn-on. And when you do, you'll bring this stuff up sensitively and nonblamingly, right? 'Cause otherwise, well, that's not the kind of punishment your partners are into.

⚡ "Casual" Sex

"Casual" generally works best as a dress code, not a relationship. It's tricky because more often than not, one of you starts feeling more…formal (see "Relapses Versus Reunions," page 55). And it's definitely hard to upgrade.

Specifically, what's tough here is the sense of going backward and filling in the step — the foundation of emotional intimacy that, according to many, should precede sex — you've already skipped over. How to go back and get it? Well, what you could do is, um, not have sex. How about a movie? A sundae date at the soda fountain? Just chatting? Give it a whirl. Otherwise, well, it may start to feel as if all your dates are on casual Friday. Don't, um, screw yourself out of a promotion.

> Dear Breakup Girl,
>
>   I love sex, I love men, I love life. I don't want a commitment; I don't want a boyfriend. My roommate disapproves of my (safe) one-nighters or casual sex relationships, saying I am dysfunctional and self-destructive. I say it's healthy . . . I have not yet met the man who deserves me. I am smart, funny, generous, pretty, confident; I need a man who can handle that and live up to some high stan-

---

**Biochemistry Corner:
THE MAGIC
OF OXYTOCIN**

Hey women, ever wonder how come, when you sleep with someone totally inconsequential, you spend the whole next day wondering if s/he's dressed warmly enough? I call this Scarf Syndrome -- and you may or may not be pleased to know that it has a basis in hormonal truth. Meet: oxytocin, a little goody that females (human and animal) release during lovemaking and, Oedipally enough, also during breast-feeding and childbirth. In fact, scientists believe that oxytocin is one of the chemical catalysts for mother-child bonding. Carnal, maternal: It's a fine line. So when you have sex, it's like you imprint on the lucky guy as if he were your bitty baby bird. Helps explain why women -- even post-trivial-one-night-stand -- may feel this bizarre, misplaced impulse to feed it, help it fly, and to want it to come to depend on them for food and warmth.

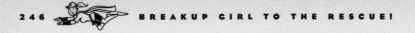
dards. Why should I give my precious time and effort to some-
one unworthy? I am twenty and I have a lot of life to live
—what's wrong with filling that life with beautiful men who
make me happy, if only for a night? Am I heading for a an
exorbitant therapy bill?
— Siobhan

Dear Siobhan,
No, you're fine. So are standards. Just make sure of one
thing: When he comes along, will you actually let him in?
Love,
Breakup Girl

THE **BIG** QUESTION: *DOES SIZE MATTER?*

Dear Breakup Girl,
I am a seventeen-year-old male. Please tell me what you think
about penis size: Does it matter? You can laugh, joke, anything,
but please let us know your thoughts on this. Please.
— Shain

Dear Shain,
Breakup Mom, didn't you leave something on the stove?
Quick, while she's gone: The only size that matters is the
size of your sincere desire to rock your partner's world.
It's not that your partner will be unsatisfied if you are
small ("small"). It's that your partner will be unsatisfied if
you *act* small.
This is information you will use when you are ready, in,
like, four years, right, Shain?
Love,
Breakup Girl

PREDICAMENT of the CHAPTER!

French Class

Dear Breakup Girl,

I really like my boyfriend. A LOT. He's the sweetest guy—he's perfect. He's also a good kisser. But. I don't want some huge foreign object in my mouth, especially someone else's huge foreign object. But I can handle a bit of tongue. In fact, I WANT just a little bit of tongue. I don't want him to be shocked or grossed out. How can I politely bump up the intensity of our love life?

—Wishing for Just a Little More!

Dear Wishing,

Oh! It is so refreshing to hear from younger folks for whom "more" is adding tongue, not . . . sex. Glad to help—especially 'cause I know it's hard to talk about these things. I mean, casual doesn't really work—"Hey, sport, what say we toss in a little tongue?" Nor does formal—"There's something I'd like to discuss with you. It's about, well, bumping up the intensity of our sex life. I'm hesitant, because I don't want to shock you, yet I feel that given our level of mutual attraction, we are ready to . . ." At this point, actually, he may stick his tongue in your mouth to get you to shut up already.

Instead, I recommend: Show, don't Tell—then Ask. Start by touching his lips with your tongue. Ask, "Um, do you like how that feels? Blink once for yes, twice for no." And so on (in). Betcha you'll rock his world. Stop kissing long enough to let me know how it goes, okay?

Love,

Breakup Girl

APPENDIX

Important Breakup Girl Maxims

Breakup Girl holds these truths to be self-evident. So should you. So should your ex, actually, but that may be asking a lot.

Breaking Up

■ **THERE IS NO SUCH THING AS "BREAKING UP WITH SOMEONE WITHOUT HURTING THEIR FEELINGS."**

Come on. Doesn't it hurt when you find out that someone you *don't* like doesn't like you? Seek to spare feelings, not to not hurt. The only way to "not hurt" is to stay in the relationship against your will. Which hurts worse.

■ **LET YOUR EX BE MAD BECAUSE YOU BROKE UP WITH HIM/HER. NOT BECAUSE OF *HOW* YOU BROKE UP WITH HIM/HER.**

Do your best.

■ **MEAN IS BAD, BUT *BLUNT* IS FINE.**

Basic breakup technique. Simple and clear (as opposed to harsh) is the cleanest, most respectful, most effective way to — literally — go.

■ **"BREAKING UP SUCKS" IS TRUE, BUT IT IS NOT A GOOD REASON NOT TO BREAK UP.**

Neither is "Because s/he is there." (Otherwise known as an "Everest Relationship.") Neither, you long-distance people, is "Because s/he isn't here."

■ **MIXED FEELINGS AFTER A BREAKUP ARE NORMAL BREAKUP AFTERMATH, NOT NECESSARILY EVIDENCE AGAINST THE BREAKUP'S WISDOM.**

Let the battery on them run down before you go and hit rewind.

■ **DO NOT ASK *WHY*.**

Yes, s/he owes you a basic explanation. But don't push it. The answer to this masochistic, self-flagellating question will not "help you understand." It will only make you say things like "*Am not!*" Or, worse, it will be exactly what you knew s/he was going to say. Don't go there.

■ **EXES DO NOT HELP EXES THROUGH BREAKUPS.**

It's too weird — like dating your therapist, in reverse — and it doesn't work. Note: Sleeping together does not count as "help."

■ **DO NOT FOOL AROUND WITH SOMEONE IN ORDER TO GET OVER SOMEONE, ESPECIALLY IF IT'S THAT PERSON.**

Bears repeating.

■ **REVENGE MAKES YOU LOOK BAD. AND WHEN YOU LOOK BAD, YOU FEEL WORSE.**

Living *better* is the best revenge. And Better People have better things to do.

■ **SOMETIMES OYSTERS (RELATIONSHIPS) HAVE PEARLS (POST-BREAKUP FRIENDSHIPS) AND SOMETIMES THEY DON'T. IF THEY DON'T, THAT DOESN'T MEAN YOU HAD A BAD OYSTER.**

Your ability to be friends with an ex is not a measure of your maturity, nor of the value of the relationship you had before. Why some exes wind up friends and some don't may forever remain a mystery of the deep.

■ **SEEING SOMEONE NEW AND HAVING MOVED ON ARE UNRELATED.**

Apples and…blue. Some people see new people outside before they've moved on inside; some people find that truly having moved on means enjoying seeing no one for a while. So don't freak if you see your ex with an insta-rebound, and don't trick your insta-rebound into thinking that you've actually moved on. And don't date someone to prove that you've moved on. That means you haven't.

■ **"OVER SOMEONE" COMES SOONER THAN YOU THINK. IF YOU LET IT.**

"Over it" doesn't mean that you don't think about your ex at all, or that it doesn't smart when you do. It means that while there may be this little

remnant of that relationship still stuck to your back in that funny place you just can't reach, well, that remnant is on your back, not standing in your way. You can leave it sitting there *while* you move forward.

■ **THE REUNION PROCESS IS MORE THAN A MATTER OF "PLEASE BE KIND, REWIND."**

If you want this to work — or if you want your re-intended to listen in the first place — do not imply that the breakup was no more than a blooper and that all it will take to get it right is to go back and recite the same lines, walk through the same motions. Paradoxically, the farther you've moved on, the healthier your comeback may be.

Relating

■ **"THE RULES," LADIES AND GENTLEMEN, ARE MANNERS.**

Don't get bogged down in he should/she should. Just ask yourself: "What would be the polite/kind/considerate move to make?" (And in the event of mishap: "What good manners will make this mess easier for everyone right now?") In a world dulled and chilled by haste and hate, trust me, manners are hot.

■ **EARLY IN A RELATIONSHIP, YOUR PRESENTS SHOULD NOT BE COMMANDING.**

Example: You give an overwhelming Christmas gift, I give your relationship twelve days.

■ **YOU CAN'T *MAKE* ANYONE DO ANYTHING.**

Love you, leave you, listen to you, whatever. Did your parents ever really make you do anything? Even if they did, did you want to when they did? The more they made you eat your rutabagas, the more you hated rutabagas, right? So don't pull a rutabaga on your intended or ex-tended. The good-news converse: Whatever s/he did is not your fault.

■ **THE ONLY PEOPLE YOU SHOULD BE HAVING SEX WITH ARE THE PEOPLE YOU CAN TALK WITH ABOUT HAVING SAFER SEX.**

This is an issue big enough (as in, life-and-death) to press someone on — and, dare I say, lose someone over.

■ DON'T CREATE SOME FOOL'S GOLD STANDARD OF FULL DISCLOSURE AND ASK EACH OTHER MORE ABOUT THE PAST THAN YOU REALLY WANT TO KNOW.

The answer will likely be: more than you really wanted to know.

■ PEOPLE ENDING MARRIAGES DO NOT SPEAK ANY SORT OF MEANING-FUL, CONSISTENT LANGUAGE TO THE PERSON THEY'RE SEEING WHILE THEY'RE DOING IT.

Take *everything* with a grain of rice.

■ NO MERCY MARRIAGES.

Perspective: There are few things harder than breaking up. Marriage is one of them.

Dating

■ WHEN CALLS ARE MEASURED BY WAIT, NOT VOLUME, SOME SETTLING MAY OCCUR. DON'T LET IT.

Don't fall into the "S / He's the *one*…who *called!*" trap.

■ YOU EITHER WANT A RELATIONSHIP OR YOU DON'T. NO ONE, NOT EVEN THE PRESIDENT, IS "TOO BUSY FOR A RELATIONSHIP" S / HE REALLY WANTS.

This is an excuse. Or, in rare cases of accuracy / sincerity, a serious problem to bring up with your boss.

■ FOR AN OFFICE ROMANCE TO BE WORTH THE RISK, YOU HAVE TO HAVE A PRETTY FIERCE HUNCH THAT THINGS COULD REALLY WORK OUT -- A HUNCH THAT COMES FROM YOUR GUT, NOT FROM YOUR FOURTH MAR-GARITA AT THE "OFFICE OLÉ!" FIESTA.

Ask yourself which you would rather face: life *without* this person as partner or the tricky — but worth-it-if-you-say-so — business of working with him / her.

■ WHEN YOU ASK SOMEONE OUT, DO NOT "BE YOURSELF."

What "yourself" would say is, "I am totally hot for you and I dream of you all the time, and you'd be crazy to go out with me since you are, like, czar of the universe, but forget all that — will you marry me?" What you really say is, "Would you like to go see *Princess Mononoke*?"

■ **WHOEVER INVITED PAYS. (ALSO BREAKUP GIRL'S DATING RULE #3.)**

Don't you dare take out (a) nice girl/boy, and then (b) a #2 pencil and a legal pad to calculate his/her share. It's not about money; it's about manners. If you can't afford a particular venue, then go someplace within your means and be equally gracious there (as our very own Paul the Intern would say: "Supersize that for the lady!").

■ **THE OPPOSITE OF *NICE* IS NOT *JERK*.**

Nice guys: Don't think you have to go "jerk" to get the girl. For every guy wondering why women go for "bad boys," there's a woman wondering where all the good guys are. Corrolary: The opposite of *jerk* is not *gay*. Plenty of gay guys are jerks. Plenty of straight guys are nice. (Might help if they had some sort of parade, though.)

GLOSSARY

Speak My Language

Bizarro World. The only place where it's possible to "break up with someone without hurting their feelings."

Boy Soy. The opposite of a boy toy. The one you actually talk to.

Brady Dating. Not: having two dates on one night, one to a costume party and one to a regular party so you have to have one wait in the den and one in the living room and then you change into and out of your vampire outfit as you pass through the kitchen. Rather: going on *dates*. One by one, maybe more than one date-ee at first. Going slow *before* "steady." *Enjoying* the impatience. Helps you know how you feel *before* you move in.

Coffee Friends. When you stay friend...*ly* after a relationship. Kosher-style. Dutchy-feely. Contact limited to occasional "Great, you?" coffee summits that prove how mature and civil (and incredibly happy) you are.

Cyberdating. An excellent place to start. But if you think it's lame to wait by the phone, try waiting by the computer.

Derogatory Purgatory. Where people who can't stop slamming their exes are destined to live out their days. Single.

Diamond in the Roughneck. What women hope to find when they date "jerks."

"Everest" Relationship. Someone you date because s/he's there. Might have been good enough for Hillary (Edmund), but it's not good enough for you.

The Flirtation Continuum. The realm of the general, flirty, fizzy buzz as an end unto itself, where no one venture is the be-all — well, end-all — of your love life as you know it.

Florence Nightingale in Shining Armor. Someone whose mission is to date people back to health. (Their issues resolved, they will then start dating someone else.)

Friend-Bound. When a recently-single seeks Everything But in a (very frustrated) new pseudomate. Also known as the Zipless Rebound.

Grecian Formula. 1 trip to Crete + 1 great little dress = 1 man out of hair.

I Can't Believe It's Not Boyfriend. Going through the motions of being "friends" while you still have the emotions of being boy/girlfriend. Tastes bad, less fulfilling.

Loftbuilder. A guy who does favors, chores, and odd jobs for the object of his affection rather than, say, asking her out. Synonym: *friend*. Ahem.

Office Romance. Tricky, but at least you know s/he has a job.

Poaching. Hitting on someone you know is taken. Illegal.

The Porch Test. How to tell if this one's *the* keeper. Can you picture yourselves together at a ripe old age, settin' together on rocking chairs on the veranda? (Results invalid if that's all you do right now; you should probably get out more.)

Pre-relationship Breakup. You've planned the wedding; s/he doesn't call.

Rebound. Chicken soup for the loins.

Relapse. Post-breakup hookup with your ex. There is, after all, no aphrodisiac like a breakup. As in: "You look great without…*commitment*."

ReZenge. The best kind: doing *nothing* in retaliation. Sends the supercilious message that Mr. / Ms. Thang has no time even to acknowledge such a petty act of lameness / evil.

Sex. The only activity in the world that makes reasonable, secure people have thoughts like, "Does darkness make me look fat?"

Snood. Also, *nosegay, alphabet shower,* etc. Terms that you will actually understand after being a member of 473 wedding parties.

Space. In a relationship, healthy distance or breathing room. As in: "I need space. So we'll sleep together; we just won't spoon."

"Why [are you dumping me]?" Don't ask.